# Language, Resistance and Revival

'This fascinating new study examines an essential part of the story of language revival and political conflict in Ireland. The interviews and analysis undertaken by the author promise to be of great interest to a wide readership.'

Dr Fionntán De Brún, Head of Irish Language
and Literature in University of Ulster

'An important contribution to our understanding of the impact of colonialism on minority languages, and attempts to revive those languages. It also explores a rarely documented aspect of the lives and struggles of political prisoners in Ireland and shows their contribution to the Irish language revival.'

Dr Féilim Ó hAdhmaill, republican ex-prisoner and Lecturer in
Sociology and Social Policy at University College, Cork

'This fascinating and most original study is to be warmly welcomed. We have here a work which should appeal to a wide readership both among the general population and among students of a variety of academic disciplines, including Irish, sociology, sociolinguistics, modern history, education, law, and conflict and peace studies.'

Dr Nollaig Ó Muraíle, Senior Lecturer in Irish,
National University of Ireland, Galway

'An excellent account of cultural colonialism in both its historical and contemporary context. While concentrating his examination on the case of Ireland, the author also places the process in an international context. He has had intimate access to sources beyond the reach of many others. This, along with his acute analytical and observational skills, has resulted in a work of real merit. A genuine treasure.'

Tommy McKearney, Former IRA Hunger Striker, historian and author
of *The Provisional IRA – From Insurrection to Parliament* (Pluto Press)

'The resistance of politically-motivated republican prisoners during the recent conflict in the north of Ireland has been well documented, but this is the first account which has the language revival as its central focus. That alone makes this a valuable contribution to knowledge. The story is a fascinating and politically instructive one which has not been told before.'

Professor Bill Rolston, Director of Transitional
Justice Institute, University of Ulster

'This book provides the perfect synthesis of insider knowledge and serious academic reflection. It benefits from extraordinary access to the ex-prisoner community, and the author shows a unique capacity to understand the historical and political complexities of their accounts. It will have an enormous impact on research seeking to understand grassroots resistance movements throughout the world.'

Professor Kristin Bumiller, Department of Political Science, Amherst College, MA, USA

'An original and thought-provoking work. The combination of an author engagé and a rich body of primary evidence has produced a study that challenges many conventional features of ethnographic research.'

Prof Gearóid Ó Tuathaigh, Historian and former Emeritus Professor of History in National University of Ireland, Galway and Member of Council of State for President of Ireland, Michael D. O'Higgins

'Profoundly personal and captivating ... Meticulously researched, eloquently and powerfully written, Mac Ionnrachtaigh's treatise is a triumph.'

Dr Bree Carlton, Senior Lecturer Criminology, School of Political and Social Inquiry, Monash University, Australia

'As a trade union, human rights and women's activist, what resonates most strongly with me in this book is the understanding of how the power of imagination sparks the self-belief that is required, within those living in the most marginalised of spaces, to challenge invisibility. The test of healthy democratic practice is how it embraces, not excludes, such challenge and change.'

Inez McCormack, world renowned Trade Union, Women's and Human Rights Activist

'A passionate and rigorous work of importance to those interested in cultural, political and social liberation in Ireland and worldwide.'

Fergus Ó hÍr, Former Civil Rights activist, founding principal of Meánscoil Feirste and current Manager of Irish Language community Radio Station, Raidió Fáilte

'At a time when the depoliticisation of culture is high on the political agenda, this work clearly illustrates the link between politics and language in a colonised land. The author's impressive research gives unique access to a significant part of recent Irish history and, by detailing the achievements of the past, gives inspiration for the future. The book's message is as relevant today as ever.'

Tomaí Ó Conghaile, Irish language activist, editor of Irish language magazine *nós* * and television/radio presenter

# LANGUAGE, RESISTANCE AND REVIVAL

## Republican Prisoners and the Irish Language in the North of Ireland

Feargal Mac Ionnrachtaigh

*To Alfie,*

*lean at des an teanga!*

**Pluto**Press
www.plutobooks.com

First published 2013 by Pluto Press
345 Archway Road, London N6 5AA

www.plutobooks.com

Distributed in the United States of America exclusively by
Palgrave Macmillan, a division of St. Martin's Press LLC,
175 Fifth Avenue, New York, NY 10010

British Library Cataloguing in Publication Data
A catalogue record for this book is available from the British Library

ISBN   978 0 7453 3227 7    Hardback
ISBN   978 0 7453 3226 0    Paperback
ISBN   978 1 8496 4845 5    PDF eBook
ISBN   978 1 8496 4847 9    Kindle eBook
ISBN   978 1 8496 4846 2    EPUB eBook

Library of Congress Cataloging in Publication Data applied for

This book is printed on paper suitable for recycling and made from fully managed
and sustained forest sources. Logging, pulping and manufacturing processes are
expected to conform to the environmental standards of the country of origin.

10   9   8   7   6   5   4   3   2

Designed and produced for Pluto Press by Chase Publishing Services Ltd
Typeset from disk by Stanford DTP Services, Northampton, England
Simultaneously printed digitally by CPI Antony Rowe, Chippenham, UK and
Edwards Bros in the United States of America

For Terry óg (1969–1998)

*a thugann spreagadh agus misneach dom i dtólamh*

# Contents

# Acknowledgements

Ba mhaith liom buíochas ó chroí a ghabháil leis an iliomad daoine éagsúla a chuidigh leis an tioncsnamh seo ón tús; murach an cuidiú, an chomhairle agus an spreagadh s'agaibh, is cinnte nach mbeadh an leabhar seo indhéanta. Firstly, I want to thank all those narrators, three of whom, Willie-John McCorry, Billy Kelly and Eddie Keenan, are sadly no longer with us, who kindly gave up their time to speak about their experiences. This book is primarily based on your story and would not exist without your valuable contributions. I want to thank all those who helped me during my time researching at Queen's University Belfast, most notably an t-Ollamh Dónall P. Ó Baoill who gave me kind help and guidance stretching over several years.

In addition, I must mention a number of others whose advice guided me along the way: Dr Nollaig Ó Muraíle, and Professors Kieran McEvoy, Bill Rolston, Gearóid Ó Tuathaigh and Mike Tomlinson. I'm particularly indebted to my friend Phil Scraton, who not only gave up his time to write a wonderful foreword, but also helped shape my intellectual journey and cajoled me to pursue this research to publication. A number of friends helpfully read drafts of this book, including my brother Niall, Ciarán Mac Giolla Bhéin, Seán Mac Bradaigh, Brian Kelly, Féilim Ó hAdhmaill and Nicola Rooney; Liam Barr gave invaluable help with compiling the manuscript. Fergal Mac Blaoscaidh was especially generous with his time and incredibly sharp analysis. My appreciation also extends to Ciarán Ó Brolcháin, who not only compiled a comprehensive index, but has also been on hand to help me with countless thankless tasks over many years. Go raibh maith agaibh a chairde.

Also, I'm eternally grateful to a number of friends and comrades who have given me invaluable practical help, not only with this book project, but also in a plethora of tasks and projects in an often hectic schedule – especially Michael McCann, Séanna Breathnach, Jake Mac Siacais, Seamas Mac Seáin, Déaglán Ó Mochain, Tarlach Ó Brannagáin, Colma McKee, Pádraig Mac Cathail, Barry Fegan, Rónán Ó Scolláin, Dónal Bairclaigh, Jim Turner, Séamas Ó Donnghaile, Breandán Ó Fiaich, Fergus Ó hÍr, Seán Mistéil, Pilib Ó Ruanaí, Orliath Nic Siacais, Conchur Ó Muadaigh, Séan Ó Corráin, Seamas Ó Tuama, Diarmuid Ua Bruadair, Cáitlín Ní

Chathail, Micky Culbert, Pól Deeds, Máirtín Ó Dochartaigh (RIP), Fionnuala Nic Thom, Cormac Ó Briain, Gráinne Nic Fhearraigh, Liam Ó Maolchluiche, Pádraic Mac Oitir, Rab Mac Siacais, Francesca Ryan, Tomaí Ó Conghaile, Ursula Ní Shionainn, Eoin Ó Broin, Tommy McKearney, Lawrence McKeown, Fionntán De Brún, Denis O'Hearn and all those from within my own community and the language movement who have shown me great solidarity and comradeship over the years – there are simply too many to mention. Most importantly, I also want to thank my entire family, for raising me, inspiring me, tolerating me, listening to me and loving me these past 30 years. Most notably my parents, Mary and Terry, who have shaped my journey; and likewise my brothers Terry (RIP), Liam and Niall and their beautiful families, and my wife Maura whose patience, understanding, support and love always kept me grounded in reality! Is grá liom sibh uilig. Go raibh míle maith agaibh, tá mé thar a bheith buíoch.

# Abbreviations

| | |
|---|---|
| AN | *Andersonstown News* |
| DCAL | Department for Culture Arts and Leisure |
| DENI | Department for Education, Northern Ireland |
| DUP | Democratic Unionist Party |
| EU | European Union |
| GAA | Gaelic Athletic Association |
| GFA | Good Friday Agreement |
| IME | Irish Medium Education |
| IRA | Irish Republican Army |
| IRB | Irish Republican Brotherhood |
| NIO | Northern Ireland Office |
| OC | Officer Commanding |
| PSNI | Police Service of Northern Ireland |
| RAC | Relatives Actions Committee |
| RIC | Royal Irish Constabulary |
| RUC | Royal Ulster Constabulary |
| SDLP | Social Democratic and Labour Party |
| UDR | Ulster Defence Regiment |

# Foreword

*Phil Scraton*

## THE POLITICS OF PRISON AND THE LANGUAGE OF RESISTANCE

Most days of the week, early morning or late afternoon, the white vans pass by barely noticed. Now an integral part of the cityscape, their uniformed drivers and rows of darkened windows are clues to their purpose. These are the vans familiar to television news watchers, chased by hopeful photographers outside courts during high profile trials, randomly flashing cameras at impenetrable glass. Moving constantly between prison and courts, between prison and prison, the vans and the routes they travel provide conduits for those detained within the criminal justice system. They are prisons on wheels, essential to the operation of the penal archipelago. Each van, with its human cargo of fear, anxiety, bravura and hopelessness, is a microcosm of contemporary imprisonment. It carries a maximum number of bodies in the minimum possible space, each prisoner confined in isolation to a locked cell the size of a cupboard. As it travels, the isolated prisoner catches glimpses of freedom lost. The van might be full to capacity but they sit alone.

With the exception of states that retain a political and ideological commitment to capital punishment, prisons and other places of detention are the ultimate sanction available for those classified 'criminal', or awaiting trial, or classified mentally ill, or assessed as 'illegals'. Places of detention also offer the possibility of internment without trial. Their high walls and fences are the physical manifestation of the prisoner's removal from her or his community, containing and punishing the ascribed 'criminal' while 'protecting' the community. The late-eighteenth-century penal reformer John Howard laid the foundations for what became identified as the 'new prison'. His aim was to promote the prison as a site where prisoners could be reformed rather than left to languish in dire conditions. The 'new prison' would emphasise isolation, silence and work as the means through which prisoners might address their misdeeds while developing 'good character'. Sparse but humane conditions would ensure the prisoner experienced a 'just measure of pain' to balance the 'gain' of her or his crimes. Reflecting on this shift from punishing the body through extreme conditions, Michel Foucault characterised this as not 'punishing less' but 'punishing better'.

Penal reformers also recognised that while not all prisoners posed the same level of threat to their fellow citizens or to the established order, protection from those considered a danger to others, or to social, political and economic stability, was a central objective of the 'rule of law'. Imprisonment provided the means for the removal of those identified as 'social' pariahs but also those who were categorised as 'enemies of the state'. The key principle underpinning the notion of 'punishing better', however, was rehabilitation. Informed by religious discourses of forgiveness and redemption, at the core of rehabilitation lay a belief that whatever the seriousness of a crime or 'sin', the individual could be reformed by understanding the harm perpetrated, showing remorse and committing to change. The confessional, a confined cell in which the sinner kneels before God and repents, is more than a metaphor in the dialogue of rehabilitation.

In design and construction, the 'new prison' was informed by reformers such as Jeremy Bentham, whose 'panopticon' design was a radical proposal for mass containment of prisoners held in individual cells. Designed like a bicycle wheel, the hub offered a central observational platform on several levels from which corridors or landings reached out like spokes, with cells housing prisoners on either side. The panopticon maximised surveillance while minimising the number of guards required. Prisoners, alone in their cells, silent in work and with little opportunity for association, were placed under constant observation. Surveillance not only monitored behaviour, it guaranteed security. Relative isolation lessened opportunities for prisoners to subvert the system and it inhibited collective enterprise. Whatever the progress of penal reform since the emergence of the 'new prison', tensions have remained consistent. Central has been the juxtaposition of the care and rights of prisoners, exemplified more recently in the World Health Organisation's oxymoron 'the healthy prison', alongside emphases on regulation, control and security.

At the turn of the nineteenth century, in a blaze of publicity and controversy, Oscar Wilde was sentenced to two years hard labour in prison, found guilty of 'gross indecency'. It was, in fact, a prosecution that went to the heart of the politics of sexuality. He served time in Pentonville and Wandsworth prisons under a regime of hard labour, virtual starvation and spartan conditions including a bed without a mattress. He came close to dying in custody and his experiences of prison were recounted with chilling clarity in The Ballad of Reading Gaol, written in France following his release. It remains a moving indictment of corporal punishment in Victorian prisons built from 'bricks of shame', exposing the relentlessness of cellular confinement – 'a foul and dark latrine' where 'all but Lust, is turned to dust / in Humanity's machine'. Children cry, frightened; the 'weak' scourged; the 'fool' flogged; 'And some grow mad, and all grow bad / And none a word may say'.

Locked in chains, 'degraded and alone', prisoners 'curse' and 'weep', while others 'make no moan'. The pain and suffering of incarceration, the discretion that permits brutality as a commonplace, the rejection of the 'hard, pitiless eye' of the guard and the irreversible damage perpetrated on the body – matched by that done to the human spirit – capture the immediacy of the personal within the routine of the institutional. Writing from prison, midway through his confinement, Wilde observed prisoners who, 'on their release carry their prison about with them into the air ... hid[ing] it as a secret disgrace in their hearts'. Having endured 'appalling punishment' the released prisoner is abandoned 'at the very moment when its [society's] highest duty towards him begins'. For Wilde, however, 'prison life with its endless privations and restrictions makes one rebellious'.

What Oscar Wilde brought into the public domain was the reality and persistent despair of the 'new prison' and its associated regimes of deprivation and cruelty. In prison he wrote a remarkable letter, later published as an essay, De Profundis, in which he reflected: 'To regret one's own experiences is to put a lie into the lips of one's life ... no less than a denial of the soul'. Throughout the twentieth century, whatever the claims made for penal reform, there was a constant flow of evidence from prisoners whose experiences testify to the cynical disregard paid to the reformist principle of 'humane containment'. Like Wilde, their accounts opened the closed gates to a process where prisoners are introduced to deprivations of incarceration: standing naked for inspection, restricted access to underwear and basic necessities, lockdown and unlock, shared cells, isolation cells, poor food, vindictive guards, the persistent threat of violence, restricted visits, inadequate healthcare, unaffordable telephone calls, mind-numbing boredom ... the list goes on.

They have written and broadcast their accounts of prisons as places where all reference points to their regular worlds are suspended, where time has no meaning other than the spyhole being opened and closed, the key turning in the lock, weekly visits with expectant loved ones, whatever work 'opportunities' or other facilities the regime has to offer. As places where all movement is restricted, monitored and questioned and where the only meaningful discretion is that held by guards, governors or disciplinary procedures; where institutional power morphs into personal power of guards on duty: 'I look from the door at who's at the desk and I know then whether I'll have an all right day or a bad day'. These are regimes in which out-of-cell time is, at most, a third of any given day and, when no work is available, prisoners are confined to their sparse cells. Reflecting on his experiences as a lone prisoner who resisted authority, Ron Phillips notes, 'all at once [the prisoner is] assailed by a realisation of his own impotence ... Most terrible of all, the value of a human being, as judged by his own value, changes out of all recognition.'

As they walk in the shadow of prison walls, those outside have scant awareness of these deprivations and their consequences. While walls are barriers to access, they are also barriers to information. Each prison operates within a custodial network under the governance of a prison service and the state's justice department. Yet each prison is a product of its distinctive history, reputation and organisational culture. Much has been written about prisoners' agency and strategies they adopt to negotiate and challenge institutional processes and practices. As individuals, however, prisoners are well aware of the limits to dissent and the discretionary scope afforded to managers and guards in their often invisible daily operation of prison regimes. Every action or sequence of behaviour is monitored, assessed and classified in determining the regime to which each prisoner is allocated, from 'basic' to 'enhanced'. Telephone access, association with other prisoners, length of visits, time out of cell and prison work are determined by the prisoner's assessed status.

Criminalisation, through which the criminal label is applied to an individual whose actions are judged to have contravened the rule of law, is a profoundly personal process in its objectification of the individual. Yet the pathological construction of the 'outlaw' masks the inherently political context in which all law is constructed and applied, all subsequent punishment given legitimacy. Entering prison, the convicted prisoner loses personal identity and civil rights. No longer a citizen, the prisoner wears convicts' clothes, becomes a number, hands over personal possessions and surrenders movement through space. In prison, the 'door' and the 'clock', central to the taken-for-granted world of everyday life, are invested with new meaning. The controlling mechanisms of the total institution function at the discretion of others. Solely on the uncorroborated evidence of guards, internal disciplinary adjudications place prisoners on restricted regimes, including solitary confinement in strip cells. The regulation of prisoners' behaviour ranges from prescribed drugs through to physical restraint, lawful or unlawful. Basic rights are traded in exchange for compliance with the regime and, in a use of the term unique within the penal vocabulary, re-presented as 'privileges'. In this process, as Erving Goffman noted, 'territories of the self are violated' and the prisoner is 'shaped and coded into an object'. Thus the 'self' is curtailed', 'mortified' and any expression of 'defiance receives immediate, visible punishment'.

## FROM JAIL TO COMMUNITY: VOCABULARIES OF RESISTANCE AND RENEWAL

The challenge for every prisoner, particularly every political prisoner, is how to survive prison intact, how to emerge from a prison undiminished, how to conserve and even replenish one's beliefs. The first task in accomplishing that is learning exactly what one must do to survive. To that end, one must know the enemy's purpose before adopting a strategy to undermine it. Prison is designed to break one's spirit and destroy one's resolve. To do this the authorities attempt to exploit every weakness, demolish every initiative, negate all signs of individuality – all with the idea of stamping out that spark that makes each of us human and each of us who we are.

Nelson Mandela (1994: 340–1)

On Robben Island there is a dazzling, white-walled quarry where Nelson Mandela and his political comrades broke stone that had no destiny. Its purpose was to serve the apartheid state's determination to 'break spirits' and 'destroy resolve'. Yet, in the fierce heat and sun's glare, the men used the quarry as an outdoor classroom to exchange ideas, consolidate knowledge and strengthen resistance. A place of hard labour, its objective submission, was reversed. This joint enterprise – political, educational, social – was in stark contrast to the individualised, silent and despairing form of incarceration described above.

Reflecting on his near-death incarceration in the H-Blocks of Long Kesh, Laurence McKeown rises above the pain and suffering he endured to reflect on a 'major lesson learned' – 'that if we stand together, no one can defeat us, whether it's in jail or the outside'. Imprisoned at the height of the conflict in the north of Ireland, a survivor of the hunger strikes, he considers his 'jail experience' as a period when he gained 'self-confidence, educating myself and getting a completely new value system, not only in terms of looking upon yourself but also how you looked upon other people, how you treated other people'. Like Mandela, Laurence McKeown identified the importance of transferring a 'lifetime's learning ... from the jail community to the wider community outside'. Freedom was not simply about release from jail, but 'people's advancement on a personal and collective level'.

The fundamental distinction between those imprisoned as individuals ascribed the label 'criminal' and those imprisoned in the context of a political movement is the strength of the collective and its defiance of the personalisation of punishment. In 1972 Long Kesh, previously a Royal Air Force camp in the north of Ireland, was established as an internment camp for Republicans detained without trial. For three years internees endured its harsh regime until, following international condemnation, internment as such ended. Long Kesh was renamed HMP Maze and those convicted of conflict-related offences were incarcerated under 'special category' status. Under this status political prisoners were accommodated in blocks according to political affiliation. As political prisoners, they did not recognise the regular prison regime, its hierarchy, its clothes, its work, its normal functions or its channels of communication.

Special category status ended in 1976 when those convicted of any offence, regardless of motive or affiliation, were reclassified as criminals. This process, criminalisation, imposed on political prisoners the routine penal regime, including prison clothes, work and authority. Accommodated in one-storey H-Blocks on the Long Kesh site, prisoners began a sustained campaign of resistance in which they were held in bare cells, naked except for a blanket. In 1978 they embarked on a 'no-wash' protest that lasted for three years. This led directly to the hunger strikes and the deaths of ten Republican prisoners in 1981. The impact of the no-wash protest and the painful deaths of the hungers strikers on British policy, military intervention, 'special powers' and policing in the north of Ireland remains contested terrain. What is not contested, however, is the strength and solidarity among Republican prisoners, men and women, throughout this period.

In recollecting the past it is tempting to focus on political struggles, particularly those of direct conflict and engagement, only in terms that are glorious and heroic. The strength and solidarity that bind young men and women together in pursuit of a just cause is remarkable and uplifting. What can be lost, however, are the deeply personal experiences of imprisonment; the infliction of suffering on close family, the fear of dying, the pains of brutality and hunger, the onset of depression and self-doubt. Reading the moving accounts of Republican women prisoners strip-searched in Armagh Jail and, later, beaten in Maghaberry Prison, the emotional and physical battering was not lessened by being shared. Their immediate control over their destiny was no greater because solidarity prevailed within and without the prison. Only those some distance from the personal hurt would suggest that in such life-threatening conditions prisoners have 'agency', making 'choices' to conform or resist. In fact, that was Prime Minister Margaret Thatcher's response when confronted with her government's policy of non-negotiation that led directly to the fatal hunger strikes.

Despite the intensity of personal suffering and loss, however, collective resistance to political imprisonment in the north of Ireland became the bedrock for resistance beyond the prison walls and the emergence of cultural renewal within Republican and Nationalist communities. It was not committed solely to removing British rule and progressing towards a united Ireland, to ending special powers and the military presence on the streets. It also projected the revival of Irish heritage and, at its core, the Irish language. What follows in this carefully researched and engaging book is the inside story of the Irish-language revival, told particularly through the reflections of those imprisoned during the contemporary struggle. It explores the dialectical relationship between the dynamics of political incarceration and resistance, and the impact and consequences of those dynamics within communities. While imprisonment has specific consequences for families and loved ones, it also has generic implications for communities. It is difficult to separate political impact, particularly at a micro level – what Michael Ignatieff refers to as the 'narcissism of minor difference' – and the emotional, profound impact on the lives and experiences of the men, women and children whose loved ones were imprisoned.

What becomes clear in reading the moving testimonies within these pages is the significance of the Irish language in developing methods and techniques of opposition within the prison, but also how it came to underpin the raising of political consciousness and cultural identity within communities. The relationship drawn readily between prison and community often focuses solely on the physical distinction between inside and outside, between captivity and freedom. Yet in the north of Ireland the territorial restrictions imposed on place, space and opportunity simply by the ascription of cultural identity created communities as virtual prisons – boundaries drawn, flagged on lamp-posts and painted on walls. Reversing the prison metaphor, the jail became the community, the resistance to the special regulatory powers of the prison inside matched by resistance to the special regulatory powers outside. It was, and remains, a dialectical discourse of defiance, but, as Laurence McKeown lucidly puts it in the above quote, the 'lifetime's learning' of prisoners' collective 'jail experience' was 'transferred outside'.

In chronicling those collective experiences, Feargal Mac Ionnrachtaigh utilises his unique, privileged position as an insider within the community and within the Irish-language revival, alongside his personal experiences of those close to him having experienced political imprisonment, including internment. The loss of his brother, Terry, murdered in 1998 by Loyalist paramilitaries, is further demonstration of the proximity of his life to death. This enables the story to be told as an insider, as a researcher whose personal understanding and political consciousness has been forged in the crucible of identity, conflict and hope. 'Being there' or 'bearing witness' includes his direct participation as a first-generation school student attending one of the pioneering Irish-medium primary schools in the north of Ireland and the first Irish-medium secondary school. Inevitably, therefore, the Irish-language narrators – political prisoners and political activists – on whose stories this book draws show Feargal Mac Ionnrachtaigh due respect in trusting him with their narratives.

However, authoritative scholarship is not only about fine storytelling. It demands rigorous contextual and structural analysis. The great achievement of this work is that it recognises personal sacrifice and the pain of confinement endured by political prisoners as individuals, locating the collective narratives within their defining contexts. While class and gender are implicit throughout, the ever present context is that of colonial rule – manifested in the dynamics and sectarianism that partitioned six of Ulster's nine counties to redraw the political boundary and create 'Northern Ireland' bordering the 'Irish Free State'. The legacy of colonisation post-partition is central to Feargal Mac Ionnrachtaigh's analysis and wider empirical project. The contemporary conflict is a manifestation of resistance to the perpetuation of the colonial imperative and the politics of decolonisation both above and beneath the surface.

It is a work of integrity, insight and reflection. The author maps the continuing story of the Irish-language revival from prison cell to community classroom. For those who gave their time to his analysis, whose personal sacrifices often remain untold, and whose endurance has contributed more to lasting change than they will witness in their lifetimes, what follows captures their experiences for all time. This is the fulfilment of what the German feminist Frigga Haug identified as collective 'memory work' through which personal struggle is recognised in its contribution to political resistance and change. Collectively it contributes to a defining debate of our time – the profound relationships between cultural identity, language revival and political transition.

As Feargal Mac Ionnrachtaigh's in-depth research demonstrates, the consolidation and expansion of the Irish language in Ireland's north is an important element within the political transformation of a society emerging from war, particularly its association with national identity. Yet the population of Ireland's six northern counties, historically and contemporaneously, is diverse. Language and nationalism should not be used as conduits towards exclusionism. As Frantz Fanon concluded, post-colonialism should be 'enriched and deepened by a rapid transformation into a consciousness of social and political needs, in other words into humanism'. It should challenge 'national consciousness' trapped by 'sterile formalism'. For, the 'living expression of the nation is the moving consciousness of the whole of the people ... the coherent, enlightened action of men and women'. Only then is there potential to move beyond shadows cast by prison walls and communities defined by inherited boundaries.

Belfast / Béal Feirste
February 2012

# Introduction

If you assume that there is no hope, you guarantee that there will be no hope. If you assume that there is an instinct for freedom, that there are opportunities to change things, then there is a possibility that you can contribute to making a better world. That's your choice.

– Noam Chomsky (1999: 6)

*Ripples of bright winter sunshine broke through dark stacks of rain-laden clouds, as the sharp wind howled up the Whiterock, nipping his face and fingertips as it rattled the shutters of the off-licence behind where he and his Ma stood shivering at the makeshift bus stop. They were always the first there, as their home in Dermott Hill was the closest; a stone's throw in the same direction as the wintry wind that blew up the crossroads of the Whiterock and Springfield Roads. Well, the closest that is, apart from the Kellys directly opposite, who still always managed to be the last to trundle down for the bus, where a patrol of heavily armed British soldiers would be hunkered on one knee among the gateways and available nooks and crevices at the top of the junction.*

*As they glared cock-eyed through the scopes of their SLRs, swarms of helicopters buzzed noisily overhead, blocking out the howling wind, as they droned in and out incessantly over Black mountain to Whiterock base, which was right beside his house and the biggest in the six counties, or so his Ma complained as the slates shook on the roof with every passing chopper. Sometimes, the Brits harassed the parents who waited with their kids for the bus, with special attention reserved for any who had been inside, like his Dad. They'd picked on him a few times, taking him from the small group and searching him with his back turned spread eagled against the graffiti-covered shutters of the off-licence. Mostly, however, especially in the frequent lashing rain, the Brits would just ignore them and they gladly returned the favour. On all four corners of the horizon, heavily fortified barracks emerged from the dense warren of streets where the community of west Belfast's Upper Springfield area lived. And the communications post at the summit of Divis Mountain, taller than the Black Mountain itself, stood sentinel over the city.*

1

*His teeth chattering and his shoulders crunched up to his ears, he watched as the lollipop man helped the throngs of children from St Aidan's cross over at the Spar directly facing them. As they entered the gates, he recognised the familiar uniform his three older brothers had worn. The youngest in the family, he had the opportunity, however, to attend 'the Irish school'. The other lads in Dermott Hill all went to the biggest local primary school, Holy Trinity in Turf Lodge. They would often wave out as they passed him at the top of the rock in their 'private school taxis'. As his schoolmates arrived with their parents, the children, impatient at the delay of the bus, broke ranks to hurdle jump the concrete blocks outside the off-licence, a task made more difficult by several layers of cumbersome clothing. In the icy air, he could hear the parents' frosty-breathed curses: 'There must be checkpoints ... a bomb-scare ... maybe even a loyalist attack?'. Inwardly, he hoped the bus wouldn't make it across from Ardoyne in the north of the city. This happened a good few times and meant one of two things. Since the parents had no access to cars for the three mile school trip to the Shaw's Road, they could either pay for a couple of private taxis (a luxury they could rarely afford) or he would get the day off.*

*Before his imagination could wander any further, he caught a distant glimpse of their huge red and white bus, ambling up past the Whiterock library. Because they had been provided with a standard city bus, there would often be a 'false alarm', as their bus could easily be confused with the local Turf Lodge bus that passed the same route just before 9 a.m. Once it passed the library, however, those with decent eyesight could easily decipher its block capital inscription: 'SPECIAL BUS'. On a few occasions, his friends from Dermott Hill had been passing in their private taxis as he stepped onto the bus. They had the best of craic upon reading its inscription. 'Do you go to a handicapped school?' they would joke when they played in the street later in the evening. When he explained that he went to 'the Irish school', they would irritate him by asking him to 'say something in Irish'.*

*Sometimes he had his doubts and wondered would it have been handier for him in the English school like his mates and his older brothers. His Ma always reminded him, however, that he was lucky to have an opportunity denied to so many others. He would be fluent in the native language 'taken from the Irish people over many hundreds of years'. His Da reassured him that he would have many advantages; he would be bilingual and part of a new generation of fluent speakers and activists who would shape the future. Kids who went to 'the Irish school' were special.*

*As the pneumatic doors of the bus hissed closed behind him, the relentless din of the helicopters and the wind's sharp wintry lick quickly melted as one of the volunteer parents directed them to the empty seats in the middle of the bus, which was now packed with children from across north and west Belfast. As he sat down on the cold hard seat, he had already forgotten about his wish for a day off and was looking forward to seeing his mates in class. He loved his school and understood that he and his mates were part of something special.*

While this book focuses primarily on the Irish language, it is not strictly a 'language book', but rather a book about people, their own history and their contribution to the Irish-language revival in the north of Ireland.[1] It aims to relate the untold story of the truly groundbreaking linguistic and educational developments that took place among republican prisoners, who taught themselves and spoke the Irish language as a means of struggle in Long Kesh prison from 1972 to 2000.[2] Significantly, it also assesses the rejuvenating impact that this struggle has had on the cultural revival beyond the prison walls. While many activists and participants in the contemporary Irish-language revival, as well as interested commentators and academics, will be aware of the link between republican political prisoners and the language revival in the north of Ireland, the details of the tale have been conspicuously absent from both popular and political narratives and 'official histories' alike. The actual story itself, including its intricacies, context, course and impact, forms the basis of the pages that follow.

This book employs a narrator-centred approach to chart the 'inside story' of the revival, utilising unprecedented and original interviews with the key protagonists to these historic developments. By allowing activists and participants to 'tell their own story', this book seeks to make sense of the relationship between the prison struggle and the language revival in the outside communities. This relationship helps explain the consequent growth and increased radicalism which the cultural revival experienced in the post-Irish-hunger-strike period. In effect, the two narratives are intertwined, in order to define and highlight the demonstrable link between the prison struggle and the community revival. Consequently, this book both answers and echoes Fran Buntman's (2003: 7) call in her study of prisoner resistance in South Africa's Robben Island, in which she extended a crucial question beyond the South African context: 'How did incarceration in political prisons affect liberation struggles, social movements, and the actors within them?' Similarly then, the research recounted in this book 'is less an intervention into an established academic discourse than' a contribution towards and 'an argument for the opening up of such an arena of research and analysis' (ibid.).

Therefore in researching this story I sought to evaluate how and why republican prisoners utilised the Irish language in Long Kesh and what role this played in prisoner resistance and the development of the overall republican prison community. What motivated defenceless and brutalised young prisoners, confined all day in a cell covered with their own excrement and with only a blanket for clothes, both to learn and to utilise the Irish language as a means of struggle? Similarly, what inspired unemployed parents in deprived working-class nationalist areas under British military siege to send their children to an Irish school as opposed to the safer option of the local English-medium primary, with the additional effort and activism this involved? Did the post-hunger-strike period witness a shift in growth and in radicalism in this community language revival and how best can it be understood? What legacy does this period have for the contemporary Irish-language movement and its future development? What ideological, political and sociological factors adequately inform our understanding of these processes? These research questions provide the basis and framework for the discussion, focused historical narratives and political analysis that follows.

Although this book began as research in an academic institution, I realised from the outset, that 'people researching and writing about social matters are inevitably influenced in the way they perceive them, as well as ... by their own social experiences and values and political commitments' (Fairclough 2001: 4). Consequently, as will be explored in more depth in the autobiographical section that follows, I write not as a detached academic researcher or 'professional' historian, if there can ever be such a thing, but rather as an Irish-language activist and human product of the story of community revival that I undertake to recount and evaluate. Nevertheless, my commitment to the language revival and the process of cultural decolonisation does not mean that 'I am writing political propaganda', because 'the scientific investigation of social matters is perfectly compatible with committed and "opinionated" investigators (there are no others!), and being committed does not excuse you from arguing rationally or producing evidence for your statements' (ibid.).

Moreover, because the narrators viewed me as an 'insider' and both a 'participant' in and a 'product' of their historical endeavour, I gained access to and won the trust of a notoriously tight-knit grouping – the republican ex-prisoner community. This permitted access to the human stories of those who could reveal what 'being there' was actually like for prisoners learning, developing and struggling in often severely oppressive conditions. Using the words of those who were central to these developments, as well as some of their many beneficiaries, this book explores what inspired them both practically and ideologically to think and act as they did in the circumstances and thereafter. Although it was and is undoubtedly my personal responsibility to construct this research and bring the history and analysis of this book to fruition, it is because I view myself as a product of these activists' ingenuity that I would prefer to describe my role as that of a facilitator in our collective historical project.

## LOCATING MYSELF IN THE RESEARCH

It would not be possible for me to explain how I actually conducted the research for this book and negotiated personal access to the testimonies of the narrators without briefly sketching my own autobiographical links to the research story. Born in west Belfast in May 1981, during the Irish hunger strikes – in many ways both the central location and the fateful year in the story and in the Irish-language revival in the north of Ireland for that matter – I was very much raised into a resurgent 'community in resistance'. I was brought up in Dermott Hill which is one of the numerous housing estates to make up the Upper Springfield area, and both my parents were actively involved, throughout my childhood and adolescent years, in a wide range of community campaigns and initiatives aimed at improving the quality of life for local residents. This included campaigns around women, prisoners, children and young people, housing, the Irish language, the environment and urban regeneration.

My father Terry Enright, one of the narrators in the research, learned his Irish while interned without trial in the cages of Long Kesh from 1973 to 1975. He and my mother, Mary, played an active role in the anti-H-Block movement in the years preceding and during the period of my birth. Both were founder members of the RAC

(Relatives' Action Committee) formed in the late 1970s by families of political prisoners to campaign for the right to political status. It was the catalyst for the hunger strike movement and was eventually renamed the National Anti-H-Block Committee (see Beresford 1987 and O'Hearn 2006). Thus from the earliest possible stage, I had made the link between the learning of Irish, community activism and the Long Kesh prison struggle.

My parents were adamant that I, the youngest of four brothers, should attend the north's first Irish-medium school, Bunscoil Phobal Feirste, in Belfast's Shaw's Road Urban Gaeltacht. Although the school was founded in 1971, it only opened its doors as a nursery school to children from English-speaking families in 1978 (Ní Phóilin 1998: 12), which meant that my two oldest brothers, Terry and Liam, who were born in 1969 and 1970 respectively, never had the opportunity to be educated through the medium of Irish.

My parents registered Niall, who was born in 1977, for the nursery school. However, he suffered anxiety attachment after being separated from my mother after her arrest at an anti-strip search protest outside Armagh Women's prison. For practical purposes, this anxiety prevented my mother from sending him on the bus to the Shaw's Road school and meant that the local St Aidan's was more suitable. This increased my mother's determination that I should go to 'the Irish school', and my registration actually pre-dated my birth. While based on the right to be educated in my native language, this determination also drew strongly from a political conviction that this new school represented a community-based manifestation of decolonising resistance worth supporting and promoting.

Although one of many children from across Belfast to attend the school in the mid eighties, I nonetheless understood that I was part of a unique revivalist project. Buses from across the city left each morning for the school and the north Belfast bus collected the dozen or so children from my own area at the top of the Whiterock Road. Notably in this period, the Upper Springfield area, like other northern working-class communities, was in the throes of a relentless political and military conflict. In these circumstances, sending their children to an Irish school took inordinate parental courage and commitment.

Many mornings, the school bus never made it across the city to collect us at our makeshift bus stop. The various reasons included military checkpoints, hijackings, loyalist attacks, and bomb scares or military operations. Whenever they could afford it, our parents, who were often unemployed, would then pay for private taxis from local firms to take us on the three-mile trip. In addition, parents usually worked voluntarily on the school buses and sat on the school committee, which invariably meant spending many evenings fundraising for the school project, including our travel arrangements. Therefore, while the Irish-language revival itself undoubtedly owes a great deal of gratitude to the unswerving diligence of these parents, so too does this book, which I would never have undertaken to research and write had it not been for my involvement in this unique venture.

My secondary schooling had a similar and yet even greater formative impact on my development as a person. In the second year of its opening in 1992, I attended Meánscoil Feirste, the north's first Irish-medium secondary school. The school was based upstairs in an old Presbyterian church on the Falls Road, which Irish-language activists had recently acquired and transformed into a cultural centre, renaming it Cultúrlann MacAdam Ó Fiaich. Many felt, even some from within the Irish-language community, that with only nine pupils in its first year and a hostile conservative government in power in Britain, the school was doomed from the outset to fail in its quest for recognition. However, it was precisely this element of 'struggle', which had been mentioned by the vice-principal at the open night, that attracted me to the school when many of my friends had chosen seemingly more 'prestigious' grammar schools.

With only 16 enrolling in my year, there was a definite feeling that all of us were part of the ensuing campaign for school recognition, parity of esteem for the Irish language, and equality for the nationalist community. In my first year as a pupil, I represented the school campaigning delegation that met the British Department of Education on the issue of recognition. I spoke Irish and had my comments translated by my teacher. It was then that I witnessed at first hand the blatant intransigence of neocolonial British administration intent on obstructing Irish-medium education. This had a massive impact on my views, personal development and determination to be part of the Irish-language revival in the following years. Our campaign to achieve recognition for the school eventually succeeded in 1996, following a national and international campaign, in which it became an issue of 'parity of esteem' for the nationalist community in the north during the peace process (O'Reilly 1999: 132–3).[3]

As the revival expanded outside the school gates, so too did my knowledge of it and how I linked it to my growing political awareness. The demonstrable link between the prison struggle and language revival remained clear to me, as the relatives of many of my classmates, including parents, either had been or were at the time in prison. In addition, a few of my most influential teachers were ex-prisoners who had learned their Irish in Long Kesh and qualified as teachers upon their release from prison before coming to work in the school.

I remained at Meánscoil Feirste, completing my A levels. It was in this period that the tragic interface of social, political and ultimately personal struggle touched my own family. On 11 January 1998 my eldest brother, Terry óg Enright, a community youth worker in Belfast of some repute, was murdered in Belfast city centre by 'loyalist' paramilitaries. His murder triggered a huge swathe of emotion among the young people and colleagues with whom he had built a relationship, and an estimated crowd of 10,000 people attended the funeral (see McKittrick et al. 1999, De Baróid 2000). Terry óg's life and the legacy of his murder, as well as the public expression of solidarity, identity and community togetherness in its aftermath, indelibly shaped my own personal and political journey. It drove my willing commitment to form a better understanding of the processes of historic injustices and structural inequality that both define and impinge on the daily lives of those on the downside of power relations, like the people of the Upper Springfield. Ultimately, it provided an additional impetus that would inspire my involvement in grassroots community empowerment projects that centred on the Irish-language revival.

In my final school years, I built a close rapport with many teachers, who are included as narrators in the research. In terms of our collective history, I had become aware of their fascinating and extremely significant personal stories. I had also consciously linked this to the huge advances in my own area of the Upper Springfield where there were now two Irish-medium primary schools that some of my nieces had begun to attend, Bunscoil an tSléibhe Dhuibh and Gaelscoil na Móna. In a ten-year period, language activists, again with ex-prisoners and ordinary parents amongst them, had completely transformed the area. In contrast with the makeshift bus stop at the top of the rock where a dozen of us had stood before travelling to the Shaw's Road, now two burgeoning Irish schools were so popular that numbers in some local English-language primaries had begun to drop significantly. The inspiration and contributing factors behind this growth interested me greatly and continued to do so as I learned more about the contemporary language revival, while becoming involved in local activism, teaching Irish classes and helping to organise cultural events, etc.

In August 1999, just prior to my enrolment in Queen's University as an undergraduate studying Irish and Celtic Studies and Modern History, I took part in a weekend crash training course for Irish teachers in the Donegal Gaeltacht area of Gaoth Dobhair. There were a number of teachers there from the republican ex-prisoners' Irish-language group Cumann na Fuiseoige, some of whom had just been released from Long Kesh. These ex-prisoners shared a commitment to the Irish-language revival and represented the various time periods in Long Kesh prison history, from the cages[4] and blanket protest to the Irish-speaking wing, Gaeltacht na Fuiseoige, in the prison's final years. Having made contact with these activists and shown a keen interest in their stories, I decided that, in the future, I would pursue their story further through research and explore how much it overlapped with the story of our language revival.

When this opportunity eventually came along, while I was working as a postgraduate researcher at Queen's, I knew from the outset that negotiating access to these activists would not be a problem considering my own background. In the first instance, the fact that my father was a political ex-prisoner and that both he and my mother were well-known community activists in west Belfast meant that my English surname 'Enright' would be recognisable to many of those I intended interviewing. Secondly, the fact that I was effectively an 'insider' when it came to the Irish-language community and considered 'one of their own' due to my Irish-language activism eroded any suspicions that I might distort or do a disservice to their historic testimonies. The fact that political ex-prisoners are structurally discriminated against in the north of Ireland in terms of employment, etc., means that they don't readily admit to or disclose their pasts to 'outsiders' (see Shirlow et al. 2010). Whereas to 'insiders' and members of their own community, their status as former political prisoners is very much considered a 'badge of honour' and something worth recounting for the purposes of historical inquiry or community education.

During this period, I had also just been trained as a part-time guide for political tours of west Belfast by Coiste na n-Iarchimí, the umbrella organisation for republican ex-prisoners. The organisation's tour programme trained a number of young people who had a good knowledge of Irish history and whose parents were political ex-prisoners, and I and a few others from my former school were suitable for that role. This further increased my status as that of an 'insider' and decreased any chance of ex-prisoners being suspicious of the research and thus reluctant to co-operate with it.

One example of this was how I avoided the 'waiting list' criteria for interviewers; due to the sheer volume of researchers from all over the world contacting Coiste seeking interviews with staff and other political ex-prisoners, they were compelled to place applications on a waiting list and place restrictions on the length of taped interviews allowed. My research, on the other hand, was exempt from such criteria and I was fully accommodated throughout, when requesting interviews and contact numbers, etc. This process culminated in in-depth semi-structured and unstructured interviews conducted with 45 different narrators. This group comprised 38 political ex-prisoners and eight language activists who were never imprisoned; this is stressed because all the participants interviewed could warrant the title 'language activist'. If the narrator was more comfortable doing the interview in Irish as their spoken language of choice, then the interview was conducted in Gaeilge. Those activists interviewed were: Eddie Keenan, Willie-John McCorry, Liam Ó Stiobhaird, Billy Kelly, Larry McGurk, Jim McCann, Eibhlín Collins (née Brady), Francie Brolly, Terry Enright, Séanna Breathnach, Daithí Mac Adhaimh, Diarmuid Mac an tSionnaigh, Cyril Mac Curtain, Jake Mac Siacais, Caoimhín Corbett, Seán Mag Uidhir, Liam Ó Maolchluiche, Donncha Mac Niallais, Eoghan Mac Cormaic, Dr Laurence McKeown, Máirtín Ó Maolmhuaidh, Dr Ciarán Dawson, Antóin De Brún, Peadar Ó Cuinneagáin, Garaí Mac Roibeáird, Pádraic McCotter, Pilib Ó Ruanaí, Michael Liggott, Michael Culbert, Caoimhín Mac Mathúna, Marcas Mac Ruairí, Seán Ó Loingsigh, Dr Déaglán Ó Mochain, Mícheál Mac Giolla Ghunna, Rosa Mac Lochlainn, Jamesey Ó Muireagáin, Rosie McCorley, Dr Feilim Ó hAdhmaill, Seamás Mac Seáin, Pádraig Ó Maolchraoibhe, Aodán Mac Póilin, Máirtín Ó Muilleoir, Bairbre De Brún, Jim Herron, Eoghan Ó Néill and Ciarán Mac Giolla Bhéin (biographies can be found at the end of the book).

In each case, my being an 'insider' meant that participants were very comfortable divulging their personal stories. That trust was mutual and usually culminated in lasting contacts and friendships with these activists, many of whom I would subsequently get to know a great deal better, often while working together in different Irish-language projects or campaigns. This book's core findings draw primarily from these interviews, as well as relevant primary and secondary sources, including archival material gathered from newspapers and periodicals, and the personal letters of participants.

Thematic and chronological considerations informed the choices of these narrators. The interviews began with a number of very prominent activists who were central to the development of the Irish language in the prison and its revival on the outside. Frequent use was made of 'snowballing', whereby one participant suggested the input of others, thus widening the research (Buntman 2003: 296). This process greatly enhanced the source base, augmenting the range, depth and detail of the narratives, and resulting in many more interviews than originally anticipated. For example, it led to the examination of the prison struggle across different areas and time periods from 1973 to 2000. These areas specifically include north, west and south-east Belfast as well as Derry City, and regions in counties Down, Tyrone and Fermanagh.

Interestingly, I also gained invaluable historical material for posterity through interviews with veteran prisoners from the 1940s and 50s – three of these activists, Willie John McCorry, Eddie Keenan and Billy Kelly have since died. In addition to the male ex-prisoners from Long Kesh, I interviewed three female political ex-prisoners about their time in Armagh and Maghaberry and subsequent language activism, and though I decided that a more detailed study of these prisons was firmly beyond the scope of this book, their personal narratives and contributions to the revival are as valuable as any other and thus merit inclusion.

Significantly, none of the participants requested any kind of anonymity and all wished to be identified with the study and by extension the Irish-language revival in the six counties. Fortunately, this corresponded with my own preferred approach, which is to acknowledge sources of history and their key roles as shapers of political events. For as Buntman (2003: 11) states, 'politics and history are not made up of inconsequential and amorphous masses, and the experiences, values, opinions, and contributions of individual human beings count'. Crucially, however, this isn't to emphasise the 'individual' over the historical–structural processes or social, political and economic determinants, but rather to recognise 'human agency' and the ability of 'social beings' to interpret, evaluate and recount their real-life experiences in accordance with 'being there' during particular historical events (Scraton 2007: 5).

## RESEARCH IN CONTEXT

> For the native, objectivity is always directed against him.
> Frantz Fanon (1961: 61)

> Washing one's hands of the conflict between the powerful and the powerless means to side with the powerful, not to be neutral.
> Paulo Freire (2005: 35)

When I began to research the history covered in this book, although initially unaware of the political, theoretical and ideological rationale of my position, it was clear to me that the 'facts' of the interrelated research stories and the accounts of the narrators couldn't possibly be understood in isolation from wider historical and structural context. Therefore, only when I began unravelling the relevant historical, politico-economic and sociocultural structures did the oral history I was gathering begin to make sense. I therefore found myself drawn towards a critical social research model which sought a greater understanding of what Scraton and Chadwick (2001) termed the 'primary determining contexts' that conditioned our daily lives. These were identified as advanced capitalism, patriarchy, neocolonialism and adulthood, wherein lay the basis for the material inequalities of class, gender, sexuality, race, sectarianism and age. According to this analytical framework, research, history and knowledge 'and its processes of definition, acquisition and transmission, cannot be separated from the determinants of "existing sets of social relations"' (Scraton 2007: 9).

The suitability of this social research model lay in the intermingling of the 'personal', the 'social' and the 'structural' in a way that engages with 'the material world, its history, its ideologies, its political economy, its institutional arrangements and its structural relations' (ibid.), irrespective of the specific area or epoch. The fact that this book bases its findings on the narratives of its participants, both prisoners and language activists, is further in keeping with the oppositionalist approach of critical social research which 'seeks out, records and champions the "view from below", ensuring the voices and experiences of those marginalized by institutionalised state practices are heard and represented' (ibid.: 10). In prioritising these previously occluded narratives, this book aims to contribute to 'an insurrection of subjugated knowledge' (Pilger 2006: 13).

These 'hidden voices' are often inaudible, because the 'official histories' of academic and state institutions both produce and consolidate 'formally sanctioned knowledge' that upholds 'the determining contexts of material power relations' (Scraton 2007: 10). Arguably, the greatest difficulty for critical researchers and historians when attempting to give voice to the historical accounts of ordinary people is that 'the discretionary use of institutional power' inhibits and prohibits their projection (ibid.: 11). The rationale behind these attempts to curtail the 'view from below' is undoubtedly seen in the 'selective commissioning or appropriation of knowledge' through which particular 'schools of thought', versions of history and academic perspectives are bestowed with 'credible status by the powerful in the context of a prevailing "politics of truth"'(ibid.).

Critical researchers recognise that knowledge construction is never 'impartial', because the accepted 'truth' is determined by power relations, manufactured within the 'mass media' and 'produced through the political processes of government' (ibid.: 10). The myth that certain forms of cultural and political representation in modern historiography and academic discourses are somehow 'objective' or 'value-free' is comprehensively debunked by critical researchers like Herman and Chomsky (1988). 'Official truths' are not arrived at unknowingly or coincidentally but rather reflect the 'manufacture of consent' the 'system of presuppositions and principles that constitute an elite consensus, a system so powerful as to be internalised largely without awareness' (ibid.: 302). Subsequently, from the outset I recognised 'that "knowledge" ... is neither value-free nor value-neutral' but 'is derived and reproduced, historically and contemporaneously, in the structural relations of inequality and oppression that characterise established social orders' (Scraton and Chadwick 2001: 72).

Therefore, the question is not 'whether we take sides', because this is unavoidable, but rather, 'Whose side are we on?' (Becker 1967). Given the structural inequalities forged by global capitalism and neocolonialism, Hall and Scraton (1981: 465) understood Becker's plea to 'take sides' as a 'clarion call to a more overt radical political commitment, with sociologists and criminologists taking up a clear, "partisan" stance'. Therefore, in confronting mainstream academic claims to 'objectivity', critical research aims to 'challenge propagandist constructions of what is published as "official history"' through pioneering 'alternative interpretations of social and political reality' (Scraton 2007: 4–5). In this context, research must transcend the 'local environments of the individual' and demands a fuller scrutiny of the 'larger structure of social and historical life' (ibid.: 6).

Therefore by privileging the oral history of republican prisoners and grassroots Irish-language activists, this book acknowledges that 'understanding a community or a culture ... means taking seriously their ways of structuring experience, their popular narratives, the distinctive manner in which they frame the social and political realities which affect their lives' (Luke Gibbons, in Cleary 2003: 28). I therefore chose the processes of colonisation in Ireland as the defining context of the research, consciously refuting the Irish revisionist argument that colonialism is 'simply a remote historical phenomenon' and insisting that it continues 'to shape developments in the post-partition periods in both the northern and southern states' and remains 'critical to the development of Irish society' (ibid.: 17).

Ireland's cultural colonisation is thus explored as part of the wider British imperial project that involved military, political, cultural and economic subjugation, which ultimately led to the demise of Irish as Ireland's spoken language in the late nineteenth century. I contend that this antagonistic linguistic policy has continued unabated until the present, merely oscillating between coercion and consent and becoming more veiled and sophisticated in conjunction with the political expediencies of the particular era. I ground this analysis in a wider understanding of cultural shift in colonial and neocolonial contexts and how this corresponds directly with the current consequences of neoliberal globalisation. In this sense, the analysis follows a comparative approach that identifies how 'comparing the histories of colonial societies around the world and their conflicting interpretations within and among cultures expands our political horizons in the present and helps us chart ways to change' (Carroll and King 2003: 15).

To this end, I argue that the consequences of colonisation inspired an ideology of decolonisation and resistance which was a central motivating factor for Irish republican prisoners and by extension for the contemporary Irish-language revival movement in the north of Ireland. The survival and development of this movement, in spite of a hostile six-county unionist regime, are viewed as practical examples of resistance-based language activism. The research also specifically focuses on the prison struggle's transformational impact on the wider 1980s language revival and its continuing legacy in ideologically shaping many regenerative cultural projects and bottom-up grassroots activist initiatives. Although, the historical analysis of this book takes account of how Irish 'social and cultural development' is 'mediated through colonial capitalism' (Cleary

2003: 43), its findings also fulfil another raison d'être: 'to develop a more critical understanding of the various forms of subaltern struggles largely written out of the dominant debates in Irish history' (ibid.: 20).

## PERSONAL AND POLITICAL JOURNEY OF A RESEARCHER

In viewing my close affinity as researcher with the research as that of 'a mutual venture of reciprocal interpersonal exchanges' (Olesen and Whittaker 1967: 274) that precipitated personal transformation and development on my part, I was drawn to the concept of 'reflexivity'. Widely used by feminist researchers, reflexivity explores the journey embarked upon by the researcher during the research period and includes the personal, political and intellectual progression of the researcher in conjunction with the work. Furthermore, my personal identification with the research story saw me arrive at a situation where 'my research interacts with my life, and both it and I myself change and go through different stages of development in parallel as the work progresses' (Greed 1990: 151).

For example, the interviews had a profound impact on me as a researcher. In addition, through 'memory work' the narrators themselves sometimes recovered both raw and proud memories for the first time. For example, on two occasions, participants broke down in tears; in one case recounting the brutality of the 'screws' in exacting 'forced washes' and 'mirror searches' during the blanket protest and secondly when a former prisoner recounted with pride the achievements of the Irish-speaking prison wing, Gaeltacht na Fuiseoige, in the late 1990s. As a researcher and especially as someone located in the research story, I found it impossible to detach myself from the powerful message at the core of these narratives, as Scraton (2007: 11) elucidates: 'It is not feasible, in the heat of such moments, to be free of moral judgement or political conviction.'

Any initial fears about my personal background and attachment to the research story being disadvantageous to the achievement of 'balanced' research was dispelled upon acquainting myself with the writings of critical social researchers and feminist activists. As Scraton posits:

> But the researcher's experiences, values and commitment are not necessarily inhibitions to fact finding, bearing witness or truth telling. If anything, critical research offers analyses of great integrity and honesty. For rather than claiming some mythical

'value-neutrality', or sanitised, controlled environment, critical social researchers position their work, identify themselves and define 'relevance'. (Ibid.)

Therefore, in developing during the research, I found that reflecting on experiences undoubtedly shaped the content of the research questions that were decided upon and the various approaches chosen to obtain answers to those questions (McRobbie 1982). Moreover, both the analysis and direction of this research were often influenced by the narratives of the activists participating in the research. A prime example of this was the fact that many of the political ex-prisoners I interviewed drew my attention to the works of radical Brazilian educationalist Paulo Freire and anti-colonial theorist and liberation fighter Frantz Fanon.

Freire's radical pedagogy espoused liberating those oppressed by colonialism through a process of 'conscientisation' and educational empowerment. Meanwhile Fanon's groundbreaking theses deconstructed the power differentials underscoring colonialism itself, before outlining a radical vision of decolonisation. The writings of both these theorists not only had a central influence on this book and its conclusions, but also played a significant role in my own ideological and political development as an Irish-language activist. These influences inspired a focused involvement on my part in various grassroots language projects and campaigns, both locally and nationally. In the process, the dual developmental role of researcher and researched was clearly evident; a facet which can be seen as a defining feature of critical social research, where '[i]t moves beyond the resources of theory into praxis, recognising the self-as-academic as the self-as-participant' (Scraton 2007: 240).

Despite committing this research to a critical framework, it was also imperative that I adhered to 'intellectual autonomy and independence' (Walters 2003: 166). To do this, I had to ensure that my research could be viewed as valid qualitative research and evidence-based history rather than easily dismissed as 'republican propaganda'. This meant being wary that my close identification with and awareness of the research story and its participants did not lead to my idealising the 'view from below' in an overly simplistic or rhetorical manner. This could be done by viewing the history of the revival uncritically and failing to take account of the inconsistencies and contradictions of given historical events.

It would also be crucial not to exaggerate the roles played by activists who participated in this research and overemphasise their achievements. I was determined to avoid this by displaying the unequivocal honesty and integrity in critical research that is referred to by Chomsky (2004: 49), when he argues that 'those who are seriously interested in understanding the world will adopt the same standards whether they are evaluating their own political and intellectual elites or those of official enemies'. While this is not to suggest that the research narrators in this book constitute 'elites', it is nevertheless to commit this work 'on behalf of those on the downside of power relations' (Hudson 1993: 6–7) to the rigours of Chomsky's plea for intellectual responsibility.

In this sense, my insistence upon colonialism as the defining and overriding context of the book was crucial in articulating a comparative and critical approach. While Irish revisionism and the modernity thesis portray the application of 'a colonial perspective after 1801' as the recuperation of 'a "seven hundred years of oppression" nationalist metanarrative that stymies serious scholarship', (Cleary 2003: 25), I consciously rejected a one-dimensional 'anti-British' narrative by viewing Irish colonialism in the global context of neocolonialism and globalisation. As Cleary points out:

> If colonialism is conceived as a historical process in which societies of various kinds and locations are differentially integrated into a world capitalist system, then it is on the basis of the comparative conjunctural analysis of such processes that debate must ultimately be developed. Cultural analysis has an important role here since it is the decisive area in which social conflicts are experienced, but it is the contradictions of the wider capitalist system that shape those conflicts, whether cultural, political or economic. (Ibid.: 44)

Thus, in exposing the reality of colonialism in Ireland, this research aims to follow Said's (2002) appeal for researchers and 'intellectuals' to become a 'voice in opposition to and critical of great power' in a way that challenges it, 'so that the victim will not, as is often the case, be blamed and real power encouraged to do its will'. Concurrently, by 'bearing witness, gathering testimonies, sharing experiences' and 'garnering the view from below', critical research concerns itself with 'speaking truth to great power' thereby recasting research itself 'as a form of resistance' (Scraton 2007: 239–40).

Therefore in recognising colonialism as context, giving voice to unheard narratives and analysing occluded history, this book is a form of 'resistance' that conforms to the view that the role of researchers is to 'change the world, not only to study it' (Stanley 1990: 15). Furthermore, from a personal perspective, I view this book as a continuation of the journey I began as a child in the early 1980s with a dozen others from my area who travelled to the Shaw's Road school. Similarly, from a political and ideological perspective, I view the research as a conscious response to Máirtín Ó Cadhain's decolonising rallying call; 'Is í athghabháil na Gaeilge, athghabháil na hÉireann agus is í athghabháil na hÉireann, slánú na Gaeilge' ('The reconquest of Irish is the reconquest of Ireland and the reconquest of Ireland is the salvation of Irish') (Ó Cathasaigh 2002: 264). Simultaneously, it is aimed as a tribute to all those who promoted and learned the language against the odds, whether they were Gaelic Leaguers in the 1890s and beyond, stalwarts of the Ardscoil[5] and Cumann Chluain Ard,[6] the innovative founders of the Shaw's Road Urban Gaeltacht, or brutalised, naked and freezing republican political prisoners in Long Kesh prison. In general terms, it is also my contention that this book will yield original historical, sociological, sociolinguistic and political lessons that aid the 'process of dismantling, understanding, and reassembling our key historical artefacts' in order to highlight 'the follies of our past and the pathway to our future' (McEvoy 2001: 359).

## CHAPTER OUTLINE

The above introduction outlines the key research questions underpinning this historical study, charts my own personal location within its story, and summarises the central political rationale of the book. Chapter 1 focuses on presenting the key concepts and ideas that inform the research, focusing on themes such as colonialism, culture, identity, power and resistance.

The following two chapters deal specifically with the relevant Irish historical context. Chapter 2 looks in depth at Ireland's cultural colonisation and the ensuing legacy of resistance and revival up to the early twentieth century. Chapter 3 reviews the retreat of the Irish language under the legislative discrimination employed by the Northern Ireland state and its remarkable survival in a 'hidden Ulster' of language activism until the late 1960s. In addition, a short fourth chapter deals briefly with the context of political imprisonment in Ireland and the role the Irish language has played historically amongst republican political prisoners. Both these historical sections are supplemented with original interview material that consolidates their analyses.

The ensuing three empirical chapters, Chapters 5–7, are based primarily on the first-person narratives of the participators as the essence of the book. These chapters are divided into sub-sections that intertwine the two stories: the learning and usage of the Irish language as a means of development and resistance amongst republican prisoners in Long Kesh, in both the cages and the H-Blocks, from the early 1970s until the mid 1980s; and the grassroots language revival in the nationalist communities outside the prison, culminating after the hunger strike in 1981, and subsequent growth thereafter. The conclusion brings together the theoretical, ideological and political rationale of the book, as well as the key historical contexts of the study, with the central research findings encapsulated in the accounts of the narrators. This is followed by a timely epilogue that explores the legacy and prospective future of decolonising activism in challenging power relations in the north of Ireland, while simultaneously assessing its potential as a vehicle for change in the era of capitalist crisis and economic collapse in the Irish Republic.

# 1
# Colonialism, Culture and Ideology

A little boy about eight years of age, addressed a short sentence in Irish to his sister, but meeting his father's eye, he immediately cowered back, having to all appearance, committed some heinous fault. The man called the child to him, said nothing, but drawing forth from its dress a little stick ... which was suspended by a string around the neck, put an additional notch in it with his penknife. We were told that it was done to prevent the child from speaking Irish; for every time he attempted to do so a new nick was put in his tally, and when these amounted to a certain amount, summary punishment was inflicted on him by the schoolmaster.

Sir William Wilde, on a visit to Ireland in the 1830s (Ó Giolláin 2000: 66)

This section provides an overview of the research story's political rationale, namely, the overriding structural context of colonialism, neocolonialism and decolonisation. It also assesses the pivotal position of language, culture, identity and nationalism within the context of Irish and international minoritised language activism. This understanding of cultural decolonisation emerged during my reflective journey, researching resistance-based activism. As such, the discourse of ideology, power and resistance lies at the very heart of the analysis.

## COLONIALISM, NEOCOLONIALISM AND DECOLONISATION

### Colonialism

The basic legitimation of conquest over native peoples is the conviction of our superiority, not merely our mechanical, economic and military superiority, but our moral superiority. Our dignity rests on that quality, and it underlies our right to direct the rest of humanity.

French Commissar-General Jules Harmond
(O'Dowd 1992: 27)

Ambitions of empire not only directed the English colonial project in Ireland, and indeed globally, but also shaped an ideology of expansionism among other 'technologically superior' western powers. Said (1993: 8) lucidly points out that 'colonialism' is 'almost always a consequence of "imperialism"', forging processes 'in which one state controls the effective political sovereignty of another political society. It can be achieved by force, by political collaboration, by economic, social, or cultural dependence.'

Imperialism represents 'the most powerful force in world history over the last four or five centuries, carving up whole continents while oppressing indigenous peoples and obliterating entire civilizations' (Parenti 1995: 1). More specifically, it fosters a 'process whereby the dominant politico-economic interests of one nation expropriate for their own enrichment the land, labour, raw materials, and markets of another people' (ibid.). Alternatively, in the words of Lenin, imperialism constitutes the 'highest stage of capitalism', where cartels and monopolies, including banks, emerge as the foundations of economic life (Larrain 1989: 63).

Nevertheless, successive empires masked this economic venture in racist terms; this reached its apex with 'the fashionable philosophy of social Darwinism', which misapplied the 'theory of evolution to the development of societies', thereby providing 'a scientific gloss to the scramble for colonies' and bigotry (Curtis 1984: 65). Numerous anti-colonial activists, notably Aimé Césaire, have analysed the human impact of colonialism and the excesses of its implementation, wherein 'millions' were 'skilfully injected with fear, inferiority complexes, trepidation, servility, despair, abasement'. Indeed, as Fanon (1961: 171) illustrates, 'deep in the minds of the natives' colonialism inculcated the belief that their pre-colonial history represented one 'dominated by barbarism'. Similarly, the Kenyan anti-colonial writer Ngugi wa Thiong'o encapsulated this psychological process:

> The real aim of colonialism was to control the people's wealth; what they produced, how they produced it, and how it was distributed; to control, in other words, the entire realm of the language of real life. Colonialism imposed its control of the social production of wealth through military conquest and subsequent political dictatorship. But its most important area of domination was the mental universe of the colonised, the control, through culture, of how people perceived themselves and their relationship to the world. Economic or political control can never be complete without mental control. (Ngugi wa Thiong'o 1997: 16)

This mental subordination is 'unleashed by imperialism' through a 'cultural bomb', which delegitimises native culture, language and identity amongst the colonised, or in the words of 1970s South African black consciousness activist Steve Biko, 'the most potent weapon in the hands of the oppressor was the minds of the oppressed'.

Equally, Freire (1972a: 151) suggests this process only succeeds when 'those invaded become convinced of their intrinsic inferiority ... [and] alienated from the spirit of their own culture and from themselves', to the extent that they 'want to be like the invaders: to walk like them, dress like them, talk like them'. Moreover, in his seminal work on colonial oppression, Alberto Memmi stresses how the assimilative experience of cultural colonisation involved a wholesale transformation on the part of its victims:

> The crushing of the colonized is included among the colonizer's values. As soon as the colonized adopts these values, he similarly adopts his own condemnation. In order to free himself, at least so he believes, he agrees to destroy himself ... just as many people avoid showing off their poor relations, the colonized in the throes of assimilation hides his past, his traditions, in fact all his origins which have become ignominious (Memmi 1965: 165).

The centrality of this assimilative aspect was never more relevant than in those colonies where 'colonised people' found themselves 'face to face with the language of the civilising nation; that is, with the culture of the mother tongue' (Fanon 1970: 14). This manifested itself in imperial education systems, where control of language epitomised the hierarchical power structures of colonialism.

This manifested itself in imperial education systems, where control of language epitomised the power structures of colonialism. Indeed, through its colonial education systems, Britain outstripped 'the other empires in the reach of its ambition, the imperial language was represented as carrying its liberal and decent qualities on to the world stage in order to take its rightful place' (Crowley 1996: 48). To quote Ngugi Wa Thiong'o (1997: 9), 'the physical violence of the battlefield was followed by the psychological violence of the classroom' where language became 'the means of ... spiritual subjugation.' In the 1950s,

> [i]n Kenya, English became more than a language: it became *the* language and all others had to bow before it in deference.

Thus one of the most humiliating experiences was to be caught speaking Gikúyú in the vicinity of the school. The culprit was given corporal punishment – three to five strokes of the cane on bare buttocks – or was made to carry a metal plate around the neck with inscriptions such as I AM STUPID or I AM A DONKEY ... And how did the teachers catch the pupils? A button was initially given to one pupil who was supposed to hand it over to whoever was caught speaking his mother tongue. Whoever had the button at the end of the day would sing who had given it to him and the ensuing process would bring out all the culprits of the day. Thus children were turned into witch-hunters and in the process were being taught the lucrative value of being a traitor to one's immediate community. (Ibid.: 11)

Unsurprisingly, proficiency in English represented the key to personal advancement and 'the measure of intelligence and ability in the arts, the sciences, and all the other branches of learning' (ibid.: 12).

Interestingly, the British had perfected compulsory Anglicisation over 100 years earlier, in their 'first colony', Ireland, drafting 'a blueprint for the consequent models of language and colonialism practised throughout the world' (Crowley 1996: 4). After 1831, the Irish national school system instituted a regime of corporal punishment in school and at home designed to prevent the speaking of Irish. The active involvement of the Irish people not only constituted psychological transformation but also facilitated the wider imperial aim of creating culturally English, indigenous, colonial elites (Anderson 1991: 93).

Conversely, proponents of modernisation emphasise the role played by the Irish themselves as evidence of individual choice over and above the sociocultural and economic context. May (2002: 3–4) criticises such simplistic readings as 'linguistic/cultural social Darwinism', which portrays language loss as an inevitable part of sociolinguistic evolution. Within this analysis, language decline represents the failure of inherently backward and archaic languages, or their speakers, to adapt to the modern world. These views clearly underestimate colonialism. Language loss does not occur in communities of power, wealth and privilege. Moreover, linguistic decline occurs within wider processes of social, cultural and political displacement often involving overt discrimination and suppression (ibid.: 4). Similarly, accounts that emphasise the 'decisions' of the 'individual' take little cognisance of the socio-psychological effects reinforcing cultural shift.

In effect, colonialism instils the belief in its 'victims' that this process is somehow 'natural' or 'legitimate', rather than engineered by the coloniser and unequal power relations. As a result, 'symbolic violence' cultivates complicity and implicit consent, encouraging 'the holders of dominated linguistic competencies to collaborate in the destruction of their [own] instruments of expression' (Bourdieu 1991:45). Predictably then, the colonised attribute greater worth to the 'dominant language', thus internalising the irrelevance of their own language, leading the victims of colonisation, by practical necessity, to become active participants in jettisoning their traditional cultures (May 2002: 310). Antonio Gramsci (1971) defined the manner in which dominant powers oscillate between coercion and consent as 'hegemony'. In analysing 'the spontaneous consent given by the great masses of the population to the general direction imposed on social life by the dominant fundamental group' (ibid.: 12), he challenged the simplistic dichotomy between domination and subordination, positing an alternative 'process of transaction, negotiation and compromise that takes place between ruling and subaltern groups' (ibid.: 10).

Although authoritarian in nature, colonial regimes were also 'interested in co-opting local elites but not in consulting them about policy', thereby excluding 'the bulk of the population from direct participation in the political system' (Gledhill 2000: 76). Interestingly, some commentators view this consensual factor and the positive interpretation of infrastructural modernisation in imperial projects as the 'exculpation of imperialism' (Ó Ceallaigh 1994b: 11). Thus, native elites operated 'oppression from within', while wider imperial processes represented a necessary global expansion that modernised human civilisation (ibid.). Andrew Roberts argues that for 'the vast majority of its half-millennium-long history, the British empire was an exemplary force for good', while John Keegan describes the empire as 'highly benevolent and moralistic' (ibid.: 20). Truly, 'revisionism is all the rage' (Pilger 2006: 18).

Similarly, in a scathing attack on Ken Loach and his Palme d'Or-winning film *The Wind that Shakes the Barley*, the Irish revisionist historian Ruth Dudley Edwards (2006) claimed: '[T]he truth is that, as empires go, the British version was the most responsible and humane of all. With all its deficiencies, it brought much of value to most of the countries it occupied', a sentiment echoed by former British prime minister Gordon Brown, who asserted that 'the days of Britain having to apologise for the British Empire are over. We should celebrate' (Pilger 2006: 20). Clearly, these views ignore the primary economic objective: 'to provide the mother country with cheap food and industrial raw materials rather than to develop an integrated modern economy on metropolitan lines' (Gledhill 2000: 77). Moreover, they represent a 'denial of the historical record' (Pilger 2006: 21), which 'would see Britain's role in the world to a large extent as a story of crimes against humanity' (Curtis 2003: 432).[1]

Therefore, 'the question of interpretation ... as well as historical writing ... is tied to the question of interests' (Said 1993: 114). To analyse relevant literature without examining 'views expressing exculpation of empire' is akin to 'describing a road without its setting in the landscape' (ibid.: 127). Unsurprisingly, Irish revisionism largely questions the validity of the colonial model, labelling it as an 'unwelcome politicisation' (Cleary 2003: 17–18). In other words, 'to assert Ireland is and has been a colony is certainly to deny the legitimacy of British government in Northern Ireland', while simultaneously questioning 'the state and governmental structures that have been institutionalised in the post-colonial Free State and Republic of Ireland' (Lloyd 2003: 48). The colonial model's counterpoint lies in the modernity thesis, which virtually ignores economic and political imperialism and locates Ireland in a 'self-contained western European context' where its own 'traditions' acted 'as a barrier to progress' (Cleary 2003: 20).

The nature of the Tudor, Cromwellian and Williamite conquests, with their associated land confiscations, dispossessions, resettlements and wholesale destruction of the native Gaelic society, means that few historians dispute the terminology of colonialism for this period. However, many analysts mistakenly replace the colonial model with a modernisation thesis after the Act of Union (1801), considering Ireland a politico-economic subunit of the United Kingdom. This analysis underplays a nineteenth-century history of forced mass emigration in the wake of a demographic disaster unparalleled in contemporary western Europe – the Great Hunger (Cleary 2003: 40).

Similarly, Whyte takes issue with Aughey's (1989) argument that the historical remoteness of Plantation and Ireland's non-colonial position under the Union, stating that

settlers from England and Scotland did come over in the seventeenth century and settle in much the same manner as their compatriots were settling in America. No one has thought to call the American settlements anything other than colonies ...

The fact that Northern Ireland is legally not a colony, but part of the United Kingdom, does not destroy the analogy; Algeria was legally part of France, and Angola and Mozambique were legally part of Portugal, but that did not stop the French and Portuguese from eventually treating them as expendable. (Whyte 1990: 178)

Northern Ireland, created by partition in 1920, spawned a settler–colonial entity in which 'boundaries were chosen to ensure a permanent Protestant majority', meaning that 'minority rights were not guaranteed and there was no possibility of alternation in office' (Clayton 1998: 50–1). In addition, the settler–colonial ideology 'arises from the need to defend interests; the fear of change; and the intransigence of fixed positions' necessitating the exclusion of the 'natives' from potential power or influence' (ibid.).

Therefore, many scholarly objections to Ireland's colonial status are analytically restrictive, ignoring wider structural realities, as they 'assume that there is such a thing as a typical colony and a standard or one-size-fits-all colonial experience against which Ireland's claims might be measured' (Cleary 2003: 31). Instead, it is necessary to interpret specific national contexts as 'the product of dislocating intersections between local and global processes that are not simply random but part of the internally contradictory structure of the modern capitalist world system' (ibid.: 45). Moreover, the heated nature of the controversy demonstrates that Ireland's colonial status 'is no antiquarian or academic squabble' (Said 2003: 177). Rather, it underpins the 'whole question of Irish identity, the present course of Irish culture and politics, and above all, the interpretation of Ireland, its people, and the course of its history' (ibid.).

## Neocolonialism

The neo-colonialism of today represents imperialism in its final and perhaps most dangerous phase and is also the worst form of imperialism. For those who practise it, it means power without responsibility and for those who suffer from it, it means exploitation without redress.

Kwame Nkrumah (1965: ix)

The term 'neocolonialism' defines the economic exploitation that former colonies endure after independence, a phenomenon that has reached an acute form under neoliberal globalisation. Western powers like Britain and France adopted neocolonialism as a strategy after the Second World War, when, bankrupt and fatigued dealing with intense popular anti-colonial resistance, they grudgingly opted for indirect economic hegemony over blatant colonial rule (Parenti 1995: 8). This entailed granting the symbolism of 'independence', while maintaining control of profitable resources. This process was formally known as 'decolonisation', arguably a 'misleading term', implying 'that Britain voluntarily gave up formal control over its colonies, when the reality was that it was forced out of many' (Curtis 2003: 236). Nevertheless, 'decolonisation' ensured that 'independent' countries 'continued to allow British companies to exploit their economic resources' (ibid.).[2]

For the imperial powers, neocolonialism had two principal advantages. Firstly, 'the removal of a conspicuously intrusive colonial rule made it more difficult for nationalist elements within the previously colonized countries to mobilize anti-imperialist sentiments' (Parenti 1995: 8). More crucially, the native government's new administrative responsibility meant that imperialist interests were 'free to concentrate on accumulating capital – which is all they really want to do' (ibid.). According to Ghanaian intellectual and anti-colonial activist Kwame Nkrumah:

> Neocolonialism is a greater danger to independent countries than is colonialism. Colonialism is crude, essentially overt, and apt to be overcome by a purposeful concert of national effort. In neocolonialism, however, the people are divided from their leaders and, instead of providing true leadership and guidance which is informed at every point by the ideal of the general welfare, leaders come to neglect the very people who put them in power and incautiously become instruments of suppression on behalf of the neocolonialists. (Nkrumah 1964: 101)

Fanon (1961) named this grouping the 'nationalist bourgeoisie', who supported the cross-class 'national liberation struggle' only to lead an indigenous replica of the exploitative colonial regime. This led to a continuing legacy of resistance by 'working people, peasantry and proletariat' against the new 'flag-waving native ruling classes' whom they denounced as 'collaborators of imperialism' (Ngugi Wa Thiong'o 1997: 2). Modern South Africa represents a case study for neocolonialism in practice: the end of apartheid brought the 'symbolic trappings' of freedom and democracy, while the majority black community suffered greater disadvantage under 'economic growth' neoliberal style (Pilger 2006; Klein 2007).[3]

However, the modernity thesis explains this poverty in terms of 'underdeveloped' traditional societies, and not as the result of centuries of exploitation (Durkheim 1984). This analysis ignores the fact that 'foreign capital is used for the exploitation rather than for the development of the less developed parts of the world' (Nkrumah, 1965: x), portraying the west as wealthy 'through its own efforts' and not due to the 'exploitative relationship' between the neocolonial west and the '"developing" third world' (Ó Croidheáin 2006: 99–100). Indeed, some commentators have even declared that 'colonialism and its aftermath are largely historical subjects today' (Betts 1998: 91). In line with this neoliberal consensus, it is assumed that 'today people are more concerned about their welfare than ideology' (ibid.).

Scraton, however, rejects such erroneous 'pluralism' and modern liberal democratic rhetoric about 'universal societal freedom in individuals' as little more than the ideological management of the structural inequalities forged by neocolonialism and globalisation:

> The cruelties of early capitalism, slavery, patriarchy were material realities. They destroyed personal lives, communities and cultures. There was no transitionary period through which their legacies were transformed, their excesses fully acknowledged and reparations realised. Capitalism, in its global capacity, has advanced, in keeping with its uncompromising objective of capital accumulation, while slavery and colonialism provided the material and cultural foundations for neocolonialism. It is not possible to analyse the material forces of globalisation without considering the economic, political and ideological dynamics of neocolonialism. (Scraton 2007: 224)

The 'end of ideology' and 'age of consensus' are illusions. The essence of this myth was that 'being materially better off and less discriminated against gave the appearance of fundamental change in structural relations' when in reality the 'redistribution of earned income through taxation presented capitalism with the scope to reconstruct, consolidate and move outwards to globalisation' (ibid.: 225).

Western claims to 'liberal governance' are essential to the manufacture of consent, where the state progressively intervenes in 'the whole sphere of ideological relations and social reproduction' (Hall et al. 1978: 303). The language of 'liberalism' is utilised to depict the 'new imperialists' as 'crisis managers, rather than the cause of the crisis' (Pilger 2006: 21). Thus, 'reasonable' and 'non-ideological' liberalism represents 'a jargon that serves great power'; yet liberal ideology is anything but reasonable, constituting the very 'antithesis of "benevolent and moralistic"' (ibid.: 22).

More significantly in the context of this book, 'Anglo-American mass culture and multinational industry [provide] the engine' for English to gain 'dominance in global culture' (Ó Croidheáin 2006: 17), a dominance secured by 'colonial conquest, imperialism and globalisation' that 'established a hierarchy of standard languages, which mirrors the power relations on the planet' and hastens 'the extinction of innumerable language varieties', stigmatising 'all but the most powerful languages' (Alexander 2003: 6). Consequently, the implicit assumption behind this co-ordinated approach is that endangered languages should simply atrophy and die, for reasons inherently political and not linguistic (May 2002: 147).

On an international scale, English linguistic hegemony strengthens Anglo-American economic and political dominance by elevating English as the language of global capital.[4] Furthermore, its monopoly of film and media, science, technology, and the information and Internet age creates a 'rationalisation process whereby the unequal power relations between English and other languages are explained and legitimated ... in favour of the dominant language'. 'English linguistic imperialism', or 'linguicism', perpetuates social, economic, political and cultural inequalities between English and other languages and their speakers (Phillipson 1992: 287–8).

The work of Michael Krauss demonstrates that at the current rate of language shift, the twenty-first century will see 90 per cent of the world's languages either lost or forced into the final stages of decline, almost overwhelmingly because of contact with a majority language defined by its speakers' superior political, cultural or socio-economic power:

> the circumstances which have led to the present language mortality known to us range from outright genocide, social or economic or habitat destruction, displacement, demographic submersion, language suppression, enforced assimilation or assimilatory education to electronic media bombardment especially television, an incalculably lethal new weapon, which I have called 'cultural nerve gas'. (Krauss 1992: 8)

Minoritised cultures and languages will 'continue so patently to play a significant (even central) part in many of the political disputes in the world today' (May 2002: 316) because global capitalism with its inherent political and socio-economic inequalities shapes this very 'linguacide'.

In Ireland, the effects of 'English colonialism ... are now compounded by ... neo-colonial international forms of cultural dominance' (Ó Croidheáin 2006: 17). Indeed, the northern settler–colonial statelet shared a border with the 'post-independence' 26-county Free State, a classic example of continued neocolonial administrative rule in indigenous form, where reactionary native elites donned 'the gowns and wigs of the British system ... employing the unmodified devices of the old regime upon themselves'. Southern Ireland suffered the customary neocolonial traits of civil war, economic dependency, a 'retreat from revolution' and the aspirations of the national liberation struggle (Kiberd 1995: 263). As a result, the Irish-language revival lost its emancipatory content, instead being utilised to redefine 'the interests of the propertied classes' and strengthen the grip of a reactionary establishment linked to the autocratic Catholic Church (Ó Croidheáin 2006: 161).

A neocolonial reading of modern Ireland, north and south, demands 'that each state's claim to the monopoly of violence within their territories be rigorously thought through in light of their own very arbitrary and violent foundations' (Lloyd 2003: 48). Notably, 'violence' here does not equate to armed insurrection, but the endemic and continuing structural legacy of neocolonialism:

> [T]he phenomenon of violence must be understood as constitutive of social relations within the colonial capitalist state, whose practices institutionalise a violence which, though cumulative, daily, and generally unspectacular, is normalised precisely by its long duration and chronic nature. Unlike insurgency, which is usually represented as sporadic and of the nature of a temporary 'crisis', the violence of the state operates through its institutions continuously, producing the material effects of poverty, unemployment, sickness, depopulation, and emigration. That these phenomena are generally not seen as state-mediated effects of capitalist and colonial violence forces us to recognise that the violence of the state belongs in its capacity to control representation, both political and cultural. (Ibid.)

This crucial control of 'representation' allows mainstream academic historiography to occlude the realities of Ireland's colonial experience, past and present, and contain it within an uncritical narrative of modernisation. The 'literally state-censored media' that 'celebrate the passage from Ireland's domination by British colonial capital to its domination by the participation in the neocolonial circuits of global capitalism' have promoted this view (ibid.). Thus to articulate a neocolonial interpretation, as this book does, not only challenges mainstream, 'official' and state-sponsored analyses but reopens the possibility of alternative futures.

## Decolonisation

> To live, the colonized must ... do away with the colonized he has become.
>
> [T]he most urgent claim of a group about to revive is certainly the liberation and restoration of its language.
>
> Albert Memmi (1965: 195, 154)

Processes of colonialism and neocolonialism invariably inspired a legacy of decolonisation. This reference to 'decolonisation', however, refers not to the process whereby colonial powers granted 'formal independence' to their colonies, but rather to 'authentic decolonisation' that engenders the strategies of survival and resistance engaged in by colonised or subordinate groups (Caute 1970: 52).

The colonial experience was typified by the predominance of 'mythical portraits', as termed by Memmi, describing the colonised as 'innately lazy, barbarous, bestial, amoral, bellicose, etc.' (Mac Síomóin 1994: 45). Hence, one of the primary first steps of any decolonising renaissance amongst the colonised was to provide an inspiring narrative to counterbalance these derogatory depictions. In appealing to 'national consciousness', this usually entailed a battle for 'legitimacy and cultural primacy', which depended 'on their asserting an unbroken continuity leading to the first warriors who stood against the intrusive white man' (Said 1993: 239).

Thus the colonised's revival of indigenous culture involved claiming continuity with the historic past in a process Fanon (1961) describes as 'hegemonic mirroring'. This was a strategy for survival in the face of the colonising power's objective to reduce the colonised to abject material and psychological poverty. It involved elevating the 'national culture' and reclaiming the native past in a 'counter-continuum that mirrors the dominant ideology in its liberal mix of myth and truth' (Ó Croidheáin 2006: 113). Fanon (1961: 172) shows that 'the passion with which contemporary Arab writers remind their people of the great pages of their history is a reply to the lies told by the occupying power'.

There were many examples of this in the Irish context, including Thomas Davis's (n.d.: 174–5) manifesto of 'nationhood', which claimed continuity with the past as evidence of a distinct national identity; Pádraig Pearse's definition of the Gael as substituted in the 'common name of Irishman' (Ó Croidheáin 2006: 113); and James Connolly's idealised account of the egalitarian pre-colonial Irish social system in *Labour and Irish History* (1983). Therefore, when anti-colonial activists like Fanon 'deliberately as well as ironically' use the language and 'tactics of the culture he believes has oppressed him' (Said 1993: 324), it should be viewed as a conscious element of decolonisation; a hegemonic mirroring of the dominant imperialist ideology.

Additionally, the importance of 'culture' to the processes of imperialism underscores the significance of cultural decolonisation and its aim to 'reclaim, rename, and re-inhabit' a 'decolonised identity' along with the closely associated 'redevelopment of the native language' (Said 1993: 273). The liberating aspect of such a linguistic revival, according to Memmi (1965: 151) stems from the willingness to make sacrifices in the process: 'he will forgo the use of the colonizer's language, even if all the locks of the country turn with that key; he will change the signs and highway marking, even if he is the first to be inconvenienced.' The spiritual and cultural emancipation of such a renaissance is presented by Ngugi Wa Thiong'o (1997), who argued that the 'deliberate undervaluing of a people's culture' had necessitated 'the conscious elevation of the language of the coloniser' as 'crucial to the domination of the mental universe of the colonised' (ibid.: 14). 'Cultural renaissance', therefore, should include 'the teaching and study of African languages' as integral to the rebuilding of pride, self-esteem and 'a meaningful self-image' amongst the colonised (ibid.: 72).

In many ways, the efforts of African cultural decolonisation had been precipitated by similar efforts in Ireland initiated by activists like Pádraig Pearse, who became the first exponent of Irish-medium education, taking innovative measures to combat the 'mental enslavement' of the national school system in Ireland, which he named 'the Murder Machine'. He argued that this system consolidated British colonialism: 'Education should foster; this education is meant to repress. Education should inspire; this education is meant to tame ... The English are too wise a people to educate the Irish in any worthy sense' (Pearse 1986: 6).

By forming Scoil Éanna and Scoil Íde in the early twentieth century, Pearse aimed to challenge those 'who no longer realise that we are slaves' and 'even think our chains ornamental' (Pearse 1986: 22). Pearse's project was a component of the Gaelic League's post-1893 programme of 'de-Anglicisation', which aimed to promote 'cultural continuity' through confronting the Irish 'colonial condition' (Ó Tuathaigh 2005: 47). Cultural decolonisation, Irish style, also included the mass reawakening of native Irish sports through the foundation of the Gaelic Athletic Association (GAA), which helped 'redress the bruising encounter with colonialism, with its persistent hallowing effect on indigenous culture' (Whelan 2005: 151).

The revitalising impact of such decolonising processes, can, according to Freire (1972a, 1972b) challenge the 'culture of silence' that has been systematically inculcated in the colonised during the colonial phase (1972a: 15). Thus, radical education can empower the oppressed to think for themselves and foster cultural transformation: 'The more the alienated culture is uncovered, the more the oppressive reality in which it originates is exposed ... knowledge of the alienated culture leads to transforming action resulting in a culture which is being freed from alienation' (Freire 1972a: 162). The process by which the oppressed attain 'critical consciousness' or 'the maximum of potential consciousness' is termed 'conscientisation' (Freire 1972a: 77–8). Thus human beings become 'conscious bodies, capable of acting ... perceiving, of knowing ... recreating' and reflecting, which enables them to combat negative self-imagery by ejecting the oppressor from within their minds (ibid.: 81).

In addition to cultural and educational elements of decolonising projects in colonised regions, many such movements throughout the world manifested their resistance through armed insurrection in 'national liberation struggles' (Said 1993). In the Irish context, for example, the cultural revival movement was the inspiration that culminated in the 1916 Easter Rising. One of its key leaders was Pearse, whose writings elevated physical force in the quest for 'nationhood': '[B]loodshed is a cleansing and sanctifying thing and the nation which regards it as the final horror has lost its manhood. There are many things more horrible than bloodshed; and slavery is one of them' (Rees 1998: 197). Fanon (1961: 74) used similar language in describing the liberating effects of the use of violence in anti-colonial struggles: '[A]t the level of individuals, violence is a cleansing force. It frees the native from his inferiority complex and from his despair and inaction; it makes him fearless and restores his self-respect.'

According to this rationale, the violence of the colonial regime against the native meant that any process of decolonisation would often precipitate violent resistance by the colonised to overthrow it. However, Said (1993: 332) points out that activists like Fanon should be understood as 'something considerably beyond a celebration of violent conflict' and strongly criticises those who represent him 'strictly as a preacher calling the oppressed to violence' (ibid.: 331). For Fanon, the emphasis on 'armed struggle' was merely tactical, a tool that could lead to the cost of colonial rule being publicly challenged and representations of imperialism eventually losing their legitimacy (ibid.: 241).

It's worth distinguishing between 'nationalist independence' phases of anti-colonial struggle and resistance and decolonisation themselves, which should be viewed as ongoing processes that often 'persist well after successful nationalism has come to a stop' and coincide with the protracted injustices and inequalities of neocolonialism (Said 1993: 257). These specific social and political struggles that aim towards more comprehensive humanist liberation see decolonisation divided into two phases: 'The first phase of this dynamic produces nationalist independence movements, the second, later, and more acute phase produces liberation struggles' (ibid.: 333).

One such example of continued adherence to the liberating aspirations of decolonisation can be found in the writings of renowned Irish-language activist and republican socialist Máirtín Ó Cadhain who, like Fanon, linked cultural struggle to socio-economic aspirations. Ó Cadhain promoted language revival through Gaeltacht grassroots groups that exposed the widespread poverty and economic inequality of the neocolonial 26-county state and the failure of successive governments to revive the language successfully:

It is the duty of Gaelic revivalists to be socialists. The Gaelic-speaking population in the Gaeltachts make up a class that is the most abandoned and the most oppressed of the Irish people. Their salvation and the salvation of the language are one and the same thing to me. But this is not possible without the reconquest of Ireland – Ireland and its productive resources to be taken back into the control of the people. To me the revolution that is necessary for the reconquest is necessary also for the salvation of the Gaelic language. Therefore any action which raises the spirit and enthusiasm of the Gaelic-speaking public is part and an important part of the reconquest. (Ó Cadhain n.d.: 14)

In this assessment, cultural reconquest is viewed as central to the completion of the decolonisation process that would 'fulfil the aims of the 1916 manifesto' and the 'revolution of the mind and heart, the revolution in wealth distribution, property rights and living standards' (ibid.: 13).

A similar linkage of cultural revival to fundamental structural change can be discerned in radical policy documents of the New People's Army (NPA) that was formed in 1969 as the military wing of the Communist Party of the Philippines (CPP) (Ó Croidheáin 2006: 304). The NPA programme for a People's Democratic Revolution proposed to extend the use of Pilipino (a cosmopolitan form of Tagalog) and argues 'that economic measures such as land reform and redistribution of wealth will solve the language issue' by promoting the 'use of Pilipino not as essentially symbolic, but rather as important in eliminating the economic inequalities created by the use of English' (ibid.). Accordingly, the debilitating effects of colonialism and imperialism on native cultures are best resolved by re-evaluating the political and economic direction of society in general.

## CULTURE, IDENTITY AND NATIONALISM

### Culture

Culture is a product of the history which it in turn reflects. Culture in other words is a product and a reflection of human beings communicating with one another in the very struggle to create wealth and to control it.

Ngugi Wa Thiong'o (1997: 14)

The concept of culture is a complex one, but can be defined as a way of life learned, shared and transmitted by a group of people who live and work together and experience a common feeling of belonging. Although culture the world over may appear stable, it is flexible and isn't inherited unquestioningly as a definitive set of customs from ancestors (Watson 2008). It evolves with the passage of time, and is always changing as people themselves change and as different generations develop ideas as to what makes up their culture (ibid.).

The importance of language to culture has been explored by Ngugi Wa Thiong'o (1997: 14), who views 'culture' as 'almost indistinguishable from the language that makes possible its genesis, growth, banking, articulation and indeed its transmission from one generation to the next'. While culture embodies the moral and aesthetic values of human societies, he stresses that 'language as culture is the collective memory bank of a people's experience in history' (ibid.). Recognising language as an integral element of culture, and therefore as much more than merely a means of communication, echoes the often quoted phrase that a person who has a 'language consequently possesses the world expressed and implied by that language' (Fanon 1970: 14).

This illustrates the rationale for what was noted earlier regarding the processes of colonisation; that the destruction or marginalisation of native languages was usually 'both a means and an end of cultural invasion' (Collins 1990). In this sense, Maori activist Tuhiwai Smith (1999: 58) argues that 'knowledge and culture were as much part of imperialism as raw materials and military strength', in that they provided the west with a framework through which to 'see', to 'name' and to 'know' indigenous communities. Whilst, at an economic level, colonialism as expressed through excesses like slavery forged new materials for exploitation and new markets for trade, at a cultural level it utilised ideas, images and experiences to shape the west's ideological claim to essential 'positional superiority' over the rest of the world (ibid.: 60).

Similarly, however, as Said (1993: 241) elucidates, 'culture' can also inspire the victims of colonialism 'to relinquish or modify the idea of overseas domination' or colonial rule, with language often playing a crucial yet subservient role:

> [T]he concept of a national language is central, but without the practice of a national culture – from slogans to pamphlets and newspapers, from folk tales and heroes to epic poetry, novels, and drama – the language is inert; national culture organises and sustains communal memory, as when early defeats in African resistance stories are resumed; it reinhabits landscape using restored ways of life ... it formulates expressions and emotions of pride as well as defiance, which in turn form the backbone of the principal national independence parties. (Ibid.: 260)

Therefore the imposition of colonial authority over all aspects of indigenous life shapes the colonised attempts at 'reclaiming, reconnecting and reordering those ways of knowing which were submerged, hidden or driven underground' (Tuhiwai Smith 1999: 69). Fanon (1961: 193) recommended that native intellectuals, including artists, writers and teachers, engage in the process of rehabilitating a 'national culture' as 'a special battleground' that can legitimate a new nationalist consciousness. This process encapsulates a three-stage development whereby native intellectuals cross 'back over the line' (ibid.: 178–9). While the first phase involves recognising that intellectuals have been assimilated into the culture of the occupying power, the second sees them returning to their roots and recalling their historic past. In the final phase, the intellectuals aim to revive and awaken their people by realigning themselves with their cause, while producing a relevant yet revolutionary national literature (ibid.).

Moreover, Fanon (ibid.: 191) argues vociferously that during 'colonial domination', any effort to awaken 'national culture' also 'means in the first place to fight for the liberation of the nation, that material keystone which makes the building of a culture possible. There is no other fight for culture which can develop apart from the popular struggle' (ibid.: 187). By interpreting cultural revival by colonised peoples as integral to the wider struggle of national sovereignty, Fanon articulated a theoretical template that corresponded with various processes undertaken in many anti-colonial struggles throughout the world. Significantly, a parallel analysis is presented by Freire (1972b: 81–2) whose concept of 'con-scientisation' depicts the 'phase of denouncing an oppressive society and proclaiming the advent of a just society' as 'cultural action for freedom'. In linking education with critical consciousness, the exploration of 'culture' by the 'oppressed' could break the 'culture of silence' in which they were taught to accept what was handed down to them by ruling elites (Mackie 1980: 4).

This unavoidable political dimension to questions of culture is notable in the Irish context, as emphasised by Gibbons, who highlights the intensifying factor of colonialism:

Faced with the invidious frontier myth from the onset of colonisation, it is not surprising that culture in Ireland became ineluctably bound up with politics. All culture is, of course, political, but in Ireland historically it acquired a particularly abrasive power. To engage in cultural activity in circumstances where one's culture was being effaced or obliterated, or even to assert the existence of a civilisation prior to conquest, was to make a political statement, if only depriving the frontier myth of its power to act as an alibi for colonisation. (Gibbons 1996: 8)

Hence, the colonial experience effectively consolidated culture as 'a consolation for injustice' that imbued it with an added transformative capacity (Whelan 2003: 90). This very capability saw culture constructed as a 'site of self-differentiation, and therefore of resistance' in the colonial context (ibid.: 95). Conversely, however, in the succeeding period culture became instrumental in the regressive manifestation of the 'post-independence' Irish Free State. Thus, rather than 'culture' being employed to embrace a 'revolutionary remodelling of Irish society', instead it 'stifled the revolutionary impulse' and strangled its potentially 'transformative energies at birth' (Whelan 2004: 182–3). By condemning the new Irish state to collapse back into a 'provincial, pseudo-Gaelic, Catholic backwater' that was constructed around the hegemonic block of the national bourgeoisie, this ultimately ushered in a successful 'counter-revolution' (ibid.).

Interestingly, the potentially conservative nature of 'national cultures' in the hands of elites who aim to enshrine their own politico-economic interests had been alluded to by commentators and activists on the left, such as V.I. Lenin and James Connolly. Lenin advocated taking 'from each national culture only its democratic and socialist elements', while opposing 'the bourgeois culture and bourgeois nationalism of each nation', which, he argued, stultified and divided the working classes (Ó Croidheáin 2006: 74). Similarly, Connolly warned how national cultures, 'apart from any intrinsic qualities they may possess', conveniently served 'in the hands of the possessing class as counter-irritants' that masked economic inequality and aimed to prevent 'class consciousness on the part of the proletariat' (Connolly 1983: 3–4).

This is evident in the Irish historical context, where the status of the Irish language and culture has often been 'dependent on the political ends or needs of elites in Irish society' (Ó Croidheáin 2006: 18). This analysis exposes the fragility of culturalist arguments in favour of the Irish language that stress the autonomy of cultural expression, asserting its primacy over wider political issues. For many socialist language activists, the future survival and development of the Irish language can only be ensured 'by questioning the distribution of resources and the ownership and control of the means of production in Ireland' (ibid.).

The linkage between culture and power has been examined by Bourdieu (1991), who conceptualises culture as the medium through which social hierarchies and power differentials are channelled and maintained. Thus culture is viewed as a form of capital, with its own 'specific laws of accumulation, exchange and exercise' that legitimate the exercise of power through a 'symbolic system' which can elicit the consent of both the dominant and dominated (Swartz 1997: 8). This analysis corresponds with the view that 'cultural hegemony' contests traditional Marxist economic determinism, which interprets cultural, social and ideological activity as 'super-structural' or simply the duplication of the forces of production (Williams 1977, 1980).

Rather, cultural hegemony has been described as 'something ... which is lived at such depth' that it actually corresponds 'to the reality of social experience very much more clearly that any notions derived from the formula of base and superstructure' (Williams 1980: 37). This elaborates on Gramsci's theory of hegemony, in which cultural processes are shaped by 'power' and a 'central system of practices, meanings and values' that uphold the 'dominant' culture (ibid.: 38). The widespread projection of such 'dominant' cultures has accelerated under the auspices of neoliberal globalisation, where the interests of American consumer culture and global capitalism forge the 'economisation of culture', which threatens to obliterate regional and minority cultures (Carroll and King 2003: 7).

Furthermore, the continued decline of minority cultures 'reflects a global system of international capitalism that seeks to homogenise markets by reducing national and linguistic boundaries, thereby increasing power and profits at the expense of the well-being and autonomy of national populations' (Ó Croidheáin 2006: 18). Consequently, struggles opposing cultural homogenisation, such as those outlined in this book, should be considered an essential aspect of any political challenge to the power of such elites, whether at national, regional or even local level. As Stuart Hall indicates, 'the return to the local can be a form of resistance, a defensive response to globalisation ... the struggles of those on the margins to reclaim some form of representation for themselves' (Mayo 1997: 159).

## Identity

Identities are the names we give to the different ways we are positioned by, and position ourselves within, narratives of the past.
Stuart Hall (Fox and Starn 1997: 123)

Like culture, identity is subject to change: 'every community must wrestle with it as best it can, and find ways of reconstituting its identity in a manner that is both deeply sensitive to its history and traditions and fully alive to its present and future needs' (Parekh 1995: 267). This significant role being attributed to history and 'the past' is also emphasised by David Miller:

> A national identity helps to locate us in the world; it must tell us who we are, where we have come from, what we have done ... the story is continually being rewritten; each generation revises the past as it comes to terms with the problems of the present. Nonetheless, there is a sense in which the past always constrains the present: present identities are built out of materials that are handed down, not started from scratch. (May 2002: 269)

Additionally, identities can become reshaped in the face of new sociocultural or structural circumstances. This is often the case in the context of colonisation or globalisation, where the fear that something is being lost, destroyed or abandoned can inspire cultural revivals. As the narratives in this book indicate, certain identities are reaffirmed, reclaimed and reinvested with extra value or meaning to suit particular circumstances (O'Reilly 1999: 172).

Though identity has multiple manifestations and markers, its inescapable links with language in ethnocultural terms have been explored by reputed linguist Joshua Fishman (1989, 1991). His analysis of the significance of language to identity shows that the association between a language and a particular culture is 'best able to name the artefacts and to formulate or express the interests, values and world views of that culture' (1991: 30). This contention that language is the 'prime symbol system to begin with' (1989: 32) is also articulated in relation to ethnolinguistic movements, in which 'the role of language ... is symbolic or iconic – that is, language is not just a means of communication but stands for a way of life or a symbol of identity' (Rahman 2001: 62).

However, it is crucial not to overstate the connection between language and identity, as is commonplace in primordial and racialised accounts of ethnicity that derived from certain nineteenth-century cultural nationalist writers. A more balanced view recognises that 'language is the contingent marker of ethnic identity and that adopting any other position inevitably involves an essentialist view of the language–identity link' (May 2002: 10). The fact that ethnic identities are social, cultural and political forms of life means that they cannot be understood in isolation from other political and sociocultural circumstances. This is epitomised by the prominent role languages play in 'the identity claims and the political mobilisation of many minority movements in the world today' (ibid.).

Languages provide such movements with legitimacy and authenticity, while also embodying the subjugation of a group's ethnolinguistic identity by an oppressive power (Fishman 1989). When constructed as part of an oppositional identity, language can be integral to the assertion of alternative histories as an important means of challenging dominant discourses and fundamental inequalities, while simultaneously providing new opportunities to reinvent identity (O'Reilly 1999: 175).

Therefore ethnolinguistic struggles that focus specifically on identity can be recast as symbols of socio-economic inequality and political discrimination, experienced by ethnic minorities in general (Khleif 1979: 349). Moreover, language becomes an indispensable rallying point when it 'has been suppressed, banned, or humiliated', thus inspiring 'its resurgence' as a 'powerful symbol of regeneration' (ibid.: 348) which 'cuts across internal divisions, vested interests, and feelings of inferiority' (Khleif 1985: 178). This reinvestment of value in a minoritised language imbues its supporters with a 'confidence in their own identity' and 'the knowledge and critical awareness to articulate their rights' that make them more 'resistant to exploitation at the hands of the dominant group' (Cummins 1995: 160).

However, it is worth noting how such resistance can subside and be assimilated in the context of an altered relationship with dominant powers in which discrimination becomes more veiled, as accounted for earlier in the oscillation between colonialism and neocolonialism. For example, Mac Póilin (1997c: 176) notes how the 'nationalist, anti-British, oppositionalist motive' to revive the Irish language 'lost much of both its function and its force in post-independence Southern Ireland ... particularly when the difficulties facing the revival could no longer be blamed on the British'. However, in the Irish example, colonialism and neocolonialism shaped a process which spawned a reactionary free-state administration that failed to promote the liberating aspirations of revival as a means of decolonisation (Kiberd 1995, Whelan 2004).

The opposite was and arguably still is the case in the north of Ireland where the realities of British and Unionist rule and subsequent 'repression of Irish identity' saw the Irish language offer 'an opportunity for people to assert their sense of Irishness' (O'Reilly 1999: 175). This tendency became increasingly marked following the 1981 Irish hunger strike, when the language was openly extolled by many nationalists, republicans and language activists as a 'symbolic weapon' of resistance in the wider struggle for national self-determination.

The colonial legacy can be seen to have had a profound impact on identity in Ireland, where long-term side-effects like 'dependency, imitativeness and negative self-image are symptoms of this residuum of centuries of cultural oppression' that continue to paralyse political and cultural development (Mac Síomóin 1994: 44). One example of this is the 'cultural schizophrenia' expressed in 26-county state surveys into 'public attitudes towards the Irish language', which 'couple widespread support for the language with widespread inability/unwillingness to learn or speak it' (ibid.: 51). A similar point about the centrality of the Irish language to claims of cultural distinctiveness is made by Irish historian J.J. Lee, who observes:

> There is in present circumstances no substitute for the Irish language. However exhilarating Gaelic football and hurling may be at their best, however exuberant the beat of the bodhrán, however enriching the great resurgence of traditional music, these are only details in the overall design of a distinctive culture. The language is now, for practical purposes, the design. (Lee 1989b: 666)

In stressing the permeation of the omnipotent Anglo-American 'mother culture' within Irish culture, Lee warns that 'without language, only the most unusual historical circumstances suffice to develop a sense of identity'(ibid.: 662).

'Identity' in the contemporary era has been summarised by renowned sociologist Manuel Castells (1997: 7), who categorises forms of resistance identity as defensive responses to globalisation's dissolution of cultural autonomy and local institutions, as well as its wholesale individualisation of social relations of production. 'Resistance identities', he argues, foster 'communal havens' that provide sanctuary from the excesses of globalisation; these invariably stagnate and become reactionary unless they give rise to 'project identities' that can utilise globalisation to their advantage as agents of social transformation (ibid.).

Ironically, the 'age of globalisation' is 'also the age of nationalist resurgence expressed both in the challenge to nation states and the widespread construction of identity on the basis of nationality' (ibid.: 27). This process has precipitated the formation of a plethora of language movements, indigenous movements and social movements worldwide, with the failure of traditionally elected political parties 'to counter economic exploitation, cultural domination, and political oppression' leaving marginalised groupings with no choice other than to organise themselves autonomously, usually in their immediate locality (ibid.: 61).

Social movements that define themselves on the basis of identity are usually organised collectively within civil society and 'may achieve social and cultural change at the grassroots of this society without any interaction with the state' (Foueraker 1995: 50–1). Although this collective identity will be shaped 'through the experience and memory of struggles past and present', it will be 'formed in some degree through political struggle and so shaped by relations of political power' (ibid.). It's as a reaction to the failure of state institutions that 'new social movements' aim to bring about change at a lower level 'through the transformation of values and personal identities and symbols' (Scott 1990: 18). These movements attempt to bring about various forms of transformation, 'not by challenging society as a whole', but instead by 'opposing specific forms of social closure or exclusion' (ibid.: 150). While critics of such localised activism will cite its limitations in delivering structural transformation, this nevertheless doesn't lessen its importance and potential to develop longer-term radical alliances when imbued with greater ideological resonance.

These social movements, though by no means inherently progressive, contain many features which reflect a 'unity of spirit and purpose' that have both appealed to and inspired indigenous groups throughout the world (Tuhiwai Smith 1999: 110). They are 'highly political' and tend to promote a 'revitalisation and reformulation of culture' that rejects globalising uniformity and demands equality for indigenous peoples (ibid.). As Tuhiwai Smith attests,

> protest actions over land rights, language and cultural rights, human rights and civil rights were taking place literally across the globe, from the very northern reaches of the Sami people in Norway, to Welsh language actions, Basque protests in Spain, to different indigenous peoples in the Middle East, Africa, North, Central and South America, the Philippines, India, Asia and the Pacific. All these national struggles have their own independent histories but the rising profile of political activities occurring on

a world-wide scale did give renewed impetus to other indigenous groups. (Ibid.)

While these groups are mobilised and maintained locally as ostensibly grassroots developments, they also develop outward, building international alliances with similar indigenous and non-indigenous groups who plough parallel counter-hegemonic furrows (ibid.).

The various conflicts these groups are involved in are 'most often precipitated' when governments and nation states 'ignore demands for greater cultural and linguistic democracy and not – as is commonly assumed – when they accommodate them' (May 2002: 17). Hence, on the basis of current trends throughout the world, it is difficult to contest the view that identity politics 'will be a relevant force for the foreseeable future' (Watson 2008: 68). Additionally, 'the ability or inability of the state to cope with the conflicting logics of global capitalism, identity based social movements, and defensive movements of workers and consumers will largely condition the future of society in the twenty-first century' (Castells 1997: 109).

## Nationalism

[W]e have seen ... that nationalism, that magnificent song that made the people rise against their oppressors, stops short, falters and dies away on the day that independence is proclaimed. Nationalism is not a political doctrine, nor a programme ... [T]o avoid regression, or at best halts and uncertainties, a rapid step must be taken from national consciousness to political and social consciousness.

Frantz Fanon (1961: 163)

Modern forms of nationalism were predated by the cultural and linguistic nationalism of the late-eighteenth-century German romantic writers, as embodied in the influential triumvirate of Herder, Humboldt and Fichte (May 2002: 57). Johann Herder (1744–1803), who influenced cultural and linguistic movements that swept Europe between the 1780s and the 1840s and beyond, advocated an 'organic' or linguistic nationalism in which culture – especially language – was viewed as central to the essence or character (*Volksgeist*) of the nation (ibid.). The idea of language as the representation of the soul or spirit of the nation is best encapsulated in the work of Wilhelm von Humboldt (1767–1835), who stated that the nation's 'language is its spirit' and 'from every language, we can refer backwards to the national character' (ibid.).

These views, which would inspire the twin theories of linguistic determinism and linguistic relativism, wherein each language is assumed to represent a different way of 'looking at the world', also promoted fervent ethnocentrism and were in direct opposition to the political nationalism of the French Revolution and its rhetorical underpinnings of equality and popular sovereignty (ibid.: 58). The most extreme of these contributions was made by Fichte (1762–1814), whose views linking the German language to 'blood and soil' as well as 'forces of nature' projected overt racialist superiority. Although most theorists of nationalism would recognise the significance of language to the formation of identity and world views, the above positions are rejected as overtly essentialist, with preference being given to more socially constructed accounts of nationalism and nationality (ibid.: 52).

Despite this, many modernist proponents of cultural nationalism, emanating from its older German romantic variant, argue that it can 'recreate the idea of the nation as a living principle' when the statist type of political nationalism has failed (Hutchinson 1994: 124). Although cultural nationalism has a politics of its own, it differs demonstrably from political nationalism in that its intellectuals and educated middle classes tend to promote the sciences and the arts and aim towards specifically linguistic and educational developments rather than the creation of a national state (ibid.).

Nevertheless, cultural nationalism can incorporate distinct political aims and often develop into political nationalisms and claims for independent statehood, as manifested in the mid 1990s in Quebec, for example (May 2002: 78).[5] The opposite can be ascertained through exploring the dynamics of Welsh nationalism, which has remained avowedly cultural in spite of its long history of political and economic incorporation into the British state (ibid.). Welsh nationalism derives largely from 'cultural continuity' and collective memory wherein the promotion of Welsh culture and particularly the Welsh language are its central tenets (Williams 1994).[6]

On the other hand, the revivifying potential of cultural nationalism in instigating national or political struggles has been detailed by Hroch (1985) whose conception of Risorgimento nationalism succinctly categorises the development of such nationalist movements in a tripartite sequence. Initially, this involved the recuperation of national identity, in which intellectuals take an interest in the culture, folklore and history of the indigenous people.

The second phase enthused a broad national reawakening, in which definitive programmes of action are drawn up that begin to redirect the revived national culture towards a more overtly political course. Finally, there was a transition from cultural revival to the harnessing of concrete political demands, which saw the creation of mass movements in which an extensive cross-section of the people was channelled into political action.

These movements were established most effectively during a crisis in social authority or state legitimacy, when the belief systems of communities could be transformed to fit models of sociocultural and sociopolitical development and change. Hroch's conceptual framework can also be applied to Ireland's late-nineteenth- and early-twentieth-century cultural revival, in which 'social processes combined with a political tendency towards the eclipse of empire'; this empowered cultural nationalism in a way that homogenised the Irish people and differentiated them from their British colonising counterparts (Whelan 2005: 147–8).

Modern nation states are products of the nationalisms of the past few centuries, beginning most notably with the French Revolution (May 2002: 6). According to modernists, nations and nationalism are sociological necessities, rooted in the advent of modernisation brought about by late-eighteenth-century European industrialisation (Gellner 1983:1). Thus the transition from traditional agrarian societies to modern industrial societies demanded centralised political control, a unitary language and state-monitored education; this created nationalism, which provided a means of shared cultural and linguistic identity (ibid.: 55). The development of this 'modern nation state' had the adverse consequence of effectively eradicating minority cultures and posing 'the keenest threat to both the identities and the languages of small (minority) communities' (Dorian 1998: 18).

Similarly, Anderson's conception of 'imagined communities' interprets 'national' entities as 'imagined', in that members may never know or meet their fellow members 'yet in the minds of each lives the image of their communion' (Anderson 1991: 6). While not suggesting that concepts of national consciousness and identity are imaginary in themselves, he nevertheless maintains that both small- and large-scale collectivities in the form of nationality 'are cultural artefacts of a particular kind' (ibid.: 4). This view conceives that 'a solid community' arose from the correspondence of industrial capitalism and print technology in fifteenth- and sixteenth-century Europe, which created dominant 'languages of power' (ibid.).

These cultivated a sense of a 'nation's' history and associated cultural symbols that could be consolidated through the centralisation of state control in the era of modernisation (Anderson 1994: 94). In addition to their insufficient cognisance of the complex intricacies of colonialism, neocolonialism and emerging global capitalism, these modernist accounts don't account for 'the ongoing persistence of nationalism in the modern world – particularly in situations where political modernisation has already been achieved' (May 2002: 68). The logic of modernist arguments suggests that the globalisation of modernising processes would eventually subsume nationalism, when in actuality the opposite has occurred, 'as the increasing proliferation of 'ethno-nationalisms' in the modern world highlights' (ibid.).

Alternative modernist views on nationalism are presented by some Marxist analysts, who view the spread of nationalism as specific to the development of capitalism, in which many traditions were 'invented' by political elites in order to legitimise their power (Hobsbawm and Ranger 1983, Hobsbawm 1990). This corresponds with the traditional Marxist view that the creation of the nation state was a necessary element of the bourgeoisie's programme for its own development via the concentration of capital accumulation. May (2002: 23) nonetheless, highlights inconsistencies in Marx's position on nationalism, citing his view that 'working men have no country', and contrasting this with both Marx's and Engels' endorsement of the nationalist causes of 'historic nations', in which the 'proletariat of each country must, of course, first of all settle matters with its own bourgeoisie'. Accordingly, such 'historic nations' never included minoritised ethnic or national groups,[7] which shapes the views of commentators who suggest that Marx and Engels were 'impatient with and intolerant of ethnic minorities' (Nimni 1995: 68).

Notably, other Marxist commentators adopt a less sceptical analysis on ethnic mobilisation, arguing that the ability of nationalism to mobilise large-scale inter-class support renders it an important agent for social change, which, though invariably populist in content, has the effect of inducting the masses into politics (Nairn 1994). In addition, some socialist commentators are critical of the reductive and simplistic Marxist views on nationalism, and posit that 'nationalism' is 'a notable black beast in the intellectual undergrowth of many socialists' who wear 'the blinkers of a bogus internationalism' (Mac Síomóin 1994: 68).

The 'narrow' views of Engels, Luxemburg, Stalin and Hobsbawm on national minorities are arguably reflective of their often 'ill-informed' backgrounds as citizens of colonising nations (Mac Síomóin 2007: 117). In this sense, oppressive colonising nationalism should be distinguished from potentially emancipatory nationalism that can mobilise suppressed minorities. Cultural revivals can form part of the 'ideological struggle between dominant and repressed groups' that unites the national and the social, as represented in the Irish context by the 'radical historical synthesis of James Connolly', which 'became in its time a programme for both national and working-class liberation in Ireland' (Mac Síomóin 1994: 70). This framework has also applied to general tendencies in the growth of anti-colonial nationalism, which functioned as a 'destabilising force in so far as it challenged the whole structure of capitalist imperialism' (Jay 1992: 202). According to Vietnamese writer Thich Nhat Hanh:

> The factor of nationalism in the small countries of Asia and Africa is an immensely important one, but it must be understood in its true character, as a manifestation of resistance on the part of these countries to conquest and domination by foreign powers, not as a form of extreme chauvinism. (P. Ó Snódaigh 2006: 7)

This nationalism is promoted by 'people who feel the need to transform themselves and in so doing raise themselves' in the context of a national or cultural identity that is being threatened with obliteration (ibid.: 14). Furthermore, it has been contextualised as a 'social, intellectual and moral revolution' that produces aspirations of democracy and personal freedom amongst subjugated peoples:

> In a world in which the strong and rich peoples have dominated and exploited the poor and the weak peoples, and in which autonomy is held to be a mark of dignity, of adequacy, of the capacity to live as befits human beings, in such a world this kind of nationalism is the inevitable reaction of the poor and the weak. (Ibid.: 15)

Although such anti-colonial nationalism has been credited with advancing 'the struggle against western domination' that succeeded 'in ridding many territories of colonial overlords' (Said 1993: 69), it has nonetheless been described as 'a deeply problematic enterprise' that could lead to a 'frozen rigidity' enshrining 'nationalist functionaries', thereby replicating the inequalities of the old colonial dispensation (ibid.: 258).

Originally inspired by Fanon (1961), this analysis shows how orthodox nationalism often implemented inequalities fostered by imperialism by appearing to concede authority to an indigenous nationalist bourgeoisie while in reality concretising its hegemony. Fanon (ibid.: 163) stresses the potential of 'national consciousnesses' as a tool for internationalising anti-colonial struggles, but warns that this will regress unless imbued with a political and social consciousness that can lead to 'a real humanism' and genuine liberation. The outworking of this prediction is evident throughout the globe in newly independent states, where nationalist elites utilise nationalism as a means to avoid dealing with social injustice and economic disparities (Chatterjee 1983). This form of 'statism' occurs when nationalism is transformed into a narrowly 'separatist even chauvinist and authoritarian conception' in contrast to 'liberationist nationalism' that promotes the 'real human liberation portended by resistance to imperialism' (Said 1993: 262).

Interestingly, Carroll and King's (2003: 6) subdivision of the various forms of nationalism is wholly applicable to the Irish context. Firstly, they identify 'emergent nationalism', as expressed in the collective project to construct a nation and protect the people's national cultural traditions. They then describe 'official state nationalism', which develops after the nation seizes state power and attains 'national bourgeois hegemony'. This contrasts with 'imperial nationalism', which is promoted by powerful and established nation states that subsequently impose their culture on other less powerful peoples and states. Finally, 'nationalisms against the state', they argue, 'are emancipatory rather than fixed in the repressive apparatuses of state formations [because of] their conjunctural relation to other social movements'. This analysis underlines the historic consequences of unreflective opposition to all forms of nationalism, as opposed to the necessary critique of repressive and authoritarian imperialist nationalisms. Moreover, political change is usually channelled through national institutions, since political movements continue to organise in forms of national solidarity, wherein the nation rather than transnational bodies inspires popular appeal (ibid.: 10–11).

A similar point is made by Irish commentator Antóin Ó Muircheartaigh:

> Nationalism is not a philosophy or an ideology ... At its most basic level, national feeling of identity springs from family and kinship. Tribes grew out of extended families, then nations, located in

a common language, a shared culture with its own unique set of traditions, values and institutions ... Their shared historical experience gives them a national identity, a national personality, distinct from other peoples occupying other territories with different languages, economies, cultures and histories. The social bonds of kinship which bind a nation together are therefore very deep and very powerful irrespective of the social system which exists at a particular time in history ... Any class which aims to dominate must identify itself with the nation, as this is the only way of mobilising people behind its aims. (Mac Síomóin 2006: 45)

Similarly, global capitalism can be resisted through national politics that 'need not be narrow but that is cosmopolitan in its support for other struggles around the globe and allows for multiple political positions, crossing the exclusionary divides of national identities' (ibid.). Hence, nationalism should neither be idealised nor dismissed uncritically without cognisance of the particular historical and politico-economic circumstances in which it develops. The practical world experiences forged by colonialism and neocolonialism, including those specific to Ireland's history, indicate both its emancipatory and regressive potential in varying circumstances.

## IDEOLOGY, POWER AND RESISTANCE

### Ideology

> Ideology is connected to power, because the assumptions that come to be accepted as common sense depend upon the structure of power in society.
>
> James Tollefson (1991: 11)

Ideology has caused more analytical problems for philosophers and social scientists than practically any other concept and has thus been contested ever since the word was first coined two centuries ago (Eccleshall 1992: 24). While ideologies can be ambiguous and embrace contradictory sets of values, they are understood primarily as belonging to the realm 'in which people clarify and justify their actions as they pursue divergent interests' (ibid.: 23). However, while ideologies aim to construct a coherent perspective through which human beings can understand, make sense of and act upon the world, they also, provide 'conflicting interpretations of society' that stand in competition with one another and represent 'rival systems of belief' (ibid.: 8).

Ideology, through forms of discourse and rhetoric as its communicative manifestation, has skilfully attempted to eliminate such 'rival systems of belief' as evidenced in post-Second World War Britain, the USA and other advanced industrial societies. The capacity of a modernised capitalist state economy to generate growth and employment that garnered political stability led many political scientists and sociologists to proclaim the 'end of ideology' (see Waxman 1968). They argued that the extremes of communism and fascism had only flourished because of high unemployment and economic recession and that ideology had declined with the growth of 'liberal democracy'.

However, this prevailing analysis was recognised as mythical by critics who exposed the emergence of an all-pervasive ideology which served the interests of dominant social groups and those elites who profited from consumerism (Wright-Mills 1959, Marcuse 1972). This lent credibility to Gramsci's view that ideological differences could be veiled by a hegemonic ideology that manufactured consent through a coalition of social forces aiming to win the 'hearts and minds of a broadly aligned constituency' (Scraton 2007: 227). This consensus was fractured in the late 1960s as civil rights groups, the anti-Vietnam war movement, revolutionary groups and social movements added to the proliferation of anti-colonial struggles already challenging the status quo (ibid.: 7).

A new consensus, however, would be lauded via the New Right agenda of Thatcher and Reagan and its consolidation of unregulated free-market economics (ibid.: 225). This would be celebrated rhetorically, as the west acquired world dominance following the collapse of the USSR, when Francis Fukuyama famously announced the 'end of history'.[8] This announcement, which has subsequently been disproved by continuing sociopolitical turmoil throughout the globe up until the present in the realms of identity, class and nationality, also highlights the key function of ideology in legitimating power imbalances.

The original meaning of ideology was fundamentally altered by the work of Marx, who argued that its material roots lay in the structure of society. Therefore ideas were not autonomous, but merely reflected the particular interests and aspirations of rival social classes who used them to further their own interests (Ó Croidheáin 2006: 37). Ultimately, according to Marx and Engels, 'it is not the consciousness of men that determines their being but, on the contrary, their social being that determines their consciousness' (Larrain 1991: 22). In this analysis, the fact that ideas that reflect the conditions of people's existence are produced in the human brain through the medium of social activity meant that ideology was a form of 'false consciousness' and served definite class interest (Ó Croidheáin 2006: 33). This view had a transformative influence on the concept of ideology, with few thinkers thereafter defining it in terms of universal truth (Eccleshall 1992: 26).

However, while ideology can be conceived in negative terms as a form of false consciousness or deception that distorts human understanding of social reality, it can also be viewed in positive terms 'as the expression of the world-view of a class' and the 'opinions, theories and attitudes formed within a class in order to defend and promote its interests' (Larrain 1979: 13–14). This positive reading of ideology was a break from the traditional Marxist conception. It derived from Gramsci's concept of 'hegemony', a more nuanced term than 'domination', which failed to acknowledge the active role played by subordinate people in the operation of power (Larrain 1991: 41). Gramsci questioned the simplistic notion that the economic base determines the ideological and cultural superstructure. Instead, he proposed that the relationship between base and superstructure be seen as reflexive and dynamic (Jones 2006: 39–40). Therefore, just as ideology is the mechanism through which the ruling class achieves hegemony, so too can it be the means for subordinate classes to become conscious of their role and attempt to reclaim their hegemony over other non-ruling classes (Larrain 1991: 82). In order for this to happen successfully, each class must create its own 'organic intellectuals', who will 'elaborate, modify and disseminate its class conception of the world', thus giving it homogeneity and awareness of its potential in the economic, political and social fields (ibid.: 84).

The various intricacies of such counter-hegemonic ideologies are theorised by George Rudé (1980) who argues that popular ideology fuses two specific elements. Firstly, an inherent 'sort of "mother's milk" ideology, based on direct experience, oral tradition or folk memory and not learned by listening to sermons or speeches or reading books' (ibid.: 28). The second element comprises 'ideas and beliefs that are "derived" or "borrowed" from others', whether political or religious ideals or philosophies. These can often overlap with the 'inherent' beliefs of one generation, becoming ingrained in basic group culture and thus inculcating beliefs 'that were originally derived from outside by an earlier one' (ibid.). The potential for such 'derived' elements to be 'effectively absorbed' depends on how well the ground has been prepared in specific historical contexts (ibid.: 35). This ideological fusion will depend on circumstances and experience as well as 'the social needs or the political aims of the classes that are ready to absorb them' (ibid.: 36).

At a micro level, the potential role of the 'subject' in ideological transformation has been emphasised by Freire (1972a, 1972b, 1992). His conception of critical consciousness or 'conscientisation' casts the subject as 'no mere spectator of the historical process', but rather someone who can 'participate creatively in that process by discerning transformations in order to aid and accelerate them' (Freire 1992: 12). Through a process of education, where oppressed groups are treated as 'knowing subjects' and not 'as recipients', they can 'achieve a deepening awareness both of the sociocultural reality which shapes their lives and the capacity to transform that reality' (Freire 1972b: 51). This process necessitates a shift from 'false consciousness' to 'critical consciousness' that can transform the subject from feelings of hopelessness and inferiority to hope and self-awareness, thereby developing his/her capacity to become an 'agent for change'(ibid.: 75).

In the context of colonialism, the development of such counter-consciousness has inspired forces to challenge powerful colonial structures. Awareness of historic struggles against a coloniser and the cultural losses this process entailed can recast indigenous languages as an essential part of counter-consciousness that helps form a highly politicised and self-aware identity (Ó Croidheáin 2006: 306–7). In Ireland, this was not only evident in the early-twentieth-century revolutionary period, but has also defined the recent dynamism and energy of the contemporary language revival in the north. Although ideology has been central to such counter-hegemonic forms, it has also been skilfully used by Irish elites, who incorporated language and culture to legitimate their own authority and disguise socio-economic inequalities (ibid.: 313). This has been the case because ideology can serve 'to bolster up individuals and groups who occupy positions of power' (Tollefson 1991: 135). Therefore to ignore the centrality of ideology would be to ignore the inequalities of wealth and power in which historical and contemporary political conflicts are ultimately grounded.

## Power and Resistance

> History is also about power. In fact history is mostly about power. It is the story of the powerful and how they became powerful, and then how they use their power to keep them in positions in which they can continue to dominate others.
>
> Linda Tuhiwai Smith (1999: 34)

> [R]esistance, far from being merely a reaction to imperialism, is an alternative way of conceiving human history.
>
> Edward Said (1993: 260)

The concepts discussed in this chapter thus far are inextricably bound with fundamental questions of power and ideology. Although language in itself could not necessarily be described as ideological, its links with the structures, distribution and deferential use of power invariably make it so. Few query the view that 'questions of language are basically questions of power' (Chomsky 1979: 191). In recognising language as significant to the production of social relations, 'the concept of ideology has very rarely figured in discussions of language and power within linguistics' (Fairclough 2001: 2). Thus mainstream linguistics has been preoccupied with presenting an 'idealised view of language which isolates it from the social and historical matrix outside of which it cannot actually exist' (ibid.: 6). Such an 'asocial' approach to studying language arguably ignores the relationship between language, power and ideology. This critique also extends to sociolinguistics, which is strong on 'what' questions relating to the facts of language variation but 'weak on "why" and "how" in terms of social relationships of power' (ibid.).

These views correlate with Bourdieu's (1991: 53) view that 'symbolic power' imposes and disguises social inequality via linguistic and cultural processes; 'all linguistic practices are measured against the legitimate practices, i.e. the practices of those who are dominant'. This analysis is endorsed by Tollefson (1991: 183), who proclaims that 'inequality is rooted in system and structure – historical, social class, economic, and political forces – which are reflected in the educational system, and therefore are not amenable to change by it'. In this regard, various kinds of language-teaching policies are another 'mechanism by which the interests of dominant socio-political groups are maintained' (ibid.: 32).

Accordingly, this process promotes the world view of the powerful, the acceptance of which 'by the less powerful consolidates the system of the distribution of power', thus elevating languages as 'the means for propagating ideologies' (Rahman 2001: 68). A clear example of this is the worldwide teaching of English as part of a 'political project' that is defined by the view that spreading one's world view effectively empowers 'one's culture; one's apprehension of reality; one's definition of what is valuable and what is not' (ibid.: 70). On the other hand, language movements tend to confront such systems of power by utilising language as a symbol of unity. Such forms of 'language resistance' often entail cultural revivals that 'resist the dominant powerful language' and rebel 'against the system, using language to create alternative systems or networks of power' (ibid.).

Foucault defines the overlap between power and resistance: 'Where there is power there is resistance and yet, or rather consequently, this resistance is never in a position of exteriority in relation to power' (McEvoy 2001: 34). However, the tendency to present power and resistance as binary opposites has been challenged by Buntman (2003: 265), who suggests that rather than viewing resistance as something that opposes power, it should be seen in its 'myriad of bodies' and 'range of operations' as an attempt by powerless groups to appropriate and produce power. In her more flexible dialectic, which stresses human agency, the 'relationship between power and resistance is closer to a continuum than a relationship between opposites' (ibid.: 267).

In theorising resistance amongst South African political prisoners on Robben Island, Buntman (ibid.: 254) divides resistance up as follows: resistance as survival, resistance as dignity and self-consciousness, resistance as open challenge, resistance as reducing state power or defeating the ends of the oppressor or dominator, and resistance as the appropriation of power or at least the attempt to acquire power. 'Resisting for survival' is usually a response to terrible physical or mental conditions in which actions that maintain sanity remain the only avenue of resistance (ibid.), while 'resistance for dignity and self-consciousness' requires an awareness of one's oppression and the capacity to organise against it collectively. The Robben Island context shows how these acts can culminate in 'resistance as open challenge', with events such as hunger strikes or escapes publicly challenging prison authorities. Conversely, longer-term resistance that aimed to reduce state or oppressor power and eventually appropriate its own power involved maintaining political organisation and a sense of community, in order to construct 'alternative institutions' that removed 'state control of the prisoners' and introduced 'self-government on a community and organisational basis' (ibid.: 265).

In distinguishing between what she terms 'categorical' and 'strategic' resistance on Robben Island, Buntman associates the former with defiant and confrontational forms of activism engaged in by the younger 1970s generation of prisoners. The latter refers to activism aiming at longer-term development of the community of prisoners in organisational and educational terms that could 'impact upon the political terrain both within and beyond the prison' (ibid.: 128–9). Neither form could be described as 'right' or 'wrong', but the two often found a tactical balance that represented the 'generational convergence achieved by political prisoners on Robben Island' and depended on the material circumstances of the particular era (ibid.: 129).

Elements of this conceptual framework are related to the prison context in the north of Ireland by McEvoy (2001: 32), who defines resistance as a concrete manifestation of political struggle. Republican prisoners, he argues, locate 'an analysis of their imprisonment within the context of an 800 year struggle against British imperialism in Ireland in which prisoner resistance has played a crucial role'. He includes 'escape, dirty protest, hunger strikes and violence' as forms of collective resistance that assert the 'political status of the prisoners' (ibid.: 44), but specifically describes the use of hunger strikes and 'dirty' protest as representing 'the transformation of the body and its waste products into symbolic sites of struggle' (ibid.: 45). His conception of educational processes, including the learning of the Irish language, as 'hidden or less overt forms of resistance' (ibid.: 33) is challenged by the accounts of prisoners in this book, who describe its transformational and very 'public' role during the blanket protest.

Although undoubtedly central to any study of history or politics that seeks to explain various forms of change, the concepts of power and resistance are particularly pertinent to the oral history explored in this book. Likewise, their wider relevance to the relationship between structure, ideology and consciousness convey their potential to influence the development of ideas and the distribution of power (Buntman 2003: 249). However, the core issue in this book is not one of deciding 'what is or is not "real" resistance', but rather one of exploring the context 'which determines the precise structural implications of particular counter-hegemonic acts' and analysing 'both their possibilities and limitations as practices contributing to systematic change' (Gledhill 2000: 93).

# 2
# The Irish Language: Conquest, Suppression and Revival, 1169–1920

This chapter focuses on the Irish historical context, dealing specifically with the history of colonial suppression and revival associated with the Irish language as central to the examination of culture and identity politics undertaken in this book.

The chapter first sketches briefly the period of the Norman invasion and subsequent Gaelic reconquest, before detailing Ireland's cultural colonisation from the onset of the Tudor conquest until the rapid demise of the Irish language in the late nineteenth century. By extension, it examines the development of both revivalist and decolonisation projects as forms of resistance to colonisation and catalysts for the Irish revolution in the early twentieth century.

The chapter conceptualises the historical fortunes of the Irish language within the context of the debilitative cultural consequences fostered by British imperialism in Ireland. The events, activities and trends of power and resistance are viewed within the context of the thematic political analysis presented in the previous two chapters.

## 'MORE IRISH THAN THE IRISH': EARLY CONQUEST AND RECOVERY

It hath ever been the use of the conquerors to despise the language of the conquered and to force him by all means to learn his.
Edmund Spenser (Ó Fiaich 1969: 104)

It is widely accepted that the Irish language has been spoken in Ireland for around 2,000 years and is the oldest written language in Europe still spoken in everyday usage. It belongs to the family of languages called the Celtic languages, a branch of the Indo-European linguistic tree, which is thought to have had its home in Europe, somewhere between the Baltic and Black sea.[1] The history of conquest and struggle associated with the language is normally traced to the centuries that followed the Anglo-Norman invasion of Ireland in 1169. In this invasion, the native culture was immediately identified as a powerful impediment to successful conquest.

The model by which the 'mere Irish' and their cultural way of life were viewed as inferior or uncivilised had its roots in the twelfth century and is epitomised in the vociferous invective of Giraldus Cambrensis (Gerald of Wales) (1180). His negative stereotyping of Irish cultural and ethnic identity initiated a tradition of ethnocentric invader superiority which has continually manifested itself over the *longue durée*, becoming most vitriolic and racist during times of conflict. Thus, by attacking the core of the Gaelic ethos, the colonising mission in Ireland was rationalised as a providential mission to civilise backward natives: 'The fact is that officially the Gaelic race, and its language and institutions, indeed its whole culture, was regarded as second class, and often depraved' (Mac Síomóin 1994: 46).

However, while Ireland inevitably experienced unprecedented upheaval in the period of the Anglo-Norman intervention, Irish remained the dominant language throughout the country three and a half centuries later (Ó Cuív 1975: 509). The efforts to promote the English language and to prevent the spread of Irish speech and habits to the non-Irish parts of the population, by the legislative enactment of statutes and other more overt military incursions, had on the whole been unsuccessful – 'with the result, that outside the towns and parts of Leinster, the people were almost exclusively Irish-speaking'.

The Irish language's survivability was officially recognised in the Statutes of Kilkenny of 1366, wherein 'the speaking of Irish in the areas of English settlement was prohibited under pain of forfeiture of land or liberty pending payment of sureties against further offence' (Lennon 1994: 10). Although the Statutes were aimed at English colonists, rather than native speakers of the language, they were indicative of a concerted policy to eliminate the language that would remain at the heart of the future colonial agenda. Ultimately, a turbulent legacy had been left behind: 'the Statutes created strife and violence in the centuries ahead, the Anglo-Irish ... had learned nothing in the 200 years since their forbears came to Ireland' (Ross 2002: 109).

The failure of legislative persecution is underlined by the fact that the descendants of the original Anglo-Norman settlers assimilated into the native infrastructure: 'Outsiders they may have been, but most of them had the good sense to adopt the language, customs, and traditions of the Gaelic Irish and to become "more Irish than the Irish themselves"' (Cosgrove 1990: 102). The extent of this assimilation is attested to by the fact that prominent colonists fell under the influence of Irish music and literature, often becoming its patrons and practitioners (Ó Huallacháin 1994: 17).

This was during the Bardic period, lasting roughly from 1200 to 1600, when the Irish language was pivotal to the maintenance of an indigenous intellectual order and many hundreds of elite noble Irish families sustained hereditary poets with honour and ceremony. The Gaelic resurgence of the fourteenth and fifteenth centuries was so comprehensive that the influence of the English language became effectively confined to a small area centred on Dublin, known as the Pale. In its aftermath, Irish indigenous elites were not seriously threatened until the sixteenth-century Tudor dynasty, which had the completion of the Anglo-Norman invasion as a principal objective.

## 'BRISEADH NA nGAEL': THE CULTURAL COLONISATION OF IRELAND

For cultural invasion to succeed, it is essential that those invaded become convinced of their intrinsic inferiority. Since everything has its opposite, if those who are invaded consider themselves inferior, they must necessarily recognize the superiority of the invaders. The more the invasion is accentuated and those invaded are alienated from the spirit of their own culture and from themselves, the more the latter want to be like the invaders: to walk like them, dress like them, talk like them.

Paulo Freire (1972a: 151)

The English imperial approach to Ireland from the sixteenth century onwards manifests a consistent pattern of hegemonic practice that assumed the superiority of English values, culture and language and also had the power to project them through various means, including military, political, cultural and economic subjugation. The means of assertion has varied in accordance with the colonial strategy pursued in successive epochs. However, the long-term aim remained the cultural subordination of the Irish within a wider expansionist project based on exploitation and economic profit. Therefore, the rise of the Tudor monarchy in the sixteenth-century colonial era not only signalled the birth of English nationalist aspirations, but also promoted an aggressive colonial model as the formative stage in the construction of a vast future empire.

Consequently, strategic imperatives in the task of colonial conquest were articulated in 'an outpouring of justifications for colonization and conquest' (Canny 1973: 581), a moral crusade to civilise the culturally inferior Irish. Moreover, striking parallels

can be drawn between the English descriptions and characteri-
sation of Irish and Native American peoples in an ideology that
justified conquest. Inevitably, the process of colonisation, whereby
indigenous peoples throughout the world have 'been consistently,
often violently, dispossessed of their cultures, languages and
lands, not to mention their very lives' (May 2002: 17), resulted
in a tradition of native resistance in Ireland. Unsurprisingly, this
provoked a reciprocal intensification of English coloniser brutality,
since the English 'were now absolved from all restraints in dealing
with' the natives (Curtis 1984: 21). This was justified through a
classic exposition of supposed native barbarity, as evidenced in the
writings of Edmund Spenser, English poet and colonial emissary to
Queen Elizabeth, who prescribed that '[t]he Gaels must be redeemed
from their wildness: they must cut their glibs of overhanging hair
(which conceals their plotting faces); they must convert their mantles
... into conventional cloaks; above all, they must speak the English
tongue' (Kiberd 1995:10).

This colonial ideology excused the wholesale process of land
confiscations and plantations, culminating in the Battle of Kinsale
of 1601 – a watershed in modern Irish history. This would leave a
bloody legacy and yield a reversal of fortunes for the Irish language
and herald 'the triumph of the English language, law and politico-
administrative institutions throughout Ireland, and the defeat of the
whole institutional edifice of the Gaelic political and social order
which had been sustained and mediated through the Irish language'
(Ó Tuathaigh 2005: 42).

Under the Elizabethan conquest, Irish effectively became the
language of the dispossessed. The acute connection between Ireland's
political defeat and the endeavour to eradicate the language was
referred to by one of the leading architects of the Ulster plantation,
Sir John Davies, who stated 'that the next generation will in tongue
and heart and in every way else become English; so as there will be
no difference but the Irish sea betwixt us' (Ó Fiaich 1969: 105). His
undue optimism underestimated the latent potential for resistance
as manifested in the rebellion of 1641, in which the natives rose
in an attempt to repossess their lands, in what 'must have been in
its early stages almost exclusively an insurrection of Irish speakers'
(ibid.: 106).

The post-1649 Cromwellian campaign ushered in an unprecedented
legacy of death, destruction and land confiscation, as evidenced by
the massive reduction in the Irish population. Cromwell's imperial
objectives had religious and racist undertones 'not far removed

from those which Nazis used about Slavs, or white South Africans use about the original inhabitants of their country'. In each case, the contempt 'rationalized the desire to exploit' (Hill 1970: 113).[2] Cromwell's campaign of genocidal devastation left Ireland in ruins; by 1653 the population had halved from 1.5 million people, with over 616,000 dead, 40,000 conscripted to serve in European armies and a further 100,000 rounded up and transported to the new colonies of the Caribbean and America as slaves (Curtis 1984: 28).

Although the Penal Laws did not specifically proscribe the Irish language, the hierarchy of the Anglo-Irish Ascendancy viewed it disdainfully as a language of backwardness and poverty. Hence the impoverishment and inequality of the Irish emerged from their linguistic, racial and cultural inferiority as opposed to the invasion, subsequent repression, and the dispossession of their lands (Williams 1992: 130). The indigenous elite's eventual defeat consolidated British imperial and political power, leading to widespread economic exploitation that cleared the ground for the imposition of capitalist social relations upon Irish society (Cleary 2003).

Against this backdrop, a process of language shift to 'English, the language of power and of all the avenues to advancement, soon gathered momentum among those who aspired to improve their condition or to progress and participate fully in the life of the country under the new order' (Ó Tuathaigh 2005: 42). Thus, by the end of the eighteenth century, Irish had 'been banished from Parliament and from the Courts of Law, from town and county Government, from the Civil service and from the upper levels of commercial life' (Wall 1969: 82).

Ireland was undergoing the initial side-effects of the classical colonial condition. The increased demand for literacy – in English – and the growing commercialisation of the rural economy contributed to the propagation of the myth that traditional customs were obstacles to survival. That the economic element was central to this campaign was epitomised by the higher pay given to Irish labourers who could speak English (Crowley 2000: 34). Naturally, many native Irish speakers who faced stark poverty were influenced more by such necessity than by choice as the process of cultural colonisation in Ireland intensified:

The colonized's mother tongue ... is precisely the one which is least valued ... If he wants to obtain a job, make a place for himself, exist in the community and the world, he must first bow to the language of his masters. In the linguistic conflict within the colonized, his mother tongue is that which is crushed. He himself sets about discarding this infirm language, hiding it from the sight of strangers. (Memmi 1965: 151)

In addition, the Catholic Church in this period also facilitated colonial assimilation in the interests of its own survival and enhanced status. From its opening in 1795, English was promoted as the language of choice at Maynooth, the national training college for Catholic priests, despite the majority of its parishioners being monoglot Irish speakers (Crowley 2000: 84). Similar tendencies were evident in the early-nineteenth-century campaign for Catholic emancipation. Daniel O'Connell, a native speaker from county Kerry, encouraged the demise of the language: '[T]he superior utility of the English tongue, as the medium of all modern communication, is so great, that I can witness without a sigh the gradual disuse of Irish' (Curtis 1994: 26).

The national school system's imposition of 'civility' saw Irish become a non-language and the Irish people effectively a non-people. This is illustrated by the notorious mandatory morning assembly recitation in national school classrooms:

> I thank the goodness and the grace
> Which on my birth have smiled;
> And made me in these Christian days,
> A happy English child. (Kiberd 1992: 29)

Irish children were thus taught that Irish damaged the acquisition of English and that their parents' lack of English represented a lack of intelligence and civilisation, thereby internalising a sense of shame about their indigenous culture and non-literate parents (Nic Craith 2001: 103). Despite the untold damage done by the national education system, according to the census of 1841 more than half the population remained Irish-speaking (Hindley 1990: 15). Rapid decline was accelerated by the catastrophic demographic impact of the Great Hunger (*an drochshaoil*), however, which 'decimated Irish-speaking Ireland through death and emigration' (Ó Tuathaigh 2005: 43).

In the period of *an drochshaoil*, which would continue for much of the nineteenth century, the well-established association between the native language, illiteracy and low social status became deep-rooted when linked with individual survival. This era was characterised by 'widespread acceptance of negative colonial stereotyping that fostered the inculcation of the seeds of shame and inferiority in the minds of Irish speakers for their own language' (Ó Conaire 1986: 6). This Irish assimilative experience mirrored indigenous experience across the wider British empire, in which the destruction or assimilation of indigenous languages was a prominent, usually calculated feature. Such cultural invasion not only created subservient and loyal subjects, but simultaneously facilitated the economic power and wealth of the expanding empire.

In assessing the 'remarkable event in Irish cultural history' represented by the 'massive abandonment of Irish as vernacular language during the nineteenth century' (Ó Tuathaigh (2005: 43), many commentators unthinkingly separate language 'choice' from the all-pervasive reality of cultural colonisation in Ireland. According to Edwards (1985: 62–3) for example, the language shift in Ireland had less to do with sociopolitical factors than with the fact that the 'mass of the Irish people' had become 'linguistically pragmatic' and made the practical choice of losing their language, thus becoming 'more or less active contributors to the spread of English'. This view is echoed by Comerford (2003:146), who believes that 'parental pressure' on Irish children reflected a widespread 'societal enthusiasm' to adapt to the modern world.

This analysis overestimates the element of individual 'choice' in this language shift in Ireland, while simultaneously marginalising the profound impact of the Great Hunger and a national school system which had more 'to do with cultural and mental colonisation' (Ó Ceallaigh 1994b:16) than with bringing modern education and literacy to Ireland. The role of starving and impoverished Irish parents in this process of language shift – which included preventing their children from speaking Irish at home – is portrayed as reflecting 'a popular and spontaneous re-evaluation of an ancient and bountiful culture', rather than considered in its essential context of the wider process of British colonialism in Ireland (ibid.).

The Irish example illuminates the inherent problems with depicting language shift as 'voluntary' in similar cases throughout the world: 'if minority languages are consistently viewed as low status, socially and culturally restrictive, and an obstacle to social mobility, is it little wonder that such patterns of language shift exist?' (May 2002: 149). The central dilemma faced by native speakers in making this supposed choice, is whether: 'to remain loyal to their traditions and to remain socially disadvantaged (consigning their own children to such disadvantage as well)' or 'to abandon their distinctive practices and traditions, at least in large part, and thereby to improve their own and their children's lots in life via cultural suicide' (Fishman 1991: 60).

Irrefutably, much Irish revisionist historiography conforms to this wider practice of rationalisation. This view is illustrated in Comerford's work, which serves as an example of the reductive analyses inherent in many academic histories:

> The commercial calculations behind the collective move to acquire English that took place about the middle of the eighteenth century among the Irish-speaking populace are reaping rewards beyond the imagining of the Anglicising generations. American domination of a globalizing world gives enormous potential to native speakers of English ... Being an Anglophone country gave Ireland a crucial advantage in attracting foreign investment that supported the economic transformation of the country in the 1990s ... These are advantages that an Irish-speaking Ireland would have never enjoyed. (Comerford 2003: 150)

This celebratory description of the 'advantages' of cultural assimilation not only ignores the traumatic consequences of such developments, but asserts in an unreflective fashion the ideology of 'English linguistic imperialism' that maintains social, economic, political and cultural inequalities between English and other languages (Phillipson 1992). In addition, it's worth noting that the extolment of bogus neoliberal 'economic transformation' would also be comprehensively disproved with the subsequent collapse of the Irish economy in 2008 (Kirby 2011).

While a thorough examination of the cultural colonisation of Ireland underpins the analysis in this book, it is also clear that 'an understanding of the language issue remains essential to any serious consideration of the cultural and political history of modern Ireland' (Ó Tuathaigh 2005: 58). The devastating consequences of colonisation in Ireland, which would shape the varying approaches of those engaged in revival, will form the basis of the next section. An ideology rooted in decolonisation and resistance would not only inspire the Irish revolution, but would also resonate as a key motivating factor amongst many in the contemporary Irish-language revival movement.

## FIRST REVIVAL ATTEMPTS: PROTESTANTS AND THE IRISH LANGUAGE

> [A] knowledge of Irish is also absolutely necessary ... [I]t is surely reasonable and desirable, that every [Irish] person should be able to hold converse with his countrymen; as well as to taste and admire the beauties of one of the most expressive, philosophically accurate, and polished languages that has ever existed.
>
> William Nielson (Hughes 2006b: 52)

In the circumstances of accelerated cultural decline in nineteenth-century Ireland, it was ironic that north-eastern Presbyterians and Belfast's radicals of the 1790s in particular would be the first to display a concerted interest in cultural revival (Ó Snódaigh 1995: 61). The Belfast Harp festival of July 1792 sought the 'reviving and perpetuation of the otherwise forgotten arts' (ibid.: 12). While in the past, many Protestants and members of the Anglo-Irish ascendancy had been attracted to the language through antiquarianism (McCoy 1997: 70), Presbyterian intellectuals in the north actively promoted the learning and use of the Irish language as a means of communication through the sponsoring of instructional classes.

There is also considerable evidence that many within the Belfast Irish-language movement of the 1790s recognised its potential to unite 'settler and native', and some members of the United Irishmen viewed cultural revival as relevant to their revolutionary ideals of 'Liberté, Égalité, Fraternité'. This is apparent in the preface to Ireland's first Irish-language magazine, *Bolg an tSolair*, which was published in October 1795, and written by Thomas Russell and his Irish teacher and County Down scribe, Patrick Lynch (Ó Fiaich 1969: 108). Its contents not only stressed the importance of preserving and cultivating the language as the 'vernacular tongue ... of every Irishman', but also strongly condemned Britain's colonial record in Ireland, hinting at the birth of the ideology of decolonisation:

> To recommend the Irish language to the notice of Irishmen ... to persuade the natives that their own language is of some importance to them, would appear quite superfluous in the eyes of foreigners; but seeing that the Gaelic has been not only banished from the court, the college and the bar, but that many tongues and pens have been employed to cry it down and to persuade the ignorant that it was a harsh and barbarous jargon, and that their ancestors, from whom they derived it, were an ignorant,

uncultivated people – it becomes necessary to say something in reply ... the Irish enjoyed their own laws and language, till the reigns of Elizabeth and James (Ó Snódaigh 1995: 64).

In chronicling the suppression of the language and the many means by which its speakers were derided as 'ignorant and barbarous', Russell and his collaborators referred to Ireland's cultural colonisation to inspire the Irish people to reclaim 'this ancient and once-admired' language.

In addition, many amongst the leadership of the 1798 rebellion learned, promoted and spoke the language, including William Putnam McCabe, Jemmy Hope, Robert Emmet, William Drennan, William McNevin and Thomas Russell (Ó Snódaigh 1998: 4–5). There is also evidence that Wolfe Tone had Irish, having written out 30 Irish airs for musicians while in France, and subsequently, along with other leaders utilised it, however broken it may have been, to propagate their message amongst the Irish-speaking masses, many of whom would have had no understanding of English (ibid.). The activities of Russell and the others were 'more than merely academic', as articulated in the strong views of Lord Edward Fitzgerald, himself a colonel in the 1798 rebellion, who is accredited with positing 'that the English language should be abolished' before encouraging 'younger and more enthusiastic' Irishmen to '[set] themselves forthwith to the study of the Irish tongue' (Ó Fiaich 1969: 108–9). While the 'Gaelic tradition in politics was not a republican one', many poets and survivors of the Gaelic literary tradition were attracted, as vocal representatives of the dispossessed and culturally distinct Catholic Irish peasantry, to any form of hope for the revolutionary overthrow of the repressive political system (ibid.).

However, this cross-religious alliance of 'politically disadvantaged Ulster Presbyterian bourgeoisie who made common cause with their Catholic compatriots against a government and an Anglican elite' in 1798 was crushed through military coercion, while English rule in Ireland was consolidated through the legislative enactment of the 1801 Act of Union (Ó Giolláin 2000: 16). While the radical revolutionary spirit of Presbyterianism largely vanished after the 1798 rising, 'cost[ing] the revival movement many of its friends and leaders in dispersal, death or emigration', ardent revivalists from the Protestant tradition pioneered the legacy for much of the nineteenth century (Ó Snódaigh 1995: 65).

Although attracted to 'the cultural, literary and artistic aspects of the language', crucially, this Presbyterian tradition promoted Irish as 'a functional language in widespread daily use at the time' (Hughes 2006b: 57). In retrospect, Robert MacAdam stands out in this era as 'the champion of the cultivation of the Gaelic language and its broader culture, both old and modern' (Hughes 2006a: 99). He would later be described as the one 'who first had the idea of "reviving the language" although he has yet to receive credit for this – he truly was "the first Gaelic Leaguer"' (ibid.: 100). However, genuine hopes of revival and the cultivation of cultural activities were severely impeded by sectarian violence, drastic population growth and the onset of industrialisation.

The arrival of poverty-stricken Irish Catholics from rural areas hoping to reap the benefits of the economic 'boom' doubled the number of Belfast's Catholics from 16 per cent of the population in 1808 to 34 per cent in 1834. Their presence flooded the labour market, intensifying competition for jobs and houses, and in periods of intermittent economic crisis the more established Protestant workers were inclined to identify Catholics as an economic threat. In this context the Orange Order orchestrated a dramatic rise in anti-Catholic sectarianism, lobbying ferociously against Catholic emancipation and repeal of the Penal laws, with the resulting tensions inevitably manifested in violent rioting and sectarian attacks. The first serious episode occurred in 1813, peaking in intensity between 1832 and 1835, and continuing periodically, with serious violence flaring in 1843, 1857, 1864, 1872, 1884 and 1886 (ibid.).

As a by-product of this growing sectarian tension, Protestant interest in the language waned considerably after 1860, as 'the Irish language began to become more associated in the public mind with Catholicism' and was 'looked upon with a certain suspicion by people who had no first-hand knowledge of it' (Ó Snódaigh 1995: 128). The integration of northern Presbyterians into the post-union political and economic order removed the basis for their alliance with excluded Catholics and reinforced the sectarian alignment aggressively promoted by the Orange Order. Their interest in the Irish language was one of the important casualties of this realignment in Presbyterian outlook in the new, highly-charged sectarian atmosphere of the industrialising north.

Cultural activism in the mid nineteenth century had also found expression in the romantic nationalism of the Young Irelanders, whose leader, the inspirational young Protestant barrister, Thomas Davis, regarded the Irish language as the key to national revival. His renowned article 'Our National Language' emphasised the historical importance of the language to a native national identity:

> A people without a language of its own is only half a nation. A nation should guard its language more than its territories – 'tis a surer barrier, and more important frontier, than fortress or river ... To lose your native tongue, and learn that of an alien, is the worst badge of conquest – it is the chain on the soul. (Davis n.d.: 174–5)

Davis's writings, which were 'inspired by the centrality of national languages to the political programmes of contemporary European cultural nationalist movements' (Crowley 2000: 34), provided Irish nationalism with its central concepts of Ireland and Irishness. While Davis's manifesto has been strongly criticised as mythological and based on 'racialist assumption' (Comerford 2003: 141), his contribution has also been conceptualised as that of Ireland's first 'radical decolonising intellectual confronting head on the difficulties of constructing an Irish identity in terms made available by the imperial power he was attempting to throw off' (Smyth 1999: 37). In this sense, Davis's decolonising voice paralleled Fanon's concept of counter-hegemonic mirroring, as his writing provided an inspiring counterbalance to the all-pervasive British viewpoint. Crucially, Davis also had an immense influence on a future generation of cultural and political activists (Ó hAilín 1969: 93).

## DE-ANGLICISATION AND THE GAELIC LEAGUE

> I have no hesitation at all in saying that every Irish-feeling Irishman, who hates the reproach of West-Britonism, should set himself to encourage the efforts, which are being made to keep alive our once great national tongue. The losing of it is our greatest blow, and the sorest stroke that the rapid Anglicization of Ireland has inflicted upon us. In order to de-Anglicize ourselves we must at once arrest the decay of the language.
>
> Douglas Hyde (1892; Crowley 2000: 187)

Owing a significant debt to the Davisite tradition, Douglas Hyde's inspirational manifesto called for widespread cultural revival. 'The Necessity for de-Anglicising Ireland', delivered as a speech in 1892, 'opened up the revolutionary perspective that reversed traditional nationalist political logic' (Townshend 1998: 39) and provided the template for the formation of the Gaelic League a year later. The League itself differed radically in its objectives from all previous societies in that it openly aimed to eradicate the inferiority generated by years of Anglicisation and colonialism through the revival of the language as a spoken tongue.

This followed hard on the heels of Michael Cusack's formation of the Gaelic Athletic Association (GAA) in 1884. The revived Gaelic Games envisaged the emancipation of the Irish poor from the 'dehumanisation, degeneracy and depoliticisation' of existing athletics clubs, as well as rugby, soccer and cricket organisations, while simultaneously providing a 'nationalizing idiom, a symbolic language of identity filling the void created by Anglicisation' (Whelan 2005: 150). By 1890, there were over 1,000 clubs.[3] The revival's popularity was testimony to a widespread sentiment for decolonisation, while in the process providing the ideological framework for cultural nationalism. Inevitably, early Gaelic League activists discovered that 'many were ashamed to admit they knew Irish, because it was associated in their minds with illiteracy, poverty and proselytism' (Ó hAilín 1969: 92–3). In this sense, this 'deliberate project of "decolonisation" ... formulated and adopted by a group of intellectuals and artists' was designed to undo 'the shame of defeat, dispossession, humiliation and impoverishment – the classic colonial condition' (Ó Tuathaigh 2005: 46–47).

The League's radical educational policies emphasised instructional classes as well as more overt political campaigning aimed at increasing the language's status. Thus by 1900 the Irish language had been accepted as a mainstream optional subject within the British National School System, to be taught during school hours. In 1904, the League's bilingual policy for primary schools in Irish-speaking areas was accepted (ibid.: 99). Arguably, the largest achievement was when Irish became a compulsory matriculation subject in the National University of Ireland after Gaelic League activists utilised its network of supporters in lobbying the university authorities (Comerford 2003: 141).

However, governmental flexibility in the early-century era of 'killing Home Rule with Kindness' (Jackson 1999: 148) demonstrated that antagonistic British policy towards the language had merely become more veiled and sophisticated:

An Conradh [the Gaelic League] continued to play a sort of game with the education authorities and the British treasury. The game went like this: An Conradh made certain demands for teaching of Irish. The British Government refused them. All shades of public opinion [were] brought to bear by An Conradh and the authorities gave in. However a short time later the Government introduced some new rule or measure which hit the teaching of Irish. An Conradh mobilised its forces again. There was another submission and a little later another wriggle by the Government and Irish suffered again. (Ó Fearaíl 1975: 30)

Invariably, the British authorities only acceded to the League's demands due to political expediency. In the aftermath of any notable concession, the authorities pursued every available avenue to neutralise the validity or implementation of the reforms.

In this period, the Irish-language movement naturally converged, as happened in numerous anti-colonial struggles throughout the world, with the growing forces of nationalism. This led to a dramatic increase in support; the number of Gaelic League branches rose from 120 in 1900 to 985 in 1906, with membership peaking at 75,000 members (Hutchinson 1987: 178–9). The revival's undoubted force in the period rested on the fact that it radically refocused popular sentiment on the issue of national sovereignty by harnessing latent anti-British feeling. In essence, the League's non-political stance was 'something of a fiction in any case', in that it fostered a false ideology whereby 'a commonality was pre-supposed' between two traditions, 'where in reality divisions existed' (Crowley 2000: 178). Ultimately, Hyde's naive hope that such a commonality could be maintained floundered on his 'blithe assumption that a movement as opposed to mainstream unionism as the Gaelic League could somehow be non-political' (Kiberd 1995: 123).

However, some commentators view the League's 'politicisation' as a disadvantage because of the resultant unionist alienation (Mac Póilin 1997b: 42–3). In truth, however, anti-Irish suspicions in the pro-union community pre-dated the League's formation. As has been stated, the unionist position had emerged from Ulster's industrialisation and political incorporation under the legislative union. This trend was copper-fastened in the campaign of opposition to the First Home Rule Bill. The ensuing political tensions, as depicted by late-nineteenth-century writer Cathal O'Byrne, left unionist interest in the language highly improbable: 'the League was never considered quite "respectable" ... by the planters. To be a Gaelic leaguer was to be suspect always' (Ó Snódaigh 1995: 85). The tiny number of unionists who, oblivious to its 'unexamined contradictions' (Kiberd 1995: 149), were attracted to the Gaelic League at the outset, found their participation gradually more untenable following the militant redefinition of unionism during the passage of the Third Home Rule Bill (Lee 1989b: 1).[4]

Notably, many revisionist historians have been deeply critical of the Gaelic Revival as reactionary, 'fundamentally sectarian and even racialist' (Foster 1988: 453). Such reductionist readings ignore the cultural revival's centrality to the Irish mass-liberation movement, attribute an uncritically positive value to Anglicisation and disregard the revival's position as a response to an established process of cultural imperialism. Arguably, such revisionist historiography should be understood as part of a trend whereby 'the debunking of Nationalism, revolution and native cultural resurgence suits conservatism both in its backward glance and current circumspection. The past must be de-radicalised to help prevent radicalisation of the present' (Ó Ceallaigh 1994b: 8).

It is crucially important to measure the 'decolonising' Gaelic League project against the context of the sociocultural trauma, political subordination and significant levels of death and displacement that were the legacy of British colonialism in Ireland. That this modest attempt to transform the situation would emerge as such a prominent factor in the Irish political independence struggle was attested to by Pearse, who wrote that 'when the seven men met in O'Connell street to found the Gaelic League, they were commencing ... not a revolt, but a revolution' (Crowley 2000: 216). In actuality, the Gaelic League's historical legacy would extend well beyond the early twentieth century; in the absence of its dedicated programme the Irish language might have taken a similar path towards extinction to that taken by languages like Manx and Cornish (Ó Riagáin 2006: 3).

## 'NÍ AMHÁIN GAELACH ACH SAOR': REPUBLICANISM AND CULTURAL RECONQUEST

A free Ireland must not only be free but Gaelic-speaking while a Gaelic-speaking Ireland must not only be Gaelic-speaking but free also.

Pádraig Pearse (Kiberd 1995: 152)

The involvement of militant nationalism and radical republicanism is recognised as a crucial factor in the evolution of the language revival movement into 'the first modern example of a great democratic movement, with the ascendant apparatus of committees and boards, under completely Irish control' (Greene 1966: 80). However, the historic precedent for this linkage is considerably less explored. In addition to the aforementioned association of the leaders of the 1798 rising with the language, the IRB (Irish Republican Brotherhood), which was founded in 1858 and subsequently became 'the epitome of militant nationalism, included a number of language activists among its prominent men' (Comerford 2003: 140).

One of the IRB's founders, John O'Mahony, was a Gaelic scholar and produced a translation of Keating's *Foras Feasa ar Éirinn*, published in New York in 1857 (ibid.). Jeremiah O'Donovan Rossa 'certainly went beyond Davis's concept of English as the language of commerce when he made Irish the language of his shop in Skibereen, even of its advertising material' (Ó Fiaich 1969: 110). Although the Fenians 'conducted their public politics, whether at home or among the Irish Diaspora, overwhelmingly in English' (Ó Tuathaigh 2005: 44), John Devoy later claimed that 'the intention to restore the language ... was as strong among the Fenians as that of establishing an Irish republic ... .Had the Fenian movement succeeded ... it would have taken prompt and effective measures to restore the language' (Ó Fiaich 1969: 110).

Despite this background, it is notable that the IRB and militant nationalism had little involvement with the Gaelic League in its early formative years. Fenians tended to gravitate towards the GAA, not only because of its insurrectionary potential, but because the organisation's accessibility and typical membership demographic better reflected the IRB's 'democratic and republican social ideal' (McGee 2005: 348–9). Nevertheless, by the beginning of the century, Fenian instrumentalist designs had clearly extended to the League.[5] With the subsequent emergence of the Sinn Féin party, the Gaelic League became a mass revivalist movement which was viewed as a conduit for the participatory separatist model. As the RIC inspector general explained: 'Gaelic classes, concerts, dances, SF clubs and GAA football matches' are 'some of the most convenient means of collecting rebels together and fomenting hatred of England' (Laffan 1999: 94).

Moreover, the enhanced interest in nationalist ideas also coincided with a developing interest in socialist ideology and Labour politics, as exemplified by James Connolly and Jim Larkin. Connolly, too, drew inspiration from the past and argued for a united ideological front that would enable the reconquest of Ireland in the future based on what he viewed as the culture, fellowship and co-operative ideals of the earlier Gaelic civilisation. Connolly's relevance rested in articulating a Marxist analysis rooted in the Irish experience. His involvement in the Easter Rising was foreshadowed by earlier initiatives that included promoting collaboration between the suffragettes, republicans, the Sinn Féiners, and the Gaelic Leaguers (ibid.). Perhaps more importantly, he succinctly provided a structural analysis of the socio-economic relations in Ireland, while providing a synthesis between the national and the social; this would form the basis for many future decolonising projects.

Connolly was not alone in being affected by the reality of unionist resistance to home rule and the wider ramifications of emerging global conflict. This shift in position was also evident within the ranks of the language movement. Radical activists like Pearse argued that 'fighting with the state for concessions could only ever take second place to the formation of a separate Irish state' (Ó Croidheáin 2006: 150). Pearse called for the arming of nationalists, stating that 'an Orangeman with a rifle is a much less ridiculous figure than a nationalist without a rifle' (Githens-Mazer 2006: 62).

An increasingly influential section began to question the rationale of the League's non-political stance. A September 1913 article by Fergus MacLede, in the IRB-controlled *Irish Freedom*, pointed out that in the context of the 'conquest of Ireland ... the work of the Gaelic League is to prevent the assimilation of the Irish nation by the English nation' (Ó Huallacháin 1994: 66):

> The Gaelic League does not stand to take sides in the political differences that separate Irishmen into different parties, and therefore it is claimed to be non-political. The claim appears to be useful, but in practice it is only misleading ... it may have misled a few unionists into the Gaelic League, and to that extent may appear to be useful; it has undoubtedly led some unthinking nationalists into great confusion. It has confused the one straight issue for them, and that issue is whether the Irish Nation or the English Nation is to predominate in Ireland ... The Irish Language is a political weapon of the first importance against English encroachment; it can never be a political weapon in the hands of one Irish party against the other. (Ibid. 66–7)

Mac Póilin (1997b: 40) states that he knows of 'no better definition' of 'the radical nationalist perspective on the language' than the concluding point in the above quote. Nevertheless, his focus is arguably restrictive: he argues 'that the function of the language movement was to assist the political movement' (ibid.), whereas, in actuality, the article intimates that the language is an unavoidable aspect of the political struggle rather than an element that can be divorced from it. It was this perspective which defined the militant republican vision of cultural reconquest that dominated the ideology of future generations of activists.

In the months ahead, tensions increased between the League's radical element and the 'right wing' led by Hyde. This tension emerged from Hyde's 'refusal to follow the logic' that 'the two aspirations' of being 'not merely Gaelic but free' were 'interdependent' (Kiberd (1995: 152). IRB and Gaelic League activist Ernest Blythe claimed that 'between 1913 and 1916 Hyde's influence as a leader of opinion underwent something like a complete eclipse' (Ó Huallacháin 1994: 63). These tensions would culminate in the IRB's takeover at the 1915 Ard Fheis. A Fenian-sponsored amendment to include the word 'free' alongside 'Gaelic-speaking' led to Hyde's resignation and replacement by Irish Volunteer leader and League co-founder Eoin MacNeill.[6]

Interestingly, IRB leader Seán Mac Diarmada had initially opposed Tom Clarke's suggestion of an IRB takeover of the League for fear that it would 'die and the death will be put down to our influence' (MacAtasney 2004: 208). The newly radicalised political circumstances, however, rendered the League's support crucial to Clarke's revolutionary objectives. Thus, the military council which initiated the Easter Rising arguably recognised that the cultural revival helped crystallise for a variety of social groupings the structural reality of British colonialism in Ireland. As a decolonising vehicle in transformational circumstances, the League held the potential for republican politicisation designed to subvert constitutional nationalist dominance and rejuvenate the tradition of physical-force republicanism.

When the Easter Rising eventually took place in April 1916, the practical extent of the linkage between the Rising and the Gaelic League was illustrated by the fact that six of the seven signatories of the Proclamation were members, and all but two of the officers of the *Coiste Gnótha* of the League were implicated in the Rising, with 16 of its members being shot, wounded, taken prisoner or disappearing (Ó Huallacháin 1994: 72). The Rising is universally recognised as a defining moment in the Irish Revolution. Similarly, few dispute the summation that 'the Gaelic resurgence was the revivifying force which made possible the Easter Rising of 1916' (Rees 1998: 211). In the aftermath, Frongoch and other prisons transformed the trajectory of the independence movement by becoming radical

schools of 'the new Sinn Féin thought' (MacArdle 1951: 201). While
the Rising and the martial law imposed by the British government
had irreparably damaged the moderate nationalism of the Irish Party
and the Home Rule cause, the release of highly politcised internees
in 1917 rejuvenated radical Irish nationalism on the outside and led
to the reorganisation of Sinn Féin.

Sinn Féin was dominated by a generation of ardent Gaelic League
activists who passed resolutions at the convention declaring that
Irish should become the language of its executive, 'imperative' for
all members, and a pre-requisite for election to the executive and the
nomination of candidates for parliament (Laffan 1999: 116). The
adoption of 'Irish Ireland' was a logical and important element in
a mass participatory separatist campaign, which sought to replace
colonial domination, both cultural and political. It was also useful
as an ideological glue to hold together what was a pan-class
movement – since it gave commonality to a struggle which could
have potentially suffered much more from intra-class tensions. This
was greatly assisted by the pro-republican and abstentionist position
adopted by the Irish Labour movement, which paved the way for
their landslide electoral victory in December 1918. However, the
potential always existed for ownership of the language to become
disputed in the counter-revolutionary stage, due to the prominence
of the cultural revival in popular mobilisation from 1917 to 1921.

The British government responded to the emergence of radical
republicanism by employing state coercion against it. All expressions
of Irishness were subject to draconian measures, including the
Gaelic League, which was declared a 'dangerous organisation which
encourages and aids persons to commit crimes' (Ó Fearaíl 1975:
45). Paradoxically, such measures actually strengthened language
revivalists' resolve. At the first public meeting of Dáil Éireann,
held at the Mansion House in Dublin in January 1919, the order
of business was published bilingually and the proceedings were
conducted primarily in Irish (Ó Gadhra 1989: 57). The First Dáil's
Democratic Programme was read out in Irish, then French, then
English thus sending out a 'powerful message to the world about
the revolutionary intentions of the new Irish Government' (A. Ó
Snódaigh 2006: 12).

Nevertheless, circumstances were completely transformed
when the British imposed the Government of Ireland Act in 1920,
which partitioned the six north-eastern counties of Ulster into
unionist control. The British government subsequently negotiated
a Treaty settlement with the Irish independence movement, which

approved partition under the threat of 'immediate and terrible war, and war within three days' (Lyons 1973: 437). Ultimately, these developments would irrevocably split both republican and Irish-language movements, thus rendering the language an 'emblem of divided Irish political allegiances' (Ó Huallacháin 1994: 83). Whilst the republican movement was split down the middle, the language became a source of competition between pro-Treaty and anti-Treaty camps as to who was most genuinely wedded to the revival project (Mac Póilin 1997b: 43).[7]

The Gaelic League itself went into sharp decline after 1922, partly because it was believed that the state would take over the revival, but primarily due to the Civil War, which tore many branches apart (Lyons 1973: 636). One Cork activist described how the enthusiasm for Gaelic League classes, augmented by the fervour of the Anglo-Irish war, subsided in the aftermath of the Treaty:

> [A]lmost overnight the enthusiasm evaporated and the classes faded away. At first we couldn't believe the classes were not going to continue ... one of the most intellectual of the students ... said 'well the enthusiasm was great because we expected to have a Republic, and its dignity would demand the native language, but now we'll still be part of the British empire, and have a divided country – not worth the effort of learning the language – English will be good enough for us.' (Ó Croidheáin 2006: 167)

The number of League branches plummeted from 700 in 1920 to 565 in 1922 (Ó Fearaíl 1975: 45). While Gaeilgeoirí such as Pearse, MacDonagh and Mac Diarmada were executed by British firing squads in the aftermath of the Rising, it was a bitter irony that radical language activists like Liam Mellows and Cathal Brugha would die at the hands of former comrades during the Civil War (Lyons 1973: 636). The anti-Treatyite defeat 'seriously weakened a revolutionary tradition', as signified in the 1922 Free State constitution, which saw 'a watering down of the much more radical Democratic Programme of the First Dáil' (Croidheáin 2006: 165).

Despite the fact that there were many genuine language activists on the pro-Treaty side, who had been instrumental in the 1915 Gaelic League takeover, and pushed the revivalist doctrine of the language movement to the forefront of the newly formed state, the unionist ascendancy and a pro-British, colonial mentality retained control of most state institutions (A. Ó Snódaigh 2006: 12).[8] The fact that the new state, which was consolidated following an effective 'counter-revolution',[9] retained the same administrative system as the inherently hostile British administration left plans for the Gaelicisation of the civil service and government bodies with little reasonable chance of success. In this state, anglicised Catholicism became the dominant Irish identity, as a 'politically conservative government battled against radical ideas in the shape of revolutionary socialism and republicanism' (Ó Croidheáin 2006: 120).

The revivalist project was placed in the hands, and lost in the sea of the bureaucracy that was the Department of Education. Motivated by the vain hope that compulsory Irish in Free State schools could reverse the negative impact of the British education model, the language was taught, often by teachers at the same level of fluency as the children, as a dead language rather than as a living, thriving language in the throes of revival (Lee 1989b: 671). Furthermore, entry to secondary schools could only be achieved by a minority upper or middle class, which did not face the structural challenge of a genuinely radical educational overhaul that could have provided the potential for language revival in the schools (ibid.: 172).[10] The Irish language was utilised as a right-wing nationalistic ethnic symbol that redefined 'the interests of the propertied classes' and strengthened the grip of a reactionary political establishment on the one hand and the autocratic Catholic Church on the other (Ó Croidheáin 2006: 161).

In addition, the rhetorical commitment given by the new state to maintain the poverty-stricken Gaeltacht areas was exposed by its failure to provide legal or administrative services to native speakers in order that they could spend their lives with self-respect in their own country (Lee 1989b: 674). Ireland in this period 'became a disturbing retreat into a conservative type of cultural protectionism', which subsequently alienated a whole generation of radical activists and intellectuals who might well have backed a more progressive cultural programme (Ó hÉallaithe 2004: 165).

This enshrined the hegemony of a reactionary Free-State administration that failed to promote the liberating aspirations of cultural revival as a means of decolonisation. As Smyth posits:

Despite the best efforts of its liberal and left wings, radical decolonisation was commandeered by a nationalist bourgeois elite which tried to arrest the process at the point where it assumed control of the state apparatus left vacant by an offshore power.

The drive towards an essential national identity in the years after 1922 actually reinforced social and political hierarchies even as it claimed to be an agent of liberation from such hierarchies. (Smyth 1999: 37)

Nevertheless, though the project of 'radical decolonisation' had not reached fruition, its pervasive ideology maintained an appeal with various remnants of the republican movement that continually reappeared, often violently, in the decades following the formation of the Irish Free State.

The ideology of cultural reconquest would often be integral to the resistance strategies employed by these republicans in their opposition to the two states when imprisoned on either side of the recently constructed border. When Dawson Bates, the Northern Ireland home secretary, vowed in the early 1920s to 'treat' republican prisoners in the six counties 'with the same severity as Mr [Kevin] O'Higgins was displaying to their comrades in southern Ireland' (Kleinrichert 2001: 216), it was clear that the Irish language could again provide those imprisoned with succour from the excesses of incarceration. In this sense, it could encompass a practical means of resistance against prison hardship and simultaneously define their principled adherence to the revivalist doctrine of decolonisation that had inspired the subverted Irish revolution.

# 3
# 'Promoting Sedition':
# The Irish Language and the
# 'Orange State', 1922–72

This chapter deals primarily with the outworking of the colonial process in the six counties following the formation of the Northern Ireland state in 1920, when the Irish language retreated in the face of systemic legislative discrimination by the unionist one-party administration. By contrast with this, the chapter goes on to recount the remarkable development, under hostile circumstances, of a 'hidden' language revival; it includes original extracts from the oral testimonies of some of the activists involved. This revival culminated in the formation of the Shaw's Road Urban Gaeltacht in 1960s west Belfast and the north of Ireland's first Irish-medium school in 1971.

## STATE HOSTILITY TOWARDS THE LANGUAGE IN 'NORTHERN IRELAND'

What use is it here in this busy part of the empire to teach our children the Irish language? What use would it have to them? Is it not leading them along a road which has no practical value? We have not stopped the teaching; we have stopped the grants, which I think amounted to £1,500 a year. We have stopped the grants simply because we do not see that these boys being taught Irish would be any better citizens.

James Craig, Stormont prime minister,
speaking in 1933 (Andrews 1997: 83)

The 1920 Government of Ireland Act which partitioned Ireland laid the foundations for the formation of Europe's first one-party state in its north-east. This was designed to ensure a permanent unionist majority and prevented Irish nationalists' access to political power, employment and housing, thereby relegating them to a subordinate, apartheid-like status (Farrell 1976). The Protestant majority in the six counties 'now effectively had their own settler state' in which 'their illegal armed forces were allowed to become a 'special constabulary' (Clayton 1998: 49). These forces implemented newly enacted draconian security legislation that oversaw 'the indiscriminate violence of loyalists against Catholics during the early years of the state's formation' (Andrews 1997: 56).

The new administration's survivalist dictum of 'what we have we hold' encompassed the destruction of militant Irish republicanism in the short term and the systemic repression of Irish nationalism, with a view to giving preferential, 'legislative force to the political and cultural priorities of unionism' (ibid.: 57). Thus, the early years of unionist consolidation saw interminable sectarian violence resulting disproportionately in mass internment, workplace expulsion and bloody pogroms directed at the Catholic minority (Farrell 1976). This repressive system left no room for any political or cultural expression of Irish nationalism which could be viewed as a threat to British cultural dominance.

The Irish language embodied one such 'threat', and by association its main promulgator, the Gaelic League, which was viewed by unionists as 'an anti-British counter-culture dominated by republican separatists' whose promotion of the Irish language was nothing more than 'the promotion of sedition and disloyalty under another name' (Andrews 1997: 56). The Unionist government seized the opportunity to marginalise the Irish language with its 1923 Education Act. This substantially negated the achievements of the Gaelic League over the previous 20 years and initiated a policy of systematic neglect and legislative discrimination.

This Act recommended that the concessions achieved by the Gaelic League, should be abolished and that Irish should be treated and taught as a foreign language, like Latin or Greek. During this early period, a number of detrimental decisions laid the ground for 50 years of state hostility towards the language (ibid.). These included: abolishing the post of organiser of Irish instruction; the reduction in the teaching of Irish as an optional subject to 90 minutes a week in Public and Elementary schools; the refusal to cater for the existence of bilingualism in the six counties, leading to the extinction of numerous Gaeltacht areas;[1] and the withdrawal of funding from established Irish-language colleges (ibid.: 65).

Additionally, a report submitted by a departmental committee of the ministry for education recommended that 'no aid be given to any school in which principles subversive of the authority of the state were inculcated; that no books should be read to which reasonable objections might be entertained on political grounds' (ibid.: 67). These proposals along with the successful demand to censor school textbooks relating to history, economics, citizenship and Irish, conformed to the 'classic colonial policy' of controlling not only the present, but also the representation of the past (Ó Croidheáin 2006: 192).[2] Ultimately, many of the reports' policy suggestions, including the call to abolish fees for Irish to below standard V in educational category, thus degrading its status to that of dead and foreign languages like Latin and French, were endorsed by the Unionist government and remained in force until recent times (Andrews 1997: 67).

Meanwhile, state repression had a crippling effect on voluntary effort on behalf of the language in the area under the jurisdiction of the Belfast government. Before the end of 1922 all branches of the Gaelic League in the South of Ulster had ceased to function, while the province organiser had to flee from the six counties in 1923, under threat of arrest and imprisonment, and to resign later that year (Ó Huallacháin 1994: 108). The League's 1926 report indicates the extent to which they had been eradicated: 'Little of the body of the Gaelic League remains after the destruction of the last three or four years. Most of the people are apathetic ... older people fight shy of Irish in case it would draw the suspicion of the Government on them' (ibid.). The rigours of the notorious 1922 Special Powers Act resulted in the internment without trial of thousands of nationalists, many language activists amongst them, thus further exacerbating the wholesale fear and alienation in the nationalist minority (Farrell 1976).[3]

Similarly, the damaging legislative restrictions placed on the teaching of Irish during school hours meant that the number of schools teaching it as an optional subject fell by over 50 per cent by the end of the decade, prompting Lord Charlemont, the minister of education, to announce that Irish 'in Northern Ireland was a dead or dying language' and that French was more useful (Andrews 1997: 69–70). Despite the fact that all special grants for the teaching of Irish were terminated and its status downgraded to as low as grade 7, the Stormont regime came under increasing pressure from hard-line loyalists to stop paying fees for the language as an extra subject. One such MP, William Grant, vehemently attacked the language in Parliament in an exchange with the Parliamentary education secretary: '[T]he only people interested in this language are the people who are the avowed enemies of Northern Ireland

– and does he not think the time has now arrived when this grant should be cut off?' (ibid.: 77).

While these extreme loyalist attitudes were motivated by an objective which was shared by the prime minister, Craigavon, and his government, they resisted calls for a complete prohibition of Irish teaching in schools in favour of a less overt and more pragmatic and gradualist form of legislative repression. This involved allowing it to continue as an optional subject, while constantly limiting opportunities and finances for its teaching. Craigavon's response to the Loyalist League demands was that his government felt it 'better to keep a control by means of regulations over activities of this character than to drive them underground where they will undoubtedly tend to germinate and exert a baneful influence' (ibid.). This view is arguably similar to the strategically expedient position taken up by the British government in its more veiled early-twentieth-century dealings with the Gaelic League – a position which would characterise the attitude of the Northern Ireland state towards the language thereafter.

Consequently, however, when the opportune moment arrived at the end of 1933 the government voted unanimously, in a parliament that nationalists had been boycotting for the previous year, to stop payment of fees for the teaching of Irish as an extra subject. While Craigavon's pragmatic repressive methodology differed in practice from the more overt persecution being demanded by extreme loyalists, these differences were merely tactical and ultimately defined by a settler ideology which depended exclusively on 'cultural racism'. This racism had its roots in cultural colonisation, which necessitated the xenophobic view that Ireland's 'inferior' native culture and all its associated features were socio-economic and practical impediments to the 'progress and humanity' of the British Empire and its dominant 'civilising' culture.

Under this rationale, those who failed to conform to the rigours of British cultural hegemony, or worse still, those who actively opposed it, were not only unworthy of its so-called benefits, but regarded as disloyal, subhuman and dangerous. Thus loyalist portrayals of nationalists as 'both inferior and dangerous' could subsequently justify their cultural, political and socio-economic exclusion (Clayton 1998: 53–4). According to this analysis, classic colonial stereotypes shaped how nationalists in the six counties were viewed:

Lazy, dirty, devious, treacherous, violent, over-fecund, irrational, emotional, inferior in education and skills, ungrateful, easily manipulated, superstitious, priest-dominated and in thrall to manipulative leaders. By contrast Protestants portray themselves as hard-working and competent, independent in deed and thought, peaceful and law-abiding, but manly and resolute. All of these stereotypes mirror those found in other settler colonies, and constitute the 'mythical portraits' of the colonized and colonizer described by Memmi. (Ibid.)

These 'mythical portraits' were manifested in institutionalised discrimination towards Catholics in employment and housing, as notoriously articulated on 12 July 1933 in a speech by Basil Brooke MP, a future prime minister, when denouncing those who employed Catholics: 'I would not have a Roman Catholic about my own place ... and I would appeal to Loyalists to employ good protestant lads and lassies' (Farrell 1976: 90).

It was precisely because the predominant Ulster Unionist psyche associated the Irish language with inferiority and disloyalty that it vociferously opposed it anytime it reared its head. For example, when a request was issued by 106 local students at Strabane technical school for an Irish class, it was refused by the unionist-dominated Strabane education committee, despite meeting the criteria of the regulations. This culminated in the dismissal of the principal of the school who had forwarded the proposal (Andrews 1997: 84). Although the government continued with its policy of pragmatic legislative repression, attitudes of intolerance and bigotry retained prominence among the political elite. This was evident when nationalist MP Eddie McAteer attempted to say a few words in Irish in Stormont in August 1945, invoking an angry interruption from the prime minister, Basil Brooke, with calls of 'no foreign language here', ending in his being forbidden to continue speaking in Irish (Mac Póilin 1997c: 184).

Therefore any attempts to gain legitimacy for the Irish language were viewed by the Unionist state as an attack on British cultural hegemony, thus igniting further attempts to eradicate the language. In 1948, discriminatory legislation was passed in the form of an amendment to the Public Health and Local Council Act which prohibited the erection of Irish street signs. This came as a direct response to the erection of Irish street signs by nationalist councils in Omagh and Newry, which caused outrage amongst unionists, who, in the words of Brian Faulkner, a future Stormont prime minister, could not 'tolerate the naming of our streets in a language which is not our language' (Maguire 1990: 11).

Furthermore, this set the scene for a barrage of draconian legislation to be introduced throughout the 1950s. The Public Order Legislation (1951) and the Flags and Emblems Act (1954) amounted to drastic emergency measures that enabled the Stormont government to subdue any cultural or political expressions of Irish nationalism by the excluded Catholic minority. The impossibility of finding an accommodation for the Irish language within the restrictive power base of the one-party unionist state is accurately summarised by Maguire:

> The Irish language was perceived in political terms by the Government, its propagation was considered a threat to the balance of power which was firmly controlled by the Unionist majority within the six counties. Schools were expected to play their part in propagating the cultural and political value system of the ruling party – a party which was to rule the Northern Ireland state continuously for 50 years. The Irish Language could not be accommodated within that tight framework. (Ibid.: 44)

## 'HIDDEN ULSTER': PLANTING THE SEEDS OF REVIVAL

Ná habair é, déan é (Don't say it, do it).
                                         Cumann Chluain Ard dictum

Despite official hostility towards the language displayed by the dominant unionist state following partition, voluntary language activists did their utmost to fill the void and take responsibility for providing Irish classes and promoting cultural revival. Their various projects created independent bastions of cultural activity, which amounted to 'a hidden Ulster of revivalism that enjoyed hardly any relations with statutory authorities and which was entirely alienated from the culture of the state' (De Brún 2006: 11). This provided an effective form of cultural expression, cultivating an established social, educational and recreational movement that was only tolerated because it neither openly undermined nor challenged the legitimacy of the unionist state.

In a perverse sense, systemic discriminatory practices implemented by successive unionist administrations, and reinforced by communal and educational segregation, forged an 'extremely effective form of passive resistance' in nationalist communities. This helped garner 'cultural, social, and sporting activities among the Catholic community' that came to be 'organised as an alternative society within the state usually on the basis of parishes' (Mac Póilin 2006: 126). Nevertheless, a combination of violent upheaval, state coercion and internment in the aftermath of partition had left the Gaelic League disorganised and demoralised, thus precipitating the formation of a new Ulster-based offshoot of the organisation named Comhaltas Uladh, which made great strides in particularly difficult circumstances.[4]

Due to the fact that it controlled the coffers, the Catholic Church dominated the Comhaltas Uladh executive. The Church was both 'an indispensable and erratic ally' (ibid.: 114), since it secured the Irish language's continued place in the education system. Comhaltas Uladh lobbied the Unionist government to reverse negative educational policies and even achieved a minor concession that saw Irish being taught instead of history as an optional subject in standards III and IV. The ferocious unionist response to the measure eventually forced the Stormont government to discontinue payment for Irish as an extra subject. Comhaltas Uladh attempted to 'continue the scheme but its finances proved inadequate and before long Irish was permanently unavailable as an extra subject' (Andrews 1991: 94).

In addition to campaigning, Comhaltas Uladh organised singing and dancing classes, lectures on Irish history and culture, a wide range of entertainments including *céilithe*, concerts, debates and excursions, with some branches even establishing Gaelic athletic teams (ibid.: 98). Although Comhaltas Uladh was clerically dominated, by those who viewed the language as a 'moral safeguard' against the 'vices' of materialism, modernism and socialism (Ó Croidheáin 2006: 175–6), it also attracted disparate factions. At a Belfast public meeting in a Catholic parish hall in 1927, the RUC noted the attendance of 'local suspects and a large number of past and present members of the IRA' (Mac Póilin 2006: 127).

Many of these disparate elements, including republicans and constitutional nationalists, were involved in raising funds for the building of the new Ardscoil premises, the Gaelic League's headquarters, in 1928. In the decades that followed, the Ardscoil became a mainstay for cultural revivalist activity, as described by republican ex-prisoner and renowned language activist Eddie Keenan:

D'oscail saol nua dom nuair a chonaic mé an t-atmaisféar Gaelach san Ardscoil don chéad uair sná mall-trocháidí. Bhí na céadta daoine óga ag dul do ranganna, céilithe agus damhsaí d'achan cinéal beagnach achan oíche. Bhí craobhacha an Chonartha ó gach cearn don chathair i láthair agus fuarthas amach go raibh na craobacha seo lán do mo chomhbhaill in Óglaigh na hÉireann! D'athraigh dearcadh s'agam ar an teanga ó shin i leith.

(A new world revealed itself to me when I first saw the 'Gaelic' atmosphere of the Ardscoil in the late thirties. There were hundreds of young people attending classes, *céilithe* and dances of every kind almost every night. There were Gaelic League branches from throughout the city in attendance and I found out that these branches were full of my fellow IRA members! My attitude towards the language changed from that point on.) (Interview with Keenan, 18 November 2004)

The language movement in this era, as it had done previously, acted as an ideological umbrella for nationalists, republicans and socialists, with many coming from working-class backgrounds. It was from this context in 1936, during a period of mass unemployment and endemic poverty, that 'two unemployed young men, Seamus Maxwell and Liam Rooney, set up Cumann Chluain Ard in an old covered gateway in Kane Street beside Clonard Monastery in west Belfast' (Mac Seáin 2006: 4). Spearheaded by local members of the O'Neill Crowley GAA club, the new Gaelic League branch never actually restyled itself Cumann Chluain Ard until 1938, by which time it had acquired new premises and two native speakers to aid its development (Mac Póilin 2006: 130).

From the outset, Cumann Chluain Ard was defined by a working-class, republican and left-wing ethos that was independent of the Catholic Church and considerably more radical that other branches of Comhaltas Uladh. Although often castigated from the pulpit by priests at Clonard Monastery, who denounced its republican and communist tendencies, this never prevented it extending its radicalism to Irish-language activities, including the original concept of Irish-only nights, which were held on Tuesdays. The project continued unabated, despite the imprisonment of many of its members during the mass internment of hundreds of nationalists and republicans during the Second World War. Unsurprisingly, Belfast's Crumlin Road prison became a centre for language activity and cultural revivalism as part of prisoners' practical continuation of their resistance during incarceration.

One of these prisoners who reached proficency during his imprisonment in Crumlin Road Jail, Liam Ó Stiobhaird, describes his return to activism on the outside:

> Hundreds of us came out of Crumlin Road Jail as fluent Irish speakers and many of us had a rejuvenating impact on the cultural activity on the outside. I got heavily involved in the *céilithe* and was *fear an* tí, all over the town. There were *céilithe* everywhere, the Ardscoil, the Bamba hall, Pearse hall in King Street, Cumann Chluain Ard, the Felons' club. There were also classes at most of these venues with the Ardscoil and Cumann Chluain Ard being the most popular, and there was definitely something of a boom in language and cultural events in the late forties and early fifties. The IRA was heavily involved along with many other committed activists from different backgrounds who generally viewed this as part of the cultural work to achieve a united, free country. (Interview with Ó Stiobhaird, 8 March 2007)

Ó Stiobhaird's account is endorsed by renowned Belfast language activist Seamus Mac Seáin, who stated, 'd'fhoglaim mise mo chuid Gaeilge san Ardscoil agus i gCumann Chluain Ard agus bhí múinteoirí agam a d'fhoghlaim a gcuid Gaeilge i mbraighdeanas sná daichaidí do mo theagasc sná caogaidí' (I learned my Irish in the Ardscoil and Cumann Chluain Ard and I had teachers who learned their Irish while interned in the forties and taught me in the fifties) (interview with Mac Seáin, 26 July 2006). Having moved to new and improved premises in Hawthorne Street in 1944, where it remains to the present day, the club defined itself with a distinctly republican and socialist ideology for much of the 1950s (Mac Póilin 2006: 131).

One of its pamphlets published around the same time had strong echoes of Connolly's politics: 'a Gaelic-speaking Ireland was not something mystical or abstract, but a definite cultural and economic objective' associated with the Irish worker's social and economic consciousness (ibid.). Furthermore, the pamphlet intimates that this ideological fusion could create an understanding 'that the revival of the language is not of only academic interest but an essential part of the age-long struggle for Irish freedom' (ibid.). The sentiments in the pamphlet represent a clear restatement of the republican definition of decolonisation. This was manifested in Cumann Chluain Ard's alliances with radical language activists from Free State Gaeltachtaí, who formed campaigning groups such as Muinntir na Gaedhealtachta and Misneach. These groups linked the survival of the Irish-speaking areas with delivery from poverty and economic exploitation, and the granting of full rights to Irish speakers (Ó Croidheáin 2006: 189). The rallying cry of one of their primary organisers, Máirtín Ó Cadhain, that 'the reconquest of Irish is the reconquest of Ireland and the reconquest of Ireland is the salvation of Irish' (Ó Cathasaigh 2002: 264), held an inspirational resonance with many of the club's more radical members (interview with Mac Seáin, 26 July 2006).

When the club took the radical decision to become an 'Irish only' club in 1953, its new philosophy forged 'an alternative Irish language movement, more outspoken than the mainstream Gaelic League, which many of them looked upon as being too mild and bourgeois' (Mac Seáin 2006: 4). Although many disagreed with the new policy and became disaffected, 'others who remained wore their dedication to the language on their sleeve and formed a cohesive group of individuals who weren't afraid of challenges' and subsequently adopted the motto, 'Na habair é, déan é', meaning, 'Don't say it, do it' (ibid.). A core of idealistic young activists who first came to the fore in the club in the late fifties took the highly symbolic step of changing their names by deed-pole to the Irish versions, thereby highlighting their dedication to language revival by proclaiming it 'to the authorities who were generally antagonistic to the language' (ibid.).

This was an overtly political statement of intent which was hugely significant for its time, signalling, as it did, the onset of groundbreaking approaches on the part of these radical working-class language activists. As Mac Seáin explains:

Comhthaisme a bhí ann go dtáinig baicle díograiseach againn fríd sán am amháin agus muid faoi thiochar leithéidí Mac Grianna agus Ó Cadhain. Mhair muid taobh istigh de theorainneacha ár bpobal féin ach ní raibh muid ag brath ar an stát agus bhí láidreacht ag baint le sin. D'oibrigh muid i múinín a chéile agus nuair a tháinig smaoineamh chugainn, chuir muid i gcrích é, rud a chiallaigh go raibh obair iontach á dhéanamh againn. Bíodh is go raibh muid bainte le hathbheochan na Gaeilge go príomha, bhí muid ag treabhadh gort an ceartáis agus muid go fóill ag treabhadh tionscnamh neamhspleáchais i gcoitinne.

(It was a coincidence that a small and dedicated bunch of us, influenced by the likes of Mac Grianna and Ó Cadhain, came through at the same time. We survived within the confines of our own community but weren't in any way dependent on the state, and there was a strength about that position. We worked with confidence in each other and when we had an idea we made it a reality, which meant we did some great work. Although we were concerned primarily with revival of the Irish language, we also worked for our rights and for justice in what was a more general project for independence.) (Interview with Mac Seáin, 26 July 2006)

These young activists were not linked to any specific political party, nor were they as overtly political as the former Cumann Chluain Ard activists. However, they were prominent in the rights-based protest politics of the sixties and affiliated with various radical Misneach initiatives. These included the campaign against the Language Freedom Movement[5] and a public week-long fast in Belfast, coinciding with a similar Misneach fast in Dublin, to raise awareness of the Irish language during the official state commemorations of the Easter Rising in 1966 (Mac Seáin 2010: 117–19). This activism undoubtedly cast them in the light of explicitly political activists like their predecessors.

What also differentiated them was their degree of success and originality, best encapsulated by their unprecedented idea of creating an urban Gaeltacht in west Belfast, which was motivated by the hope that they could

construct a set of values and an institutional framework that could bring a modern independent Irish-speaking society into existence, using what remained intact and worthwhile of pre-colonial Gaelic Ireland. [The] preservation and development of the Gaeltacht [was based] ... on the establishment locally of a variety of Irish-speaking institutions in the belief that they may coalesce, creating the nucleus of this new society. (Andrews 1991: 98)

This decolonising project was organised by working-class people against an unfavourable socio-economic backdrop in an area crippled by political discrimination and social injustice (Maguire 2006: 138). However, these very conditions fostered a strong 'sense of cohesiveness' and community solidarity that had the power to imbue a steely confidence, independence and determination in members of this disaffected community (ibid.). This confidence inspired the Gaeltacht scheme, in which a number of young married couples, who had met at Cumann Chluain Ard, raised and borrowed the money to purchase a piece of land on Belfast's Shaw's Road before building their own houses and subsequently Ireland's first urban Irish-speaking neighbourhood (Mac Seáin 2006: 4). Although the planning and delivery of this initiative took nine years in all, eventually reaching fruition in 1969, the core group who spearheaded it 'never wavered in their determination to realize their goal' and succeeded 'without one penny of grant aid or government subvention' (ibid.).

This revolutionary self-help initiative represented a successful example of localised cultural reconquest and radical decolonisation in practice. It occurred in an era in which the nationalist minority in the north had raised its voice against structural discrimination and socio-economic inequality through the Civil Rights movement. The new-found confidence which manifested itself in marches demanding human rights also defined the determined philosophy of the Shaw's Road Gaeltacht activists. This confidence is articulated in the letter announcing the scheme sent to the families, which stated, 'without a community like this we cannot demand our rights as citizens; for no corporation, county council or government can administer to a language community which is interspersed within communities who do not share their demands' (Foras na Gaeilge 2007: no pagination).

Their evident sense of purpose and solidarity was transposed to the wider community at the onset of the political and military conflict in the north in the summer of 1969, when the Shaw's Road activists rebuilt the houses of Bombay Street off the Falls Road that were burned out by loyalist mobs facilitated by the RUC (Mac Seáin 2006: 4). Their practical skills and philosophy of self-reliance came to the aid of the defenceless nationalist residents when the local council refused to rebuild the houses. This act of selflessness taught activists like Mac Seáin, 'nár leor streachailt Gaeltacht Bhóthar Seoighe ann féin agus gurbh éigeán dúinn dul i measc an phobail in am an ghátair. Rinne muid seo mar Ghaeilgeoirí, rud a d'ardaigh stádas na Gaeilge sa phobal' (the struggle for the Shaw's Road Gaeltacht wasn't enough on its own and we needed to go amongst the community in its hour of need. We did this as Irish-language activists, which raised the status of the language in the community) (interview with Mac Seáin, 26 July 2006).

In addition, the Shaw's Road activists had succeeded in setting up the north's first Irish-medium nursery school for their children in 1965, following this up by meeting with the Stormont authorities to explore the possibility of setting up an Irish primary school (Mac

Seáin 2006: 4). They received a threatening letter saying 'that teaching through the medium of the Irish language would not be deemed to be proper instruction for young children' and that if the school was formed then 'the law would be allowed to take its course' (ibid.).

This threat, however, was duly ignored and the north of Ireland's first Irish-medium primary school, Scoil Ghaeilge Bhéal Feirste and later Bunscoil Phobal Feirste, was established on the Shaw's Road with nine children in 1971. The unionist state's preoccupation with the ensuing political conflict may have rendered them unable to carry through their threat of legal action against those involved in the school. As Aodán Mac Póilin, a former chairperson of the school, states, 'chiallaigh an éigeándáil pholaitiúil go mbeadh sé bomanta ag an rialtas dul fríd leis an bhagairt chun an dlí a chur ar an scoil. Chomh maith le sin, bheadh sé míphraiticúil agus muid i lár *no-go area*!' (the political crisis would have rendered it stupid for the government to carry through with the threat to impose the law on the school. It would have also been impractical considering that we were living in the middle of a no-go area.) (Interview with Mac Póilin, 6 October 2006).

Following the fall of Stormont and the imposition of Direct Rule from London, the Ministry for Education became a department for education directed by civil servants. While the policy of pragmatic repression towards the Irish language continued unabated, the reversion to the United Kingdom context from the former settler–colonial state forged an even more implicit methodology. This applied to their dealings with the Shaw's Road Gaeltacht, as Mac Póilin states:

Bhí *direct rule* níos oscailte don tionscnamh s'againn, de bhrí nach dtiocfadh leo diúltú glan a thuilleadh mar go raibh scoileanna Breatnaise maoinithe sa Ríocht Aontaithe. Measaim go ndearna siad difear idir muidinne agus lucht Breatnaise mar gur mheas siad i gcónaí go stairiúil go raibh an Ghaeilge bainte le bagairt, náisiúnachas agus poblachtánachas. Ar ndóigh bhí doicheall mhillteanach orthu ó thaobh na Gaeilge a bhí fréamhaithe i naimhdeas agus de bharr go raibh sé chun saol an státséibhísigh a dhéanamh níos cásta. Rinne siad meancóg, áfach, nuair a bhunaigh siad an cás inár n-éadan ar uimhreacha. Dúirt siad go mbeadh 200 páiste de dhíth le haghaidh aitheántais, rud a bhí dodhéanta le pobal beag s'againne ach ar a laghad thug siad sprioc dúinn do nuair a d'fhás an scoil sa todhchaí. D'fhéadfadh siad an cás s'acu a bhunú ar chaighdeán mar a rinne na hAondachtóiri agus bheadh muid san fhaopach.

(Direct Rule was more open to the project because they could no longer refuse us completely due to the fact that Welsh schools were being funded in the UK. I feel they differentiated between us and the Welsh community because historically, they've always associated Irish with danger, nationalism and republicanism. Obviously, they had an extreme reluctance regarding the Irish language stemming from hostility and because it would make the civil servants' job more complicated. They made a mistake, however, when they based their case against us on numbers. They said that 200 children would be needed to achieve recognition, which was completely impossible in a small community like ours with so few families, but at least they gave us a target for when the school grew in future years. They could have based their case on the standard of education as the unionists did, which would have put us in a predicament.) (Ibid.)

This methodology, however, did not deter the Shaw's Road language activists from making increasingly audacious demands on the state as the 1970s progressed, and their remarkable achievements set the benchmark for the language revival in the north of Ireland. Moreover, the formation of the north's first Irish-medium school in 1971, against all the odds, 'would propel the Irish language onto a dynamic and exciting course that would contribute to a language shift in Ireland during the remainder of the millennium' (Nig Uidhir 2006: 140). This was the defining aspect of the original Shaw's Road decolonisation project, which planted a seed that would flourish in the 1980s with the transformational impact of republican prison protests in Long Kesh.

# 4
# Imprisonment, the Irish Context and the Language

Prison robs you of your freedom; it attempts to take away your identity.

Nelson Mandela (1994: 321)

This brief chapter draws on the historical context of political imprisonment in Ireland and takes a cursory glance at some themes relating to prisons and imprisonment in general. It outlines the crucial role of political imprisonment in influencing the political strategy of various governments tasked with maintaining 'law and order' in Ireland, while simultaneously shaping resistance movements and their political struggles outside the prison walls. The context of colonisation and the ideologies of resistance that stemmed from it are viewed as key motivating factors in successive generations of republican prisoners learning and using the Irish language as a 'language of struggle' while incarcerated. In tracing these developments, the chapter also draws on original oral history material from some of the aforementioned narrators.

## 'PAINS OF INCARCERATION': IMPRISONMENT

Punishment is as old as society ... But when a policeman or prison guard in his official capacity as a representative of the governing body punishes a man, society itself is involved in its historical, political, economic and sociological vision.

Donald Clemmer (1958: 81)

Although this book deals specifically with politically motivated republican prisoners, there is a general commonality amongst people held captive against their will regardless of the judicial process in use (McKeown: 1998: 24). The manner by which prisoners understand and cope with the experiences of their imprisonment can depend on a multiplicity of factors. These include: the reasons for their imprisonment, their personal and psychological make-up, the specific culture of the prison community, their political ideologies and beliefs, how they spend their time in prison, and their relationships with the outside world (ibid.). While the nature of political imprisonment in Ireland has always been dictated by the necessities of British colonialism itself, any understanding of its wider remit, including the question of who can be forced to accept the rules and concepts of others, becomes a matter of the possession and contestation of politico-economic power.

Prisons and imprisonment can be linked with the very nature of the authoritarian state itself and represent a coercive weapon in the state's use of discretionary power:

> All forms of incarceration imply the use of force. Regardless of the outward appearance of compliance few people taken into custody would accept their loss of liberty so willingly if the full potential of state coercion was not handcuffed to their wrists. (Scraton, Sim and Skidmore 1991: 61)

By extension, criminalisation itself can be defined as the 'application of the criminal label to a particular social category' in a process that 'depends both on how certain acts are labelled and on who is doing the labelling' (Hall and Scraton 1981: 481). Therefore, the power of states or governments to 'label' is crucial in justifying political containment; it functions as a weapon in the hands of the authorities, which can mobilise popular approval and legitimacy behind the state (ibid.). The highly political nature of crime and its various constructions are manifested in the power differentials of such 'labelling', whereby 'damage, victimisation, exploitation, theft and destruction when carried out by the powerful are not only not punished, but are not called "crime"' (Cohen and Taylor 1972: 624).

Many sociological analyses on prisoner strategies to deal with the difficulties of imprisonment argue that resistance itself can constitute an effective coping strategy (Clemmer 1958; Sykes 1958). This can be achieved through collectivist attempts at forging solidarity amongst prisoners:

> A cohesive inmate society provides the prisoner with a meaningful social group with which he can identify himself and which will support him in his battles against his condemners – and thus the prisoner can at least in part escape the fearful isolation of the convicted offender. (Sykes 1958: 107)

Resistance has been depicted as a coping strategy in the prison experience by commentators on 1960s and 1970s American prisons 'where general adjustment had long since given way to "active co-ordinated resistance"' (Cohen and Taylor 1972: 131). This rationale can be applied to the context of the north of Ireland, in which 'the assertion of political status and the political character of the conflict' effectively 'places the activities of politically motivated prisoners ... firmly at the resistance end of the spectrum' (McEvoy 2001: 31).

These forms of prisoner resistance can involve 'endemic and intense forms of conflict' between prisoners and prison authorities that stem mainly 'from social structural factors external to the prison itself'. This sociological construction applies to the republican political prisoner community, who are often 'guided by a shared political ideology, motivated by common interests and values' and 'a shared sense of comradeship geared towards the mutual benefit of all' (McKeown 1998: 26).

## POLITICAL IMPRISONMENT IN IRELAND

There was no sense of guilt on the part of political prisoners, only one of resistance to oppression.

James Daly (McGuffin 1973: 144)

Political imprisonment has always played a crucial role in shaping resistance movements and their methods, while simultaneously influencing the political strategy of various governments tasked with maintaining 'law and order' (Buntman 2003: 2). While the chosen method of punishment has presented successive governments with seemingly intractable political and diplomatic problems, imprisoned revolutionaries have utilised and exploited numerous opportunities to politicise and intensify their liberation struggles on the outside. Nowhere have these themes recurred more acutely than in Ireland, where the issue of political prisoners has had deeply emotive connotations in the Irish nationalist and republican psyche. As Tomlinson posits:

Since the emergence of modern prison systems in the nineteenth century, penal policies and prison regimes in Ireland have been strongly influenced by the containment of political disorder, specifically militant Irish nationalism and republicanism. While it is quite possible to describe the prison systems of Northern Ireland

and the Republic of Ireland in administrative and managerialist terms ... this would miss the extent to which contemporary prison systems have been shaped by the political struggles of a range of movements concerned with ending British sovereignty in Ireland. (Tomlinson 1995: 1–2)

This predicament plagued British governments for over two centuries, during which the British failed to formulate consistent policies to deal with Irish political prisoners. Their policies varied depending on the particular circumstances of the time and were conditioned by political expediency (ibid.).

At the epicentre of this predicament was the choice between according Irish prisoners 'political status' or treating them as 'common criminals'. The governments' decisions were dictated by legal and constitutional factors as well as British public opinion, which usually failed to comprehend the stark differences between the two. As McConville points out:

> An ordinary offender enters the criminal process shamed, isolated and vulnerable. The political offender, should his or her group of supporters and sympathizers be large and confident enough, embraces and transcends captivity. To know that one is cherished and respected revivifies the prisoner and directs a confrontational energy on the many irksome restrictions of institutional life. (McConville 2003: 9)

Unsuccessful attempts at criminalisation constructed a battleground in various prisons, where the resistance of Irish political prisoners, who rejected the legitimacy of British rule in Ireland, often galvanised their supporters on the outside by implicating the entire cause in the attempt to attach the stigma of criminalisation. State authority could thus be challenged from within the prison walls, successfully symbolising opposition to British rule (ibid.).

Between 1801 and 1921, the British government introduced 105 separate coercion acts in its efforts to maintain control of Ireland. Furthermore, in the nineteenth century it was rare that the country's jails and penal colonies in Australia did not contain some Irish political prisoners (Farrell 1985: 5). Irish political prisoners from the Fenian movement, which has been described as the 'most enduring and successful revolutionary secret society in Europe' (McConville 2003: 114), were the first to be subjected to special regimes in English prisons between the 1860s and 1890s that were specifically designed for their mental and physical torture. Jeremiah O'Donovan Rossa's (1967: 68) personal account of Pentonville prison tells of solitary confinement, 'bread and water' diet punishment, and the denial of the right to physical exercise.

O'Donovan Rossa and his fellow Irish prisoners were given exceptional treatment: 'We were to be treated as ordinary prisoners with no difference between us and any other convicts, yet the ordinary rules were set aside and special instructions received to treat us worse than the thieves and murderers of England' (ibid.). This ill-treatment, 'which went beyond the bounds of legality, as well as decency', involved O'Donovan Rossa's hands being manacled behind him for a period of 35 days (McConville 2003: 179).[1] However, O'Donovan Rossa's election success (while imprisoned) in Tipperary in 1869 (O'Donovan Rossa 1967: 216) proved the potential of political imprisonment to move public opinion in Ireland, while his 'indomitable spirit' (ibid.: 7) set a precedent that would inspire future prisoners.

Thomas Clarke and the treason-felony prisoners known as the 'special men' suffered from an even more 'scientific system of perpetual and persistent harassing' (Clarke 1970: 13) in Chatham prison in the 1880s. The physical and psychological torture of the prisoners became part of the warder's daily routine and involved sleep prevention by banging the latch on the cell door at hourly intervals and an imposed 'silent system' which meant the prisoners could not speak without permission. These modes of torture, which lasted for almost seven years, succeeded in driving the majority of the Fenian prisoners insane (ibid.). Despite the efforts of the authorities, Clarke and two others maintained sanity and overcame seemingly insurmountable odds. In Clarke's own words:

> Some of us realised the situation early in our imprisonment, and saw that the mercilessly savage treatment was meant to smash us and three of us Daly, Ryan and myself set ourselves to defeat the officials' design. It was a fight against dreadful odds. On the one hand were the prison authorities with all the horrors of the prison machinery, relentlessly striving to accomplish its objectives with unlimited ways and means at their disposal. On the other side were the prisoners, each standing alone and friendless, but resolved never to give in, with nothing to sustain him but his own courage and the pride he had in being an Irish Fenian. (Ibid.: 21)

These two opposing forces remained in conflict for the next century, while Clarke's powerful code of self-sacrifice defined the mentality of republican prisoners throughout the twentieth century. Similarly, the tendency to view Irish political prisoners as a threat from the inside – which requires special control – while being encouraged and incited by supporters on the outside is a common feature of their history (McKeown 2001: 12).

Prison protest intensified after the turn of the century and was altered dramatically by the Easter Rising of 1916, when mass imprisonment became the order of the day. The radicalisation of prisoner resistance intensified in this period, whether against imprisonment, internment or military detention: 'the war outside the prisons was matched by a life and death struggle inside the prison. The hunger strike became the dominant form of protest' (Tomlinson 1995: 245). Different circumstances necessitated a new response from the government, which contrasted sharply with their treatment of the Fenians in the nineteenth century (McKeown 2001: 13). Demands for free association by day and night, free access to newspapers, food parcels, and the right to organise their own daily activities were granted to those interned after 1916 in England and in Wales (Figgis 1917; O'Mahony 1987).[2] The British government's change in policy was influenced by the difference in prisoner numbers from the Fenian era and also the increase in popular outside support for their political cause.

Before the change in policy, the British had already lost the propaganda battle at home and in Ireland: 'the daily ventilation of the specific and general grievances of the internees had done much to revive and spread the cause of republicanism and to change the political atmosphere in Ireland' (McConville 2003: 497). The success of the prisoner campaign for 'political status' also created a favourable electoral platform for the emergence of Sinn Féin in 1917, which ran the imprisoned Joseph McGuinness as a candidate in South Longford under the famous slogan, 'Put him in to get him out'. The Lewes prisoner's slim victory signalled the first of many electoral victories for Irish political prisoners in the twentieth century and prompted the *Manchester Guardian* to describe it as the 'equivalent of a serious British defeat in the field' (Coogan 1980: 20). To the dismay of the British government, prison issues had been magnified and skilfully exploited from both the inside and outside. British policies were 'either naïve or disingenuous' in their inherent assumption that they could imprison thousands of Irish people and 'not expect them and their friends to make politics from the incidents of their confinement' (McConville 2003: 475).

Further development on this point is evident in the assessment of the Frongoch internment camp in Wales, whose revolutionary potential the British had arguably failed to consider:

> If the execution of the leaders [of the Easter Rising] was a major mistake by the British in their reaction to the rebellion, the second major mistake was Frongoch. Here [were] housed 1,900 of the finest of their generation and it became a veritable political university and military academy, aptly described elsewhere as a 'University for Revolutionists'. (O'Mahony 1987: 58)

Frongoch and other prisons transformed the political situation by significantly energising the independence movement with the ideology of 'the new Sinn Féin thought' (MacArdle 1951: 201). Nationalists of all shades of opinion were trained in the emerging ideals of militant republicanism, armed struggle and cultural revival, subsequently returning home as dedicated activists who would spearhead the Anglo-Irish war of 1919–21 against British rule in Ireland (ibid.).

Their imprisonment was merely another chapter in what they viewed as a continuous 'liberation struggle' and thus became an enduring badge of honour, as 'prison contests grew to be an invaluable part of the national struggle, preserving the morale of prisoners, convincing the authorities of the sincerity and determination of the Irishmen opposed to them and inspiring the Irish people with a new self-confidence' (MacArdle: ibid.). The post-Easter Rising prison campaigns laid the policy foundations for future Irish political prisoners, whose demand for 'political status' defined their resistance. They succeeded when the British resolved the issue by conceding de facto political status, in a similar way to that in which William Whitelaw, the British secretary of state, would grant 'special category' status to internees years later in 1972 .

In the absence of a favourable resolution, Irish political prisoners often resorted to the tactic of hunger strike in order to obtain their demands. Inconsistent government responses varied between force-feeding, which caused the death of Thomas Ashe in 1917,[3] and allowing the prisoners to die, as happened with Terence MacSwiney, lord mayor of Cork, in 1920[4] and Bobby Sands MP and nine fellow prisoners in 1981. Paradoxically, British unwillingness to grant the 'concession' of political status in these instances usually backfired, with widespread public sympathy conferring martyr status on the dead prisoners, thereby politicising their cause. Surprisingly, successive governments learned very few lessons from history, as political imprisonment and mass internment without trial reappeared throughout the decades, often having a consolidating effect on republicanism and sporadic campaigns for national sovereignty.

It is worth noting, however, that such campaigns for political status were fought not only against British administrations in Ireland. For example, when the IRA divided over the issue of the Anglo-Irish treaty in the summer of 1922, the largest number of republican prisoners ever was rounded up by the Irish Free State, and by the new administration in the six counties of Ireland, and either interned or sentenced to penal servitude.[5] Political recognition was withheld from this group of prisoners from the outset, and their numbers peaked at 12,000 or 13,000 in late 1923 (Coogan 2002). Amongst the protests they engaged in during the period was a mass hunger strike agitating for release of all prisoners in October and November 1923, which at its peak involved thousands of prisoners (O'Malley 1978).

Four republican prisoners died during these protests, but some advancement was secured on the release of republican prisoners, with women prisoners playing a particularly significant role in securing this (ibid.).[6] These patterns of imprisonment, resistance and protest for political recognition continued in various British and Irish jails in the 1920s, 1930s and 1940s, and again during the IRA's border campaign in the north of Ireland in the late 1950s and 1960s. In each situation, there was a common approach, involving the organisation of a cohesive republican structure, usually on military lines, and the expression of the demand for political status in circumstances in which the wider political struggle was not recognised, or treated as a 'criminal conspiracy' (Coogan 2002).

These features have also been replicated in the most contemporary phase of intensified prison struggle in the north of Ireland. The most striking parallel of this reprised passage in history was the intensive prison protest and outside political struggle which ensued from the removal of special category status by the British government in 1976, to be replaced by the policy of criminalisation. Long Kesh became the political battleground on which the issues of the right to wear their own clothes, to deal with prison administration through an elected officer in command, refusal to do prison work and segregation from 'criminal' elements inspired the resistance of a new generation of Irish political prisoners. Their protracted campaign, which culminated in the death of ten republican prisoners on hunger strike in 1981, is widely recognised as a watershed in modern Irish history, synonymous with increased popular support for the republican political struggle in the north of Ireland and the subsequent revival of the Irish language.

In order to fully understand the political psyche of imprisoned Irish republicans, we must grasp their practical and symbolic affinity with their historical legacy. In McConville's words:

> A large part of modern Irish republicanism is the assertion of claims of legitimacy based on historical continuity. The history of Irish political imprisonment is central to the education of republican activists and their self-assumed obligation to keep faith with the past. To many the remembrance of the penal servitude of the Fenians ... the death of Thomas Ashe and the hunger strike of Terence McSwiney are wholly familiar events, cornerstones of their own political edifice. (McConville 2003: 10)

Attempts to define these prisoners as 'criminals' rather than 'political prisoners' radicalised them by tarnishing their entire political cause and simultaneously strengthening their shared bond with the revolutionary tradition of the imprisoned Irish. Incarceration was transformed into a new arena for political resistance that undermined state power by influencing and politicising events and activities outside the prison walls. This tendency is not specific to Ireland, as evidenced in the South African context, in which political-prisoner resistance underscored 'the paradox of a site of repression being used to undo the material and symbolic origin of the power of the repressive apparatus' and prove 'that events and patterns within prisons can and do shape political dynamics beyond the prison walls' (Buntman 2003: 8).

## 'AN GHAEILGE FAOI GHLAS': THE LANGUAGE IN IRISH PRISONS

> On board the *Argenta* we all go to school,
> The subject is Gaelic we learn as a rule,
> The tools that we work with were rough and were few,
> Pencil stubs, greasy paper, we had to make do.
> Sean Nethercott, Argenta prisonship internee<br>(Kleinrichert 2001: 139)

One critical aspect of Irish political-prisoner resistance was its continued emphasis on political and academic education as a collective means of cultural expression. Acquisition of knowledge became a practical form of power that successfully challenged the prison authorities and, by extension, the validity of British rule in Ireland. The development of cultural revival as a central tenet of the Irish independence struggle at the beginning of the twentieth century inspired imprisoned nationalists and republicans in the post-Easter Rising period to utilise the Irish language as both an educational expression of their identity and a means of struggle while incarcerated. It was also used as a means to distinguish them from 'common criminals' and their prison captors and warders, by creating both a psychological and a practical sense of separateness that helped redefine their existence. A historical precedent was set that continually re-emerged in various prisons for new generations in different phases of history.

In the aftermath of the Easter Rising, hundreds of Gaelic League activists were interned amongst thousands of others in Frongoch in Wales and in English prisons. In Frongoch republican prisoners had political status and spent much of their time doing military drilling and training as well as political education and various mainstream academic subjects (O'Mahony 1987). Furthermore, both the teaching and learning of the Irish language was seen as central to the daily life of prisoners, as William Brennan-Whitmore points out:

> [I]n the civilised studies, the major portion of our time was devoted to the Irish language, which was only as it should be. The classes in Frongoch were ideal in that we had a large number of highly qualified teachers and a considerable number of native speakers. (Brennan-Whitmore 1917: 40)

Brennan-Whitmore also states that prisoners had ignored the camp officials' initial opposition to the learning of Irish in the camp. However, the head of Frongoch camp would not 'tolerate the names of the workshops or dormitories to be posted in Irish. When we pointed out that the Germans were allowed to post them up in German, he replied that he understood German, but he didn't understand Irish' (ibid.).

Despite the discriminatory practices of the prison regime, the prisoners successfully set up a branch of the Gaelic League, which was named Craobh na Sróine Deirge,[7] derived from the meaning of the Welsh place name, Frongoch (O'Mahony 1987). The success of the branch and the programmes of language teaching in Frongoch were referred to in the work of another of its prisoners, Seamás Ó Maoileoin:

> Bhí ollscoil don scoth againn. Bhí gach ábhar léinn ar chlár na scoile sin. Bhí scoth na múinteoiri ann agus bhí ollúna as gach ollscoil in Éirinn agam. Ní nach ionadh gur tugadh Éirí amach na muinteoiri ar sheachtain na cásca. Ar na hoidí, bhí Liam Ó Briain, Liam Gogan, Micheal Ó Droighneáin, Seamas agus Seosamh Uí Thallamháin ... bhí cúrsaí oideachais ann do gach sort scolaire agus is beag duine nár bhain tairbhe astu. Chuir idir mhúinteoirí agus scolairí a gcroí san obair ... ní fhaca mé aon scoil ó shin i leith ina raibh córas múinte chomh ciallmhar is a bhí i bhFrongoch ... da múinfí an teanga lasmuigh mar a mhuineadh sa champa í agus dá ndéanfá an teanga agus stair na tire a cheangal mar a rinneadh thall, bheadh an Ghaeilge slán sábháilte againn faoi seo.

> (We had a great university. Every subject was on the school programme. No wonder they named Easter week, the teachers' rising. Amongst the teachers were Liam Ó Briain, Liam Gogan, Micheal Ó Droighneáin, Seamas and Seosamh Ó Tallamháin ... education was provided for every kind of student ... and everyone got something out of it. Both teachers and students put their hearts into the work ... I've never seen a school since with such a sensible teaching system as there was in Frongoch ... if the language had been taught on the outside as it was in the camp and if it was linked with the history of our country like it was over there, the language would have been safe and sound before now.) (Ó Maoileoin 1958: 81)

Thus the language took on a special significance in this period of mass republican imprisonment and was very much linked to the symbolic revivalist discourse of decolonisation. This is illustrated in what Frongoch internee Mattie Neilan decribes as one of the camp's most prominent mottos: 'The language of the conqueror on the lips of the conquered is the language of the slave' (O'Mahony 1987: 82). In this period, many prisoners carried their language activism to the outside and inspired an increase in Gaelic League activity, with many Sinn Féin branches also organising Irish-language classes and classes based on song and dance, while some even set up lending libraries (Laffan 1999: 205).

The Irish language played a similarly rehabilitative role amongst political internees in the six-county context in the 1920s, though in much harsher prison conditions. The internment of over 700 nationalists on board the prison ship *Argenta* in Belfast Lough from 1922 to 1925 marked the first official use of the draconian Special Powers Act by the fledgling unionist state (Kleinrichert 2001: xv). Amongst those interned were many schoolteachers, who 'were very vulnerable' because 'they possessed respected employment and a higher education'; especially targeted were those with 'the love of teaching the Irish language and culture to schoolchildren' (ibid.). These teachers were meticulously labelled by the local police and constabulary as 'ardent and active IRA propagandists at school' (ibid.).[8] These teachers, including six or seven 'Frongoch graduates' (ibid.: 278), were said to have 'encouraged a sense of spirit and intellect' by 'reminding their fellow internees of the reasons for their captivity', engaging 'them in Irish classes to keep their sense of unity and purpose in mind' (ibid.: 147). Initially, learners of the language had to make do with 'only pencil stubs and greasy butter wrapper papers', until several strikes saw the governor relent and allow paper and pencils (ibid.).

Nevertheless, the governor of the *Argenta* was opposed to the organisation of Irish classes and discouraged them by transferring teachers to Derry Gaol, where 'six weeks' punishment, bread-and-water diets, and restrictions on camaraderie awaited those who were transferred into the solitary cells of Derry's confines' (ibid.: 148).[9] However, antagonism by the prison-ship regime towards the language tended to have the opposite effect, with many internees actually achieving the gold fáinne, the badge of fluency or proficiency bestowed on Irish learners, under the stewardship of teachers Jim Kelly and Patrick Mullarkey (ibid.). Many prisoners also engaged in creative writing and poetry as a further educational form of resistance. One such poetic monologue by Belfast internee Joseph McAtanney refers specifically to the role of the Irish language on the prison ship:

*Prologue*
It is better to have a language, without freedom
Than freedom, without a language

*An Teanga*
Erin, my country, pride of past ages
The emerald gem of the western sea

Blest Ireland, of scholars, of saints, and of sages
Arise in your glory, awake and be free
The shackles of slavery, so cruel, so galling
Are loosened forever, your duty is plain
Your own Gaelic language, upon you is calling
To cherish, embrace it, receive it again.

*Epilogue*
Belfastmen on board the *Argenta* you cannot now fight for Ireland
as soldiers in arms, but you can prepare to fight for Ireland by
carrying and spreading the light of our own Irish tongue through
our own city, so in God's name and for Ireland's sake, join and
learn the language of our own Milesian forefathers. (Kleinrichert
2001: 148)

As was noted earlier, after the Easter rising, the influx of fluent
speakers released from the *Argenta* would have a rejuvenating
influence on the outside language activist infrastructure, though
many Gaelic League activists would have to go into hiding for
fear of attracting suspicion from the unionist administration
(Ó Huallacháin 1994).

On the eve of the Second World War, both the northern and
southern regimes moved to intern republicans who had begun
a bombing campaign to disrupt Britain as it prepared for war
with Germany (Coogan 2002). Northern detainees were held in
the Crumlin Road prison in Belfast, on the Al Rydah prison ship
in Larne harbour and, later, in Derry Gaol (ibid.).[10] Republican
prisoners in these prisons maintained a disciplined organisational
structure, arranging their own education classes (MacEoin 1997:
450). During this period, over 500 republican prisoners were held
in the Curragh camp in County Kildare, where internees tended
to experience better conditions than sentenced prisoners, whose
short-lived hunger strike to right this imbalance ended rapidly
because official censorship ensured that the public was unaware
of it (ibid.).[11] Despite immense difficulties under often unbearable
conditions, the main emphasis in the Curragh camp was put on
educational development: '[T]here were the traditional activities
of all prison camps. There was a newspaper, *Barbed Wire*, and a
sports programme ... concerts and dramas ... [and] more than all the
other Curragh events ... what would be remembered from the futile
years would be the [education] classes' (Bowyer Bell 1991:102–3).

While the prisoners knew it as the 'Irish Siberia' because of how cold it was, the Curragh camp nevertheless became a focal point for two Irish-language or 'Gaeltacht' huts, in which the Irish language was taught and used as the medium of communication (Ó Maolbhríde 1981: 13). At the forefront of Irish-language development in the camp was activist Máirtín Ó Cadhain, who had been imprisoned in 1940, and promoted the language amongst the prisoners as part of his wider ideological project of cultural reconquest (Ó Tuathaigh 2007: 174). The language was taught successfully in the camp despite the lack of teaching resources; as Ó Cadhain pointed out, '[w]e had no instruments of course. Whatever instruments of any kind there were in the Curragh, had to be pressed into tunnelling service' (Ó Cathasaigh 2002: 83).

However, it was not only teaching materials that were lacking in the freezing conditions at the Curragh – food itself was said to be so scarce in certain periods that Ó Cadhain once ate food that another prisoner had thrown up (ibid.: 82). Nonetheless, in the daily battle against hunger and the elements, he savoured his teaching of the language as his most worthwhile memory of his prison experience:

A hidden Ireland scene, in a dirty, cold, badly lighted hut in the centre of the bleak Curragh. A hope-bereft slum of raggy, hungry, fagless internees from bogs and city gutters, not one of whom was ever past a national school ... And these lads gobbled up the syllabic metres of middle Irish! ... And I would face a concentration camp again for the renewal of that experience, if for nothing else. (Ibid.: 84)

Teachers and pupils alike were motivated by the fact that they perceived the language as integral to the wider republican struggle. This motivation was described by Ó Cadhain when referring to the teachers: 'Ba é a gcuid Éireannachais an spreaga ... daoine nárbh í an mhúinteoireacht a ngairm ach a mheas gur seirbhís d'Éirinn é an Ghaeilge a mhúine, go díreach mar a dhéanfaidís saighdiúireacht neamhcheirdiúil le seanghunnaí d'Éirinn' (Their Irishness was their inspiration ... people who weren't teachers by profession but who felt teaching Irish was a service for Ireland, just as they would commit themselves to Ireland as unprofessional soldiers with old guns) (ibid.). One such prisoner, Willie John McCorry, who was taught Irish by Ó Cadhain, describes his experiences:

In the Curragh, there was about 20 huts all in, each containing about 30 men. We were free from 7 am till 9 at night ... there were Irish classes in the morning and in the evening ... Máirtín had organised them from early on but only really taught me a few times because a lot of his time was spent with the top class preparing the teachers to take all the various classes from beginners right up ... He was always very busy because he was also attempting a dictionary at the same time ... I was in the Irish hut with Máirtín and there was only one rule there, no Béarla (English), and we all stuck to it ... I remember once during the classes in the hut when Máirtín and Seán Ó Tuama[12] were taking a class, Seán's brother gave us and our Irish classes a mention on the radio on the outside, of course the staters then stopped us listening to the transmission after that ... There were lots of fluent Irish speakers and teachers in the camp, there were even native speakers who assessed us for fluency with the fáinne ... It was amazing, you really could have had a university education there. (Interview with McCorry, 23 January 2005)

It is noteworthy that there was a split amongst republican prisoners in the Curragh,[13] with the Irish language playing an equally important role on both sides of the camp, as evidenced in the account of ex-prisoner Eddie Keenan:

Tháinig mise isteach sa champa cupla seactaine i ndiaidh an scoilt agus chuaigh mise le daoine as Béal Feirste a raibh aithne agam orthu ... chuaigh mé isteach sa bhóthan Gaelach agus thosaigh mé ag foghlaim Gaeilge mar is ceart don chéad uair ... Bhí rang sa mhaidin, sa trathnóna agus san oíche sa chabán ... d'eist mé le daoine ag caint Gaeilge an lá ar fad ... labhair muid í an lá ar fad, bhí orainn ar ndóigh, ní raibh cead Béarla ar bith a labhairt. Bhí a lán múinteoirí maithe ann agus chríochnaigh mise líofa ... d'fhoghlaim muid a lán amhráin Gaelacha a chuidigh linn; d'fhan siad liom go dtí an lá inniú ... bhí a lán ábhair eile ar fáil fosta. Ceann de na jabanna a bhí agamsa ná a dul thart le liosta de na ranganna ag bailiú na n-ainmneacha, bhí sé dochreidte, bhí ranganna Gearmáinise ann, ranganna Rúisíse, accounting ... gach sort rud ann.

(I came into the camp a few weeks after the split and went with people from Belfast who I knew ... I went into the Irish hut and started learning Irish properly for the first time ... There was a class in the morning, in the afternoon and one at night ... I listened to Irish being spoken all day, we spoke it all day, we had to because you weren't allowed to speak in English. There were lots of good teachers there and I ended up fluent ... we learned lots of Irish songs that helped us; I still know them to this day ... there were lots of other subjects available as well. One of my jobs was to go around with a list of the classes collecting lists of names, it was unbelievable, there were German classes, Russian classes even accounting classes ... all sorts of things.) (Interview with Keenan, 18 November 2004)

When the camp eventually closed in 1945, Ó Cadhain and others were of the opinion that around 300 or 400 prisoners left it as fluent Irish speakers (Ó Cathasaigh 2002: 84).

During this same period, internment in the north saw hundreds of nationalists and republicans imprisoned in Belfast's Crumlin Road Jail, where the Irish language played a similarly regenerative role amongst the prisoners. One of the activists who were central to these events in the prison, prominent Irish writer Tarlach Ó hUid, described them in his autobiography, *Faoi Ghlas*:

Is é an fonn a bhí orm le fada an lá a insint faoin dóigh ar éirigh linne, an seisear nó mórsheisear i measc na gcéadta braighdeanach a raibh conamar beag cheana féin Gaeilge againn, an teanga sin a chur i réim i sciathán de phríosún i dtuaisceart na hÉireann agus suas le cúig chéad fear-buachaillí as cúlsráideanna Bhéal Feirste, a mbunús a chur a labhairt na Gaeilge mar ghnáth-theanga laethúil i ngach aon ghné dá saol, má ba shaol cúng idir ballaí príosúin é.

(For a long time I've wanted to tell the story of how we, the six or main six amongst the hundreds of internees who already had a little bit of Irish managed to Gaelicise a wing of a prison in the north of Ireland with the majority of up to five hundred young men from Belfast's backstreets using the Irish language as their normal daily language in every aspect of that life, even if it was a life confined within prison walls.) (Ó hUid 1985: 9)

An Irish-language club was formed in the prison, as was a branch of the Gaelic League, while mass and confession were provided in Irish (ibid.). There was also a highly successful 'Lá na Gaeilge' (Irish day) every week where only Irish could be spoken in addition to many oral and grammar classes (ibid.). Amongst the prisoners who

successfully learned Irish in the prison during this period was Liam
Ó Stiobhaird who gives a personal account here:

> I was on D-Wing and we learned Irish every day there. It was a
> great means to occupy your mind and give you something to focus
> on in prison ... we achieved our spoken fluency by doing the'siúl
> thart' (walk around) each morning between ten and twelve, when
> we would walk around the yard with a teacher practising our
> spoken Irish ... we also organised lots of social activities through
> the language like dramas and concerts and so on ... people like
> Terry Wilson, Liam McGratton and Moscow Jack Brady[14] deserve
> a lot of credit as they were very prominent in these developments
> ... I got my gold fáinne on D-wing, which I still wear to this day
> ... they were made in the prison from gold sovereign then sent
> outside to be welded with tin ... the Gaelic League on the outside
> organised that for us ...
>
> I definitely saw the language as part of my Irish identity and
> our cause of Irish freedom ... I returned to republican activity
> on the outside when I was released, I stuck to my principles, the
> Special Powers Act and Dawson Bates[15] didn't knock the spirit
> out of me ... we stayed quiet for a while but came back strong
> in the districts, I was very much involved in republican activity
> in the late forties and early fifties ... promoting our culture was
> part of this, such as organising the *céilithe*, I done this all over
> the town. (Interview with Ó Stiobhaird, 8 March 2007)

Ó hUid (1985) maintains that by the end of 1942, the Irish
language had developed into the primary means of communication
in D-Wing of Crumlin Road Jail and summarises this achievement:
'Bhí ár gcuid féin á déanamh againn ar son na hÉireann, nó bhí an
Ghaeilge á leathadh agus a neartú go buan i Sciathán D' (We were
doing our bit for Ireland as we were spreading and strengthening
the language permanently in D-Wing) (ibid.: 271).[16]

Much of this same educational structure and emphasis on
Irish-language learning was re-employed by interned prisoners in
Crumlin Road Jail in the late 1950s during the border campaign,
when hundreds were again imprisoned without trial under the
Special Powers Act (Coogan 2002). Irish-language activist Larry
McGurk explains how he learned Irish during this period:

> Bhí ranganna Gaeilge againn achan lá sa halla mór agus gach
> maidin ach amháin Dé Satharn agus Dé Domhnaigh. Bhí a lán

múinteoirí cumasacha ann ar nós Tómas Ó hEanáin, Liam Mac Maoláin agus Paddy Joe McClean, Seán Ó Cearnaigh, Prionsíos Ó Mianáin, Art mac Cathaigh. Rinneadh liosta d'fhoghlaimneoirí agus cuireadh tús le rangana taobh amuigh fán spéir ... d'úsáid muid an córás 'siúl thart' fán chlos iná raibh muinteoirí agus foghlaimneoirí ag súil thart i mbeirteanna ag cleachtadh cainte le chéile ... mhair seo seachtain agus ansin athraíodh an mhúinteoir le cinntiú nach labhráitear leis an mhúinteoir céanna i gcónaí. Bhí leasainm ar na ranganna, ná walkie-talkie classes agus ag deireadh na bliana, achan bhliain, bheadh scrúdú béil curtha ar na ranganna.

(We had Irish classes in the big hall every day and every morning except Saturday and Sunday. There were a lot of very capable teachers there, like Tómas Ó hEanáin,[17] Liam Mac Maoláin and Paddy Joe McClean, Seán Ó Cearnaigh, Prionsíos Ó Mianáin, Art Mac Cathaigh. A list of learners was made out and we started classes outside ... we used the 'walk around' system in the yard, where teachers and pupils went around in pairs practising their spoken Irish ... this lasted a week and the teacher was changed to ensure that you weren't always talking to the same teacher. These classes were nicknamed the 'walkie-talkie' classes, and at the end of the year, every year, the classes were put under oral examination.) (Interview with McGurk, 27 January 2005)

Similar memories are relayed by Billy Kelly, who contextualises his experiences within the realities of the period:

I had a good bit of Irish from school, where I had learned it from the Christian Brothers in St Mary's, Barrack Street. I was amongst the first to do the 11-plus and passed it and then went to St Mary's. There was only about two others in the prison who went to Barrack Street. The other schools didn't do Irish because it wasn't on the school curriculum ... we done two 40-minute Irish classes a week and had to come in to school on a Saturday morning to make up the lost time spent on Irish because it wasn't recognised by the state. We usually done P.E. on a Saturday morning but the odd time, we had to do maths or something ...
   In the Crum [Crumlin Road Jail], the 'siúl thart' was the most effective way to learn the language, two hours solid walking around the yard and practising your spoken Irish, we also had a wee classroom in the yard in a hut where we kept our Irish books

and stuff, which was also handy ... our conversational Irish came on leaps and bounds, you learned not to translate from Irish into English, but instead you began thinking directly in Irish without translating anymore ... eventually, I got my gold fáinne there, which Conradh na Gaeilge sent in for us from the outside. It was all very above board as we had two examiners from the outside interned with us Tom Heenan (Ó hÉanáin) from Belfast and Nelson McWilliams from Omagh ... Plenty of internees came through with Irish on D-Wing but A-wing was a different story altogether. Our John[18] was sentenced there and they got no books or nothing, locked up all day, had to wear uniforms, the whole heap. They went on hunger strike but it didn't make a difference when you had no support on the outside, it was a whole different ball-game in the 50s, nobody really cared outside the families ... have to say, there wasn't much interest in the language on the outside when I was released outside of the Ardscoil and the Cluain Ard ... I went over the odd time, but it wasn't till the 80s that it really took off with the Irish schools and that ... I also taught a few classes at this point then in the New Lodge that some of the younger ex-prisoners had organised. (Interview with Kelly, 27 January 2005)

These accounts relate the practical and symbolic importance of the Irish language to various sets of republican political prisoners whose stories alternate in accordance with the political circumstances of the era and the conditions of their incarceration. As is evident, the tendency amongst republican prisoners to learn and use Irish was often viewed unfavourably by unsympathetic British administrations, who suppressed it while in conflict with the prisoners over issues of conditions and 'political status', etc.

Various British prison-authority attempts to undermine the long tradition whereby republican prisoners learn the language as a central tenet of their republicanism only served as an inherent recognition of its importance in the political-prisoner psyche. While this general assessment becomes somewhat more limited when dealing with Irish prisons in the post-Civil War Irish Free State, where former comrades and even language activists often administered imprisoned Irish republicans,[19] the motivating factor that inspired the prisoners' interest in the language remained the same.

Their ideological analysis of Ireland's colonial experience rendered the language a vital 'political weapon' that could challenge 'the colonial ideology of the British empire' during their imprisonment

(Ó Croidheáin 2006: 156–7). It formed an integral part of the political and academic education programmes that defined their resistance to demoralisation and maintained prisoner cohesiveness during extreme hardship and inhumanity. The tumultuous history of twentieth-century Irish prison battles is littered with examples of cultural regeneration as central to the struggle of the prisoners against various regimes, as is summarised by ex-prisoner Eoghan Mac Cormaic:

> In Frongoch, in Lewes, in the Curragh, in Derry prison and in Armagh, in Mountjoy and in Portlaois, in prison ships and in prison camps, in Crumlin Road and in Long Kesh; the Irish language was a foundation-stone of the prisoners' culture. (Mac Cormaic, in O'Hagan 1991: 17)

# 5
# 'Na Cásanna': The Cages of Long Kesh, 1973–84

[R]epublican political prisoners held in Long Kesh [have] a culture of resistance to British colonial rule in Ireland ... they understand their imprisonment as just one more arena of struggle in which they can wage war against the British. The war doesn't end with their capture. Prison is a place to educate and politicise themselves for the day they will once more be on the outside.

Lawrence McKeown (1998: 45–6)

This chapter is based primarily on the memories and contributions of ex-prisoners who spent time incarcerated in the cages of Long Kesh prison. It begins by briefly outlining the political context of internment and imprisonment in Long Kesh, before examining the role of the Irish language in the prison amongst both interned and sentenced prisoners.

## CONTEXT

Long Kesh prison retains an exceptional resonance in the history of twentieth-century imprisonment in Ireland, in that it functioned for over 30 years in what was the longest sustained military and political conflict in contemporary British and Irish history. In this conflict, republican prisoners in Long Kesh spent more than three times as long in prison on average as any other republican prisoners in Irish history (McKeown 1998). In addition, loyalist and unionist prisoners were also held in Long Kesh, while the longest and most intense republican prison protest for political status, which would culminate in the deaths of ten hunger strikers, also took place there. It was also the site of the largest prison escape in British penal history (ibid.).[1]

Therefore, as has been evident in previous periods, Long Kesh played a central role in the political conflict in the north of Ireland, with events within its walls impacting on outside political events and vice versa. In the perception of republican prisoners, the prison regime itself was a microcosm of the opposition they faced in their wider political struggle, in that its staff consisted predominantly of members of the loyalist and unionist community, many of whom had a background in the armed forces, while a number of senior management were English (ibid.: 27). This inevitably meant that conflicts within the wider community relating to political, cultural and social issues were perpetuated through the internal social relations within the prison itself (ibid.).

One of the consequences of these processes is the importance of the Long Kesh story itself in the popular nationalist and republican mindset, whether it be synonymous with internment without trial, the hunger strikes, the 'Great Escape' or the revival of the Irish language in the north of Ireland (ibid.: 26). As is evident from the interviews I carried out with the narrators, they perceive their imprisonment in Long Kesh as a 'badge of honour' rather than a stigma, a fact which no doubt stems from the social, material and political support they received from their communities on the outside, who held them in high esteem. It is in this context that Seán O'Mahony (1987: 58) makes the comparison between Long Kesh and the earlier prison struggle in the aftermath of the Easter Rising: 'It seems reasonable to compare Long Kesh to Frongoch as it had a similar politicising effect in the present struggle in the Six Counties.'

Since the formation of the Northern Ireland state in 1920 and the subsequent enshrining of the Special Powers Act, the unionist administration utilised internment as a means to suppress potential political opposition within the nationalist and republican community in every decade up until the 1970s, when it was again introduced (Coogan 2002). This use of internment 'provided an example of unfettered ministerial discretion and highlighted the political nature of the struggle. The state's involvement in suppressing political opposition was clear and unequivocal' (Hillyard 1987: 284). The immediate backdrop to its most recent usage was the campaign of the Civil Rights movement in the north of Ireland in the late 1960s, whose demands could be summarised thus: 'one man, one vote in local elections; no gerrymandering of constituency boundaries, fair distribution of local council houses, the repeal of the Special Powers Act, the disbanding of the 'B' Specials[2] and a formal complaints procedure against local authorities' (Lee 1989b: 420).

Marches organised throughout 1968 and 1969 by the Civil Rights association and the more radical People's Democracy were consistently met with state coercion in the form of the 'B' Specials and the RUC, as well as violent loyalist mobs led by Ian Paisley (ibid.). These attacks culminated in the loyalist pogroms of August and September 1969, which saw over 3,500 people driven or burned from their homes, with over 3,000 of these coming from the nationalist and republican community (ibid.). With the unionist state in disarray and its spate of limited reforms amounting to 'too little, too late', the British government sent over 10,000 British army troops to ensure the survival of the one-party regime (Farrell, 1976). The essentially malevolent colonial function of the British army was typified in July 1970, when it imposed a 36-hour curfew in the Falls Road area of Belfast to facilitate arms searches; a practice they would intensify significantly in 1971 when they carried out over 17,262 house searches (Lee 1989b: 433).

When the new unionist prime minister, Brian Faulkner, eventually did introduce internment on 9 August 1971, the majority of the 342 nationalists arrested from across the six counties had no involvement in the reorganised IRA.[3] After a month, this number increased to more than 800 interned, the overwhelming majority of these nationalist, while over 2,357 people were arrested in the first months with 1,600 being released after interrogation (ibid.: 439). Internment dramatically backfired on the British and Unionist governments by having the opposite effect to that intended in nationalist and republican areas, as Farrell states (1976: 284): 'IRA membership soared ... northern Catholics now felt the Northern Ireland state was irreformable. Their objective was not to reform it but to destroy it ... By any standards, internment had been a disaster.'

Internees were brought to Crumlin Road Jail and the *Maidstone* prison ship in Belfast Lough, where they quickly articulated their demand for political status; this was initially denied to them in May 1972 (McKeown 2001). Consequently, the republican leadership in the prison challenged this decision through a hunger strike in June which was embarked upon by Billy McKee. With pressure mounting 35 days into the strike, and in the context of outside political negotiations taking place between the IRA leadership and the British government, the secretary of state for Northern Ireland, William Whitelaw, announced that all prisoners would have special category status because of the political conflict in the six counties (Beresford 1987).

The prisoners were eventually brought to the cages of Long Kesh, while female prisoners were incarcerated in Armagh women's prison.[4] This de facto political status, which effectively conferred classical 'prisoner-of-war' legitimacy on republican prisoners, had a significant influence on various forms of political imagery espoused by both the prisoners and their supporters, as was manifested in an increased popularisation of verse and song (McKeown 1998: 46).[5] This imagery was undoubtedly enhanced by the physical appearance of the cages, where prisoners were held in tin Nissen huts, surrounded by British soldiers in sentry boxes and 15-foot wire fences (Collins 1987).

## INTERNMENT CAMP, 1973–75

> We must face the fact that in Northern Ireland, normal standards do not apply.
>
> > Merlyn Rees, British secretary of state,
> > who closed Long Kesh internment camp in 1975

As is recounted below, there was considerable Irish-language development in the section of the cages where sentenced prisoners were held. However, the circumstances of their incarceration differed greatly from those of the prisoners interned without trial in the internment section of the camp, where educational development was much more difficult to organise and sustain. As Terry Enright explains:

> The internment camp was pandemonium when I arrived there in 1973 ... you had over 90 guys in a hut sometimes even much more than that depending on the circumstances ... I was in cage 4 initially and there were no classes of any kind there ... most people tended just to do their own thing to get by even though there was a hut OC and a cage OC who were usually oul hands, the republican traditionalist type ... they installed a very militaristic regime, but their drilling and military lectures, etc. only applied to IRA volunteers and therefore oftentimes, most of the hut weren't involved in this ... the old guard really struggled with the young lads who came in who had no republican background in the traditional sense, they supported soccer teams, listened to pop music and had long hair, etc. ...
>
> After that, I was in cage 22 which was a newer cage and more spacious ... the old guard would have tried to take classes of all kinds but grew frustrated because of the lack of interest in the younger lads. I can only talk, of course, about the hut I was in, but Irish was definitely seen as something that would be considered a chore ... something the younger ones just couldn't be bothered doing and couldn't be ordered to do it, they would have rather

played football and done their own thing. (Interview with Enright, 30 March 2007)

A similar point is made by Billy Kelly, who was interned again in 1974, and as a member of the camp staff, pointed to more acute problems in trying to raise the general educational attainment levels of some of the young people interned:

Internment was an absolute holiday camp compared to what I had been used to in the Crum in the 50s ... even still, this worked against us as well when we were trying to coax the young lads into classes ... we ended up breaking it down individually with a lot of them because they'd no education at all ... I mean some of them couldn't read or write never mind getting them to do Irish classes ... these lads would have been 16 or 17 and had probably not been to school for a few years with all the rioting and that, the whole education system fell apart in the 70s ... so, we rounded up some of the teachers in the camp, and there was quite a few especially from the country ... I mean guys who were teachers on the outside, and got them to do one-to-one stuff with some of the young lads giving them basic literacy and maths and so on. (Interview with Kelly, 27 January 2005)

On the other hand, there were some successful Irish classes in the internment camp, as Enright indicates:

I had always wanted to learn the language and my breakthrough came with Francie Brolly. He was a teacher by profession and his classes were very well attended and when I say that, I mean 9 or 10 people out of 80 or 90 people ... he'd have taken one class a week, sometimes two and taught us Irish through the Gaelic songs which made it more interesting, I still remember most of them today ... the camp staff had fought for us to get Irish books and stuff in, they were prevented at the start, but I think the prison authorities ended up thinking books would be a kind of pacifying force in the internment camp ... a few of us who stuck at it got our silver fáinnes, which was a big achievement for many of us who had no Irish at all originally. (Interview with Enright, 30 March 2007)

These developments were identified by Francie Brolly who explains them against the wider difficulties of promoting educational development in the circumstances of internment:

> My Irish class wasn't very well structured, I tried to stick to conversational Irish and the songs and so on to keep the enthusiasm ... the idea was that we would use the classes to organise the young fellas' time productively while they were interned, but there wasn't a great interest I must admit ... the fellas who stuck at the classes and achieved a decent level of fluency were the ones who had a real interest in learning it ... the main issue, of course, was the lack of continuity or permanence in the camp ... it was crazy, internees didn't know whether they were coming or going, and in that context it's almost impossible to motivate people to apply themselves to any kind of educational pursuit ... we'd much more success with the Gaelic games, we had a mini-league with ten-a-side because the pitch was small and it was very well-organised and competitive ... it usually ended up the city team versus the country team and we'd some great players at our disposal who were interned ... county players and the like. (Interview with Brolly, 8 November 2006)

This point is echoed by Enright who contrasts their situation with that of the sentenced prisoners:

> The major difference between us and the sentenced prisoners was the date for release. For example, after my original tribunal I knew that it would be at least a year until my next one and this gave me something to aim at with the Irish. In the sentence end, they'd have been much more settled and organised, which brings that extra discipline and focus ... any modest classes and stuff that we had managed to maintain were completely dismantled after the fire in '74[6] ... our cage, 22, was burned to the ground and a long process ensued after that where the Brits beat the shite of us and used the CS and CR gas, etc. ... it was rough after for 6 weeks or so, we'd only a few rounds of bread to eat a day for this period ... after that, I was separated from the likes of Francie and you had no choice about which cage you were going to ... the Brits just started to release big groups of people totally unannounced so any semblance of discipline or structure totally disappeared after that. (Interview with Enright, 30 March 2007)

Internment was ended by the secretary of state, Merlyn Rees, in 1975: it was phased out in Armagh Prison in April 1975 and in the cages of Long Kesh in December of the same year, when the remainder of the internees were released (Ryder 2001:152).

## SENTENCED CAGES, 1974–84

Gaeilge más féidir, Béarla más gá (Irish if possible, English when necessary).

Motto of Gaeltacht hut in cage 11

In contrast to the internment camp, prisoners in the sentenced cages of Long Kesh were organised in a very strict military style, with strict emphasis on discipline, hygiene and regular compulsory army drilling (McKeown, 2001). However, it is worth noting that this highly disciplinarian approach was eventually challenged by a younger generation of activists who took over command of IRA prisoners in the cages in 1977, after much tension and internal wrangling, before subsequently implementing a more egalitarian organisational approach (McKeown 2001).[7] As is demonstrated below, the intricacies of some of these more general developments did not noticeably impact on the nature of Irish-language activity amongst the prisoners in the sentenced cages. The extent to which the hierarchical disciplinary regime was enforced varied from cage to cage, as did Irish-language development, which was often defined by the presence of specific individuals.

This is evident in Séanna Breathnach's description of his early experiences in the cages:

Bhí mise 16 nuair a bhain mé na cásanna amach i 1973 agus bhí fáinne airgid agam cheána féin de bhrí go raibh suim agam ann ar scoil, chuaigh mé chun na Gaeltachta agus eile..so chríochnaigh mé le fáinne óir taobh istigh de sé mhí agus mé faoi thionchar leithéidí Phrionsias Mac Airt ... seanfhundúir traidisiúnta bhí ann a bhí go príomha taobh thiar de chúrsaí Gaeilge. D'fhoglaim seisean a chuid Gaeilge i mbraighdeanas sna caogaidí so bhí an córas céanna foghlama i bhfeidhm aige linne leis na fáinní agus an-bhéim ar fad ar an ghramadach. Chuir Cyril Mac Curtain ó Luimneach go maith le seo go háirithe leis na hamhráin a chuidigh go mór linn. Bhí Proinsíos mar leascheannfort ar an champa, rud a thug deis do bogadh ó chás go cás rud a chiallaigh go dtiocfadh leis an ardrang a glacadh sna cásanna uilig ... san ardrang, bhí seisean ag ullmhú na múinteoirí go búnusach chun daoine ar chaighdeán níos isle a theagasc ... bhí mé féin i measc na múinteoirí seo de bhrí go raibh mé líofa ...

Bhí córás righin míleata i bhfeidhm sná cásanna ag an am ach bheadh sé ag brath ar an chás ina raibh tú ... bhí muidinne i gcás a 11 áit ar bhunaigh muid bothán Gaeltachta ... bhí sé measartha réchúiseach ó thaobh an stuif míleata ach lán le daoine óga, tíomónta do chúrsaí polaitíochta ... léigh muid fá réabhloidí frithchóilíneacha fud fad an domhain, léigh muid fá Vietnam, Algeria agus Angola, Meiriceá Láidíneach ... spreag seo ár gcuid fealsúnachtaí pholaitiúla féin agus chuir seo lenár suim sa teanga sa chaoi gur nasc muid é ar fad le chéile le streachailt s'againn féin.

(I was 16 when I first reached the cages in 1973 and I already had a silver fáinne because I had an interest in it in school and went the Gaeltacht and so on ... I ended up with a gold fáinne inside six months under the influence of the likes of Prionsíos Mac Airt, who was an old traditionalist who was to the forefront of Irish-language development. He learned his Irish while interned in the fifties and implemented the same teaching system with ourselves where you worked through the fáinnes with a massive emphasis on the grammar. Cyril Mac Curtain from Limerick added to this well with the songs, which were a big help to us. Prionsíos was the vice OC of the camp, which gave him the chance to travel around the cages taking the higher class in each cage ... in these classes, he was basically preparing the teachers to teach people at a lower level ... I was amongst these teachers because I was fluent ...

There was a strict military system in place in the cages but it depended on which cage you were in ... we ended up in cage 11 where we formed the Gaeltacht hut ... it was pretty laid back in terms of all the military stuff but full of committed young people with a major interest in politics ... we read everything going about anti-colonial revolutions all around the world ... we read about Vietnam, Algeria and Angola, Latin America, and all this shaped our political philosophies and also added to our interest in the language, in that we really began linking it all together with our own struggle.) (Interview with Breathnach, 23 July 2003)

This highly politicised enthusiasm amongst the younger activists in cage 11 is described by Cyril Mac Curtain, who acted as one of their teachers:

Daoradh mise i 1974 agus bhí Gaeilge agam ón scoil i gCo
Luimnigh óna caogaidí, chuir mé snas air seo fosta nuair a
d'fheastal mé ar Chumann Chluain Ard nuair a tháinig mé go Béal
Feirste i '71 ... bhí plean agam ranganna a thoiseacht agus cuireadh
iad as a riocht nuair a dódh an áit ... ach ansin tógadh cupla huts
nua agus bhí a lán lads óga díograiseacha sa hut liomsa..Bobby
Sands, Géaróid Ó Ruanaí, Séanna Breathnach, Jim Gibney, Tom
Boy Loudan agus a lán eile ... bhí siad ag iarraidh ormsa an teanga
a mhúineadh leo, ní raibh aon cháilíocht agam nó cleachtadh
sa mhúinteoireacht agam ach bhí fonn millteanach orthu í a
fhoghlaim mar gur thuig siad í mar dhóigh eile le taispeáint do
na Sasanaigh go raibh an cogadh fós ar siúil ... gléas troda a bhí
ann ... bhí ranganna againn achan lá san iarnóin, bheadh daoine
ag traenáil agus ag rith ar maidin agus ansin bheadh orainn dul
ag mairseáil agus eile so i ndiaidh am dinneár a bhí forsteanach
do na ranganna ... bhí stádas againn agus neart leabhar agus eile
... *Progress in Irish* is mó a bhí in úsáid againn ... rinne muid an
litríocht Ghaeilge leo fosta leabhar ar nós *Cith is Dealán*, *Rotha
Mór an tSaoil* ... Chuir sé iontas orm cé chomh tapaidh agus a
d'fhoglaim cuid do na lads óga an teanga ... daoine ar nós Bobby
Sands, bhí a fhios agam láithreach go raibh bua na teanga aige,
bhí sé an-díograiseach faoi ... bhain siad ar fad an-phléisiúir ar
fad as ... is mar gheall air seo a bhunaigh muid an Ghaeltacht
sa deireadh ... bhí ídéalachas ag baint leis an teanga, bhí daoine
spreagtha faoi mar gur chuid d'fhís agus aisling pholaitiúil s'acu
a bhí ann.

(I was sentenced in 1974 and had Irish from school in County
Limerick in the fifties, I improved this when I attended Cumann
Chluain Ard when I landed in Belfast in '71 ... I had planned
to take classes and these went awry after the fire ... but then a
few huts were built and I ended up in a hut with a lot of really
diligent young lads. The likes of Bobby Sands, Géaróid Ó Ruanaí,
Séanna Breathnach, Jim Gibney, Tom Boy Loudan, and lots more
... they wanted me to teach them Irish; I had no qualifications
or experience as a teacher, but they had a real desire to learn it
because they understood it as another way to show the British
that the war was still going on ... it was a weapon ... there were
classes every evening, people would be out training and running
and that in the mornings and then we would have to go and
march and so on ... therefore after dinner was the best time for
classes ... we had status and plenty of books ... *Progress in Irish*

was the most used ... we also did Irish literature with them as well, books like *Cith is Dealán*, *Rotha mór an tSaoil* ... It amazed me how quickly they learned the language ... people like Bobby Sands, I knew instantly that he'd a knack for languages, he was very committed ... they all really enjoyed it and because of this we formed a Gaeltacht in the end ... there was an idealism about the language, people were really inspired about it as part of the overall political vision.) (Interview with Mac Curtain, 10 March 2007)

The impact of this idealism and newly inspired commitment to learn the language on other activists and prisoners cannot be underestimated. In this regard, Jim McCann's account is highly pertinent: he not only explores how he learned the language and the role it played in the cage 11 Gaeltacht, but also explains this in the context of his own personal ideological development:

I was lifted in '73 and hadn't a word of Irish, and had no interest at all in trying to learn it ... then I was moved to cage 17, which later became cage 11 in '75, and was influenced by great people around me who had great politics ... my interest in the language grew as I became more political and I then started to listen to Irish music as well ...

One of the things we set down was as soon as you got the green fáinne, which was knowledge of the 11 irregular verbs, you then became a teacher to someone who didn't have this much ... gradually, you moved up the ladder ... silver fáinne was next and you had to have a degree of conversation skills and it was difficult, and the gold fáinne was at a very high standard, almost at the same level as the examiners were at, and the pressure was unbelievable – the gold fáinne meant you were fluent. But once you reached a certain standard you became a teacher and you had to be prepared to teach as well as learn, and you had to be prepared to help other prisoners at any time ... this summed up our approach in cage 11, it was about helping each other and learning together ... it moved away from the heavy compulsory, anti-English language mentality ... our motto in the Gaeltacht was inclusive and simple, Gaeilge más féidir, béarla más gá (Irish if possible, English when necessary) ... At this stage with all the classes you were taking yourself and with helping others we were doing up to 13 hours a day learning the language ...

A lot of our Irish was raw and grammatically incorrect, so we began selecting teachers to go to the different cages (we found this out by meeting Cardinal Ó Fiaich, and he suggested we polish our language skills). It worked out to the extent that there was a steady stream of people taking up the learning of the language. But after 1975 there was an explosion in terms of the language and everybody wanted to learn it. There was a range of reasons why people wanted to learn it and it wasn't necessarily leadership driven ... but our main motivation was our politics, because we knew how political the language was in cage 11 ... I don't want to exaggerate, but we recognised the lengths the imperialists went to destroy the language and from this reasoned that it must be important. When you look at imperialists all over the world the first thing they try and do is destroy the culture of the nation and attempt to replace it with their own as it makes the people easier to manage!

In my eyes a lot of this was down to luck and the sheer calibre of people and Irish-language activists we were sentenced with in cage 11, great men like Bobby Sands ... but also, we had a great deal more certainty than the likes of the internees. For example, there were thousands of prisoners in the Kesh in 1975, but I reckon if you compare and contrast the levels of Irish spoken and learned in both camps it would be night and day ... they had no certainty and little to aim at whereas we could sit back and analyse ourselves and had time to develop our politics ... towards the end of my time in prison, our Gaeltacht had developed amazingly ... I mean, between 1977 and '79 I really never spoke English at all except when I had to, we even began doing all our political and theoretical discussions in Irish ... but when I actually look back on it now, I realise that I wasn't a political person until about two years into my time in prison. I always joked that it wasn't until that time that I actually became a republican, before that I would have said I was nationalist by birth and a republican by instinct. Republicanism actually only revealed itself to me when I was in jail, not only did I learn the language, but I learned why I had went to jail and what was keeping me in jail and more importantly we learned how to begin breaking all these things down. (Interview with McCann, 12 March 2005)

Notably, the language was developing and inspiring greater interest in other cages during this period as well. Jake Mac Siacais, for example, learned his Irish in another Gaeltacht hut in cage 10, where there was a more traditional and rigid organisational approach:

> Ba léir domsa go raibh an-tábhacht leis an Ghaeilge nuair a bhain mise na cásanna amach. I gcás a 10, bhí na briathra néamhrialta scríofa i litreacha ollmhóra ar na ballaí adhmaid sna bothán. D'fhoghlaim tú iad seo de ghlánmheabhair mar chuid don bhunrang agus ansin chláraigh tú leis an meánrang. Bhog tú ansin go dtí an t-ardrang agus ansin ar aghaidh chuig an treasrang. Thaispeáin an 'treasrang' go raibh forbairt déanta agat agus go raibh tú réidh le dul i dtreo na Gaeltachta. Bhí cnámharlach na teanga agat, ní raibh de dhíth anois ach líofacht labhartha. Mhol an mhúinteoir thú ach bhí liosta feithimh ann agus ní bheadh ach leathbhóthán in úsáid rud a d'fhág nach raibh ann ach thart ar 20 leaba ann ... bhí siad an-dian ar fad ar an Ghaeilge sa Ghaeltacht. I gcás a 10, cuireadh amach thú más rud é gur labhair tú i mBéarla agus bhí liosta daoine réidh d'áit a ghlacadh!

> (It was clear to me how important the language was when I reached the cages. In cage 10, the irregular verbs were written in large letters on the wooden walls in the hut. You learned these off by heart as part of the beginners' class then registered with the intermediate class. You then moved to the higher class and from there to the advanced class. After this, you had developed enough to go to the Gaeltacht. You had the fundamentals of the language; all you needed then was spoken fluency. Your teacher nominated you, but there was always a waiting list and only a half of a hut was used which left only around 20 beds ... they were very strict on the language in the Gaeltacht in cage 10 ... you were thrown out if you spoke in English and there would be a list of guys waiting to take your place!) (Interview with Mac Siacais, 18 July 2003)

In addition to generating an increase in interest in the Irish language amongst prisoners in the cages, a number of key language activists in the prison began to show a greater cognisance of cultural developments outside the prison. This involved writing out and telling family and friends of their linguistic exploits in the prison, as well as encouraging them to learn, support and promote the language. As Breathnach explains:

> Bhí muid ag iarraidh cuir ina luí ar ár dteaghlaigh nach rud sórt téibí acadúil í an Ghaeilge ach rud praiticiúil, riachtanach

a d'fhéadfadh siad foghlaim ach an iarracht a chur isteach ... D'éirigh muid an-tógtha fosta fá chuid de na rudaí a bhí ag dul ar aghaidh ar an taobh amuigh fosta. Is cuimhin liom go raibh tionchar ollmhór ag Gaeltacht Bhóthar Seoighe orainn. Ar ndóigh, ní raibh barúil againn faoi agus muid ar an taobh amuigh ach léigh muid faoi sna nuachtáin agus eile ... is cuimhin liom go maith Bobby ach go háirithe ag scríobh amach ag iarraidh ar dhaoine tacú leo.. ag an phointe sin, bhí seisean ag maíomh gur chóir dúinn tuilleadh Gaeltachtaí agus scoileanna agus eile a chuir sa tsúil.

(We wanted our families and friends to realise that the language wasn't some abstract, academic thing that was impossible to learn but something practical and relevant and could be learned if you put the effort in ... We also got really excited about some of the stuff happening on the outside. I can remember the Shaw's Road Gaeltacht having a major impact on us. Of course, we knew nothing about it when we were outside, but we began reading about it in papers and stuff ... in particular I remember Bobby writing out about asking people to back the project ... at that time, he was saying that we should set up more Gaeltachts and schools.) (Interview with Breathnach, 23 July 2003)

In one such letter, written in Irish by Bobby Sands in the prisoners' own magazine *Ar nGuth féin* (*Our Own Voice*) in 1975, he praises the vision of those who founded the Shaw's Road Gaeltacht and demands that others have the confidence to follow their example in creating culturally independent and empowered Irish-speaking strongholds:

Sílim go bhfuil thart fá cúig teach déag ann [Bóthar Seoighe] comh maith le sin tá naíscoil beag acú, agus tá na paistí ag foghlaim gach rud trí Gaeilge agus bíonn siad ag caint i nGaeilge i gcónaí agus a dtuismitheoirí freisin agus tá cultúr féin acú ... Cad tuige nach bhfuil níos mó na Gaeltacht amháin i mBéal Feirste? Bhail leis an firinne a insint sílim go bhfuil na Gaeilgeoirí rófhallsa, chuala mé a lán leithscéal cosúil le seo, níl na daoine le Gaeilge ábalta Gaeltacht a dhéanamh de thairbhe nach bhfuil aon airgead acu, ní fíor é agus ní leithscéal é. Thig leo Gaeltacht bheag a dhéanamh ina sráideanna féin fhad as tá gach duine toilteanach. Ní raibh mórán airgid ag na daoine eile nuair a thosaigh siad, ní raibh ach rud amháin acú, bhí misneach laidir acú agus sin an rud is tábhachtach. Rinne na daoine eile scoil, agus tá fhios agam ní ach scoil beag í ach is scoil lan Ghaeilge í ...

Tá fhios againn nach bhfuighidís aon lámh cuidiú ó Rialtas ar bith, thuaidh nó theas choíche, agus sin an tuige go gcaithfidh muid é a dhéanamh muid fhéin ... sula ndéanann tú aon rud, tá eolas de dhith ort ar an rud a mbeidh tú ag déanamh agus an tuige, comh maith le sin tá misneach láidir de dhith, agus le sin thiocfaidh leat aon rud a dhéanamh.

(I think there is about 15 houses there as well as a nursery school [Shaw's Road] where all the children are learning everything through Irish, and they speak Irish all the time with their parents too and they have their own culture ... Why isn't there more than one Gaeltacht in Belfast? Well, to tell you the truth, I think Irish speakers are too lazy, I've heard a lot of excuses like, people can't do it because they have no money; that isn't true nor is it an excuse. They can form Gaeltachts in their own streets as long as people are willing. The others never had much money when they started out, all they had was great courage which is the most important thing. They also formed a school and it isn't just any school but an all-Irish school ...

We know that we won't get any any help from any government, north or south, and that is why we have to do it ourselves ... before you do anything, you need to know what you are doing and why ... as well as that, you need great courage and with that, you can do anything.) [This article was kindly provided courtesy of Denis O'Hearn.] (Sands 1975)

The complexion and dynamics of the cages would be dramatically altered, however, by macro-political developments at the beginning of 1976, when the British government put the finishing touches to a new strategy of 'criminalisation' that brought political status to an end for any prisoners sentenced after the 1 March. As Coogan states:

Britain now had an embarrassing number of political prisoners to account for before the bar of world opinion and related to this there was the affront to domestic right-wing unionist opinion reading about and sometimes seeing on television, 'terrorists' with Prisoner of War status holding parades and classes, and maintaining their own system of discipline in the barbed wire enclosed compounds which had been built in Long Kesh to house the internees. A new look at the problem was required. (Coogan 1980: 55)

This new policy came in the form of 'criminalisation', which meant that Irish political prisoners arrested after the March deadline would be treated as 'criminals'. While it did not affect already sentenced prisoners in the cages, all newly sentenced prisoners would henceforth be incarcerated in a new, state-of-the-art cellular prison on the same Long Kesh site, called HMP Maze; the prisoners would refer to this prison as the H-Blocks (ibid.). In the circumstances, 'the abolition of special category status created the anomalous situation in which hundreds of prisoners who had committed similar offences, but at different times, were serving their sentences with special category status in compounds in the very same prison' (Hillyard 1987: 298).

Amongst the prisoners to be sentenced to the cages immediately prior to the deadline was Seán Mag Uidhir, who accounts for the fortunes of the Irish language during his time there:

Bhí scaifte againne a daoradh thart an am céanna, mé féin, Caoimhín Corbett, Liam Stone (Ó Maolchluiche) a chaill an spriocdáta i Márta '76 le cúpla seachtain, rud a chiallaigh go mbeadh stádas againn sná cásanna ... nuair a bhain muidinne an áit amach, bhí an Ghaeltacht i gcás 11 i ndiaidh bás a fháil tar éis gaeilgeoirí ar nós Bobby Sands, Séanna Breathnach agus Tom Boy Loudan imeacht óna chásanna ... ní raibh mise ann ag an am ach chuaigh mé ann cupla uair le freastal ar ranganna Jim McCann as Uachtar Chluanaí a bhí chomh greannmhar sin gur mheall siad a lán daoine ... ach thuig Jim nach mbeadh forbairt ceart ann gan an Gaeltacht a athbhunú so mheall sé Daithí de Paor ón Tra Ghearr a bhí líofa agus cupla duine ó chás a 9 a bhí ag iarraidh a Ghaeltacht féin a bhunú agus bhí athbhuanú cás a 11 faoi lán seol arís ... d'eagraigh siad ócáidí sóisialta ar nós seachtain na Gaeilge agus d'fhreastal muidinne ó chásanna eile air seo agus ina dhiaidh seo shocraigh mé go raibh orm bogadh, bíodh is nach raibh mé ag iarraidh cuid do mo chairde a fhágáil, b'éigean dom dá mba mhaith liom an teanga a shealbhú i gceart ... sa deireadh, chaith mé cúig bhliain go leith ann, áit iontach a bhí ann, bhí múinteoir ag achan bheirt nó triúr, thiocfadh leat cúig rang a dhéanamh san aon lá amháin agus sult a bhaint astu, d'imir muid cluichí ar nós bingo as Gaeilge, rinne muid díospóireachtaí pholaitiúla i nGaeilge ... spreag seo uilig cimí eile, nuair a chonaic siad gnáthchimí cosúil linne ag labhairt na teanga, bhris seo an mhiotaseolaíocht a bhain leis agus chreid siad go dtiocfadh leo í a fhoghlaim.

(There was a crowd of us sentenced around the same time – myself, Caoimhín Corbett, Liam Stone who just missed out on the March '76 deadline by a few weeks, which meant that we had status ... when I reached the place, the Gaeltacht in cage 11 had died out after Irish speakers like Bobby Sands, Séanna Breathnach and Tom Boy Loudan had left the cages ... I wasn't there at the time, but went there a few times to attend Jim McCann from the Upper Springfield's classes that attracted people because they were so funny ... but Jim understood that there wouldn't be proper development unless the Gaeltacht was reformed again, so he brought in Daithí de Paor from the Short Strand who was fluent and they attracted another few from cage 9 who were looking to set up their own Gaeltacht and the re-establishment of cage 11 was up and going strong again ... they organised things like Irish-language week and people from other cages like ourselves could take part ... after that I decided I was going to move there, even though I didn't want to leave my mates, but I knew I had to if I wanted to learn the language properly ... I ended up spending the next five and a half years there, it was an amazing place, you had a teacher for every two or three people and you could have ended up doing five classes in one day and really enjoying them all ... we played games like bingo in Irish, we had political debates in Irish ... all this inspired other prisoners when they saw ordinary prisoners like us speaking the language, it broke down a lot of the mythology for them and they began believing that they could also learn it.) (Interview with Mag Uidhir, 17 February 2005)

This capacity for activity in the Gaeltacht hut to inspire others who previously had little interest in acquiring the language is evident in Caoimhín Corbett's account:

Nuair a landáil mé féin sná cásanna, ní doigh liom go raibh suim agam i rud ar bith seachas popcheol b'fhéidir! ... d'amharc mise ar chuid de na Gaeilgeoirí mar sórt zealots ... ach chomh luaithe agus ar bunaíodh an Ghaeltacht, d'ardaigh sin próifíl na Gaeilge go millteanach mór agus cuireadh a lán ranganna sa tsiúl i mbótháin eile de bhrí go raibh daoine ag iarraidh cuid mhaith Gaeilge a fhoghlaim agus ansin bogadh ann ... bhí an áit fhisiciúil ina spreagadh mór ag daoine ... chomh maith le sin, d'athraigh an Ghaeltacht an dóigh ar teagascadh an teanga fiú ... de gnáth, bhí an-bhéim ar an ghramadach agus córas daingean foghlamtha leagtha amach ... Briathra neamhrialta, réamhfhocail ... struchtúr na teanga agus eile ach ansin bhog an bhéim ar fad chuig an Ghaeilge labhartha ... bhog mise chuig an Ghaeltacht i '79 agus cuid mhaith don struchtúr seo agam ach ní raibh mórán muiníne agam sa chaint ... is cuimhin liom go raibh an chéad trí seachtaine an-olc ar fad, bhí fonn orm iarriadh as mar go raibh gach duine ag caint Gaeilge liom an t-am ar fad agus shíl mé go raibh siad ag magadh orm agus eile, bhí paranoia olc orm ach d'fhan mé leis agus murach sin, tá mé cinnte nach mbeadh Gaeilge agam inniu ... mhéadaigh mo chuid suime sa teanga de réir mar a d'fhoghlaim mé í agus a d'ardaigh mo chuid féinmhúiníne chomh maith, thosaigh mé ag léamh sa teanga agus ag smaoineamh as Gaeilge, rud a bhí soiléir dom i ndiaidh mo chéad bhrionglóid a bheith agam as Gaeilge sa Ghaeltacht! ... bhí mé ann ar feadh ceithre bliana agus duine iomlán difriúil a bhí ionam sa deireadh.

(When I landed in the cages, I don't think I had any interest in anything except probably pop music ... I looked on the Irish speakers as zealots ... but when the Gaeltacht was formed, it raised the profile of the language in a major way and lots of classes were started in other huts because people wanted to learn a good bit before moving there ... the physical place really created the inspiration ... as well as this, the Gaeltacht changed the way the language was taught, usually, there was a huge emphasis on grammar and a strict system of learning laid out ... Irregular verbs, prepositions, the structure of the language, etc., but then the emphasis moved to the spoken language ... I moved to the Gaeltacht in '79 and had a lot of the structure, but very little confidence in my spoken Irish ... the first three weeks were terrible, I felt like jacking it in because everyone was speaking Irish to me the whole time and I thought they were joking about me and the like ... I was really paranoid ... but I stuck with it and if I had not have, I'm sure I wouldn't have Irish today ... my interest in the language increased the more of it that I learned and self-confidence grew as a result ... I started to read in Irish and think in Irish which became clear to me when I had my first Irish dream in the Gaeltacht! ... I was there for four years and was a completely different person at the end.) (Interview with Corbett, 2 February 2005)

Although the republican prisoners in the cages had political status, which meant that they controlled matters within their own cages, with the warders and Army on the opposite side of the wired fencing, they nevertheless were not altogether free from occurrences of inter-prison conflict. Prison authorities often manifested their sense of control through 'security searches', as Liam Ó Maolchluiche attests:

> Chuir siad 'Cuartuithe Slándála' orthu ach i bhfírinne, bhain siad úsáid as sin mar leithscéal le cimí a chiapadh agus an Ghaeltacht i gcás 11 a scrios. Rinneadh an léirscrios agus an dámáiste is mó ar bhothán s'againne de bhrí gur Ghaeltacht a bhí ann. Bhris siad na háiseanna teagaisc, an cheardaíocht láimhe agus stróic siad na leabhair Ghaeilge as a chéile ... Chuir an teanga agus an bothán Gaeltachta isteach go mór orthu; mar gur ráiteas polaitiúil a bhí ann á rá gur Gaeil sinne agus ní thiocfadh leo déileáil leis seo ... ach theip glan ar bheartaíocht s'acu agus bhí a mhalairt de thionchar aici ar toil na bpríosúnach agus stádas na Gaeilge féin ... D'ardaigh na cuarduithe clú agus cáil na Gaeltachta agus tugadh gríosú polaitiúil do thuilleadh cimí an teanga a aithint mar ghléas streachailte.

> (They were supposed to be security searches, but they were also used to annoy us and to wreck the Gaeltacht in cage 11. They seemed to do the most damage and destruction in our hut because it was a Gaeltacht. They destroyed teaching materials, handicrafts, and they ripped up Irish-language books. The Gaeltacht hut must have really annoyed them; essentially we were making a political statement that we were Gaels and they could not handle that ... but their tactics completely failed and had the opposite effect on the will of the prisoners and the status of the language ... the searches increased the popularity of the Gaeltacht and gave political inspiration to more prisoners to recognise that the language could be a means of struggle.) (Interview with Ó Maolchluiche, 28 June 2003)

This sense of 'struggle' and hostility towards the administration was exacerbated by the fact that the prisoners' comrades in the H-Blocks were engaged in an intense 'blanket protest' for political status, while at the same time the cages were stagnating, with no new prisoners coming in. As Ó Maolchluiche explains:

Ní raibh aghaidheanna ar bith nua ag teacht isteach sna cásanna agus d'éirigh an saol cinéal leadránach agus uaigneach in amanna ... chuidigh an agóid sna blocanna linn cimí a spreagadh i dtreo na Gaeilge sa chaoi gur thuig siad cé chomh lárnach agus a bhí an teanga sa streachailt in éadan coirpeachta ... d'fhéach siad air mar cineál gléas dlúthpháirtíochta ach ag an am céanna, bhí a lán frustrachas agus fearg ann de réir mar a d'imigh rudaí chun donais ... mhothaigh muid neamhchumhachtach so chaith muid a lán ama ag ullmhú ceachtanna Gaeilge daofa chun spiorád s'acu a thógáil go háirithe nuair nach raibh áiseanna acu ... chuir muid fríd na sagairt iad agus bheadh orainn bheith dearfa cinnte gur Gaeilge beacht, foirfe a bhí ann ar eagla gur scaip muid meáncóga thart ar na blocanna. Taithí maith a bhí ann agus chuidigh sé go mór le Gaeilge s'againn.

(There was no fresh blood coming into the cages at all and life became even more tedious and repetitive ... the protest in the Blocks helped us inspire people towards the language, in that they understood how central the language was to the struggle against criminalisation, they looked on it as a means of solidarity, but at the same time there was a lot of anger and frustration as the situation worsened ... We felt totally powerless whilst the struggle against criminalisation was going on in the Blocks ... we sent down Irish-language grammar lessons with the priests to raise the spirits of the lads, especially when there they had no access themselves to any type of resources ... we had to be absolutely sure that we were sending down the proper material, otherwise we would have been responsible for spreading bad Irish grammar throughout the Blocks. It was great practice for ourselves and developed our own standard of Irish.) (Ibid.)

This tension and powerlessness amongst the prisoners in the cages increased during the hunger strikes as their fellow prisoners were dying to assert their right of political status. This raised serious contradictions for many, according to Diarmuid Mac a tSionnaigh:

Bhí muid gníomhach ag cuidiú tacú le streachailt na mblocanna chan amháin ó thaobh na Gaeilge de ach chomh maith leis sin ag scríobh na mílte litreacha fud fad an domhain ag iarraidh aird daoine a dhíriú ar an stailc ocrais ... bhí daoine scriosta agus iomlán fríd a chéile nuair a fuair Bobby [Sands] bás, bhí cuid de na daoine feargach le ceannaireacht an champa, nár dhóigh

muid na cásanna chun bogadh chuig na blocanna in éineacht leo
... ach bhí an cheannaireacht dubh in éadan mar go raibh stádas
againn cheana, díreach an rud a bhí siadsan ag troid fána choinne,
ní fhaca siad go raibh aon chiall sin a tabhairt ar shiúl ... bhog
daoine aonaracha chuig na blocanna cibé, cuireadh ansin thú da
mba rud é gur rugadh ort ag iarrraidh éalú rud a rinne cuid de na
daoine chun deis a fháil bogadh anonn chuig na lads ar an agóid.

(We were very active in supporting the struggle in the Blocks,
not only through the language, but writing thousands of letters
throughout the world to focus people's attention on the hunger
strike ... people were totally wrecked and all over the place when
Bobby [Sands] died, they were angry with the leadership in the
camp for not burning the cages in order to join up with the Blocks
... but the leadership was totally against this idea because we
already had status which is what the lads were fighting for, they
felt it was senseless to give this away ... individuals moved to the
Blocks anyway, you were sent there if you were caught escaping
which is what some people did in order to get moved over to join
the lads on the protest.) (Interview with Mac an tSionnaigh, 20
April 2005).

In the aftermath of the hunger strike, a more long-term and
strategic approach was embarked on by the prisoners in the cages,
which involved reviewing their opposition to taking part in the
formal prison education processes[8] which had been in place since
political status had been removed in 1976. Ó Maolchluiche explains
the rationale behind this:

D'athraigh stráitéis s'againne i ndiaidh na stailce ... níor
chomhoibrigh muid ariamh le córais oideachais an phríosúin
mar gur mhothaigh muid nár chóir dúinn aitheantas ar bith a
thabhairt daofa ... ach thiontaigh muid seo bunoscionn agus
shocraigh muid go mbainfeadh muid úsáid as córais s'acu go
stráitéiseach agus go fad-téarmach ... chuidíodh an t-oideachas
le forbairt pearsanta s'againne agus mar sin de le forbairt na
streachailte féin ... d'éirigh linn O Level Gaeilge agus neart ábhar
eile a fháil agus muid ár n-ullmhú féin don obair pholaitiúil a bhí
romhainn nuair a scaoileadh saor muid.

(Our strategy changed after the hunger strike ... we had never
co-operated with the prison education system, because we didn't

want to give them any recognition ... but we transformed this and decided to use their system strategically and in a more long-term way ... the education would help our own personal development and thus help the development of the struggle itself ... we succeeded in getting O Levels in Irish and other subjects and were preparing ourselves for the political work in store for us when we were released from prison.) (Interview with Ó Maolchluiche, 28 June 2003)

The cages and the special category status retained by its prisoners continued until 1987, when the remainder of the prisoners were transferred to the H-Blocks (McKeown 2001). The central role that the language undoubtedly played during this period and its transformative impact on many prisoners and subsequent future events are aptly summarised in the words of Mac Curtain:

Bíodh is go raibh Gaeilge agam sula ndeachaigh mé isteach ann, is i rith mo chuid ama sna cásanna gur thuig me cumhacht na teanga i bhfírinne, an chumhacht athbheochana sin ... bhí mé páirteach i nGaeltacht eile a bhunú i bpríosúin Phort Laoise ina dhiaidh sin agus tá mé ag obair leis an teanga ó dhubh go dubh ó scaoileadh saor mé ... bhí ré ar leith i gceist sna cásanna, am spéisialta a bhí ann ... Cuireadh síol cumhachtach ann agus gabhadh roinnt do lads óga go gearr i ndiaidh bheith scaoilte saor agus do ghlac iad an Gaelachas leo istach sna Blocanna agus amuigh chuig an saol mór ina dhaidh sin ... d'éirigh go geal leo agus iad ann ... bhí toradh iontach ar a gcuid díograis ... tháinig bláth ar a gcuid iarrachtaí in am an ghatair ... bhí toradh millteanach mór air sin.

(Even though I had Irish before I went in there, it was during my time in the cages that I really began to understand the power of the language, that power of revival ... after that period, I was involved in setting up another Gaeltacht in Port Laoise prison and I've been working constantly on the language from when I was released ... it was an exceptional era in the cages, a special time. A powerful seed was planted there and some of the young lads were arrested a short time after being released and brought their language activism into the Blocks with them and to the outside world after that ... they did brilliantly there ... there was a great product from their diligence ... their efforts blossomed in terrible circumstances ... it had a massive impact.) (Interview with Mac Curtain, 10 March 2007)

# 6
# 'Ar An Phluid': The H-Blocks, the 'Blanket Protest' and the Aftermath, 1976–85

In the circumstances I was surprised that the morale of prisoners was so high. From talking to them it is evident that they prefer to face death rather than be classed as criminals. Anyone with the least knowledge of Irish history knows how deeply rooted this attitude is in our country's past. In isolation and perpetual boredom they maintain their sanity by studying Irish. It was an indication of the triumph of the human spirit over adverse material surroundings to notice Irish words, phrases and songs being shouted from cell to cell and then written on each cell wall with the remnants of toothpaste tubes.

Cardinal Tomas Ó Fiaich, 1978 (Coogan 1980: 159)

This chapter recounts the experiences of ex-prisoners who spent time incarcerated in the H-Blocks of Long Kesh. At the outset, it briefly underlines the political context of the policy of criminalisation in the north of Ireland as a backdrop to the use of the H-Blocks, officially named HMP Maze, as the prison for the detention of politically motivated prisoners. It specifically accounts for the central role played by the Irish language as a 'means of struggle' during the prisoners' five-year blanket protest from 1976 to 1981. In addition, it also relates the changed fortunes of the language in the prison in the aftermath of the 1981 hunger strike.

## CONTEXT

The political decision taken by the British government to change its policy in relation to political prisoners in the six counties was shaped by the specific needs of its political and military offensive against the armed republican campaign (Coogan 1980: 55). This tactical shift is best understood in the context of the more general strategy of the time, 'Ulsterisation, criminalisation, and normalisation' (ibid.). This involved localising the political and military conflict in the north by absolving the British Army of its immediate security responsibilities and allocating the prime responsibility for policing to the RUC and the locally recruited British army regiment, the UDR,[1] in an attempt to portray the conflict as a sectarian one between 'Catholic and Protestant warring tribes', with Britain as the neutral broker (McKeown 1998: 17). This portrayal effectively detached the conflict from the historical processes of British colonial and sovereign control of Ireland, its subsequent partition and the 50-year one-party rule under the unionist administration at Stormont (ibid.).

As had been the case in previous phases of British political imprisonment in Ireland, their approach tended to be dictated by immediate political expediency. From this point on, British government spokespeople and popular media outlets represented republican/nationalist opposition as a 'criminal conspiracy' rather than a 'political threat' (Beresford 1987: 25). Thus, the removal of political status from prisoners in Long Kesh was a central component of an overall strategy in which the H-Blocks became the primary battleground (Coogan 1980: 55–6). This process was facilitated by a radical overhaul of the legal and judicial mechanisms governing arrest, detention, interrogation and the courts in the six counties (Hillyard 1987).

Republican supporters described this new system as the 'conveyor belt system', which saw large numbers of people arrested under 'emergency terrorist legislation' – held at Castlereagh interrogation centre for seven days, charged and imprisoned for a period on remand in Crumlin Road Jail, and then brought in front of a Diplock Court (a special court without a jury or right of appeal) before being sentenced to the H-Blocks (McKeown, Campbell and O'Hagan, 1994). It is estimated that as many as 80 per cent of convictions in this period were based on 'confessions' extracted during intense interrogation, in which many prisoners alleged they were subjected to various forms of brutality and torture (Hillyard 1987). The contradictory nature of the controversial process leading to criminal convictions saw those who fell victim to it 'considered as political in the courtroom but criminal for the purposes of punishment' (Tomlinson 1980: 193).

This key function of 'criminalisation' as a predominant justification for overtly political forms of containment, which aimed to engineer popular support for repressive state action, is explained by the fact 'that people are more likely to support state action against a "criminal" act than they would the use of the law to repress a "political cause"' (Hall and Scraton 1981: 489). Consequently, the new propaganda discourse adopted by the British government in this period, whereby political prisoners became 'gangsters' and 'criminals', was integral to a co-ordinated political strategy. This conscious project had international precedent, as Schubert (1986: 189) elucidated when referring to the German context: 'The criminalisation of political enemies and the denial of their existence as political enemies is an essential element of a consciously waged psychological war of isolation and destruction.' The ingrained historical precedent amongst republican prisoners to oppose individual and collective criminalisation by successive British administrations shaped their understanding of themselves as political. Additionally, the fact that they had already been afforded such status in the cages, while also having this belief reinforced by the communities they came from, shaped their strong opposition to the policy of criminalisation (McKeown 1998: 64).

In the republican prisoner perspective, their incarceration was as a result of the exceptional political situation in which they found themselves, which saw 'special' legislation in order to 'clean' republicans from society, to delegitimise their political objectives and identity and thereby dismantle their community cohesion and solidarity as well as their subsequent lack of guilt at their actions (ibid.). Accordingly, as increasing numbers of people from the nationalist and republican community became by-products of the processes of 'criminalisation', its epicentre in Long Kesh invariably took on a much wider significance. As ex-prisoner Brendan McFarlane attests, 'Our refusal to submit to criminality became more than simply an internal jail issue. The battle against it became a crucial factor in the overall struggle for self-determination' (McKeown, Campbell and O'Hagan 1994: 104).

## THE H-BLOCKS, 1976–81

> I'll wear no convict's uniform, nor meekly serve my time, that Britain might brand Ireland's fight, 800 years of crime!
> Francie Brolly's 'H-Block song'
> (McKeown, Campbell and O'Hagan 1994)

The first republican prisoner imprisoned in the H-Blocks under the new system in September 1976 was Kieran Nugent from Belfast, who immediately refused to wear the prison uniform, declaring, 'if you want me to wear your criminal garb, you are going to have to nail it to my back' (Coogan 1980: 79) and thus igniting the prisoners' battle for political status. Séanna Breathnach, who was

arrested and imprisoned only a few months following his release
from the cages, depicts the beginning of the protests:

Caitheadh muidne caol díreach isteach i lár na hiarrachtaí a bhí
Rialtas na Breataine a dhéanamh lenár streachailt a mhilleadh le
lipéad na coirpeachta. Ní raibh 'master plan' againn, bhí muid
ag déileáil leis ó instinct ... Ar an mheán, bhí an mhórchuid de
na cimí 17 nó 18 bliana d'aois agus cinéal saonta ... Cibé ar
bith, thuig muid gur phríosúnaigh pholaitiúla a bhí ionainn agus
nach raibh muid ag dul éide phríosúin a chaitheamh. Nuair a
caitheamh isteach sa chillín muid lomnocht, thóg muid an phluid
thart orainn ... Ní raibh a fhios againn ag an am go raibh Tomás
Ashe ar an phluid nuair a fuair sé bás ar stailc ocrais i 1917 ar
son stadas polaitiúil agus go raibh poblachtánaigh eile ar phluid
sna daichidí don chúis chéanna ... ach lean muid an traidisiún
gan smaoineamh ... ar ndóigh, is mar gheall air seo a bhí muid
faoi ghlas sa chillín an lá ar fad gan cead aclaíochta, bíodh is
go raibh cead againn amach ag an tús gach maidin ar feadh
deich mbomaite le haghaidh níocháin ... bhí cosc orainn leabhair,
páipéar nó pinn a bheith againn ... thuig muid gur chuid é seo
don phlean chun muid a bhriseadh ó thaobh na síceolaíochta de
le go n-éireodh muid as an agóid ... ach d'éirigh seo níos deacra
acu agus níos mó daoine ag teacht isteach sa phríosúin agus ar an
agóid ... bhí muid diongbháilte sa troid ina gcoinne agus bheadh
an teanga níos lárnaí ná mar a bhí ariamh sa chath seo.

(We were thrown into the middle of the British government's
effort to besmirch our republican struggle with the label of
criminality. We had no master plan, we reacted instinctively ...
on average, most of the prisoners were 17 or 18 years of age
and somewhat innocent ... anyway, we understood that we were
political prisoners and that we were not going to wear a prison
uniform. We were thrown naked into our cells and wrapped
ourselves in the blanket ... we were unaware at the time that
Thomas Ashe was on the blanket when he died on hunger strike
in 1917 for political status and that other republicans had been on
the blanket in the forties for the same reason ... but we followed
the tradition without realising it ... of course, it was because
of this that we were locked up in the cell all day long without
exercise, although at the beginning we were allowed out for ten
minutes in the morning for a wash ... we were prevented from
having books, papers or pens ... we understood that this was all

part of the plan to break us psychologically so we would come off the protest ... however, this task of theirs became more difficult as more people came into the jail and on the protest ... we were determined to fight against this and the language was more central than ever before in this battle.) (Interview with Breathnach, 23 July 2003)

While the Irish language would take on added significance in these circumstances, its development was nevertheless dependent upon the arrival in the H-Blocks of a number of fluent Irish-speaking activists who had previously learned Irish in the cages. One of these activists, Jake Mac Siacais, highlights this point:

Tháinig mise isteach sna blocanna leath-bhealaigh fríd 1977 agus bhí dream beag againn le taithí na gcásanna taobh thiar dúinn cheána féin ... mé féin, Séanna Mór [Breathnach], Bobby [Sands] agus b'fhéidir ceathrar nó cúigear eile a bhí i ndán ranganna oideachais agus ranganna Gaeilge a chuir ar siúl sna sciatháin eagsúla ... bhí seo iomlán luachmhar sna coinníollacha millteanacha iná mhair muid chun spiorad agus féinaithne na leaids a thógáil ... Dúshlán ollmhór a bhí ann de bhrí go raibh muid faoi ghlas sna cillíní an lá ar fad gan áiseanna ar bith. Bhí 'scairteoir' in achan sciathán agus scairteadh seisean na ranganna amach an doras ag an hinse i bpróiseas fadálach foghraíochta. Thosaigh an Ghaeilge ar bhonn slándála agus chríochnaigh sé mar theanga labhartha na mblocanna ... ar ndóigh, bhí sí úsáideach ag an tús chun rudaí a choinneáil faoi cheilt ar na gnáthbhairdéirí ach is cinnte i mo bharúil gur chuir údaráis an phríosúin, dá mba rud é go raibh ciall ar bith acu, gléasanna éisteachta isteach chun ár gcuid teachtaireachtaí a aistriú agus eile ... so ní sin an phríomhaidhm a bhí aicí, an tógail féiniúlachta is mó a bhí taobh thiar di ... Bhí an dul chun cinn dochreidte ar fad, déanta na fírinne. Ag an tús, ní raibh ach seachtar nó ochtar de bhunadh na gcásanna le Gaeilge agus cupla leaids óga eile a fuair ar scoil í ar nós Eunan Brolly, dearthair Francie agus Gerry Mc Conville a dtugtaí Gerry O air de bhrí go raibh O Level Gaeilge aige ón taobh amuigh, rud a bhí éisceachtúil ag an am ... ach taobh istigh de bhliain go leith bhí 300 cimí le Gaeilge ar a dtoil.

(I came into the Blocks half way through 1977 and there was a small group of us with the experience of the cages behind us ... myself, big Séanna [Breathnach], Bobby [Sands] and maybe

four or five others who could start the education classes and the
Irish classes on the wings ... this was totally invaluable in the
terrible conditions to lift the spirit of the lads and help build
their identity ... it was a major challenge in that we were locked
up all day without any resources. There was a 'shouter' on each
wing, who would shout the classes out the door at the hinge in
a slow phonetical process. Irish took off on the basis of security
and ended up as the spoken language of the Blocks ... of course,
it was useful at the outset to conceal information from ordinary
screws, but there was no doubt, in my opinion, that the prison
authorities, if they had any sense, planted listening devices in
order to decipher our messages ... so that wasn't its main function;
the building of identity was its main function ... to tell you the
truth, the progress was unbelievable. At the beginning, there were
about seven or eight of us from the cages who had Irish and a few
young lads who had it from school like Eunán Brolly, Francie's
brother, and Gerry McConville, who was known as Gerry O,
because he had an O Level in Irish, which was exceptional at the
time ... and within a year and a half, there was 300 prisoners with
fluent Irish.) (Interview with Mac Siacais, 18 July 2003)

This progress in language-learning was achieved through
replicating the cages model of informal education, which saw the
'pupil' become the 'teacher' after arriving at a particular level of
fluency. This process is underlined by Breathnach:

Ag an tús, ní raibh againn ach an chrois naofa, a raibh cead
againn caitheamh ar ár muineál, le haghaidh na ceachtanna a
scríobh ar na ballaí sna cillíní ach níos moille, ghoid muid an taos
fiacla a d'fhág na báirdéirí taobh amuigh dona doirse, agus iad
ag iarriadh taispeáint do chuairteoirí san NIO nach raibh muid
sásta glanadh agus eile ... so ghoid muid iad agus rinne muid pinn
luaidhe ó bhun an taos fiacla ... le himeacht aimsire, fuair muid
ceachtanna gramadaí is eile óna cásanna fríd na sagairt nuair
a thosaigh muid ag dul ar aifreann ar an Domhnach; níor fhag
muid an cillín ach amháin ansin agus don chuairt uair amháin
sa mhí; chuidigh seo linn ábhair teagaisc breise a fháil isteach
agus a scaipeadh fríd na píopaí ag bun an chillín ... go praiticúil,
d'fhorbair teagasc na teanga trí chórás pirimide; theagasc daoine
le Gaeilge mheasartha daoine le beagán Gaeilge agus theagasc
daoine le beagán Gaeilge daoine gan Gaeilge ar bith agus d'fhás

sé mar sin cé nach raibh ach dornán beag daoine ag an bharr le Gaeilge líofa acu. Rinneadh múinteoir d'achan duine ...

Bíodh is gur modh foghlama éifeachtach a bhí ann, scaipeadh a lán meancóga agus drochnathanna foghraíochta ... mar shampla, bhí claonadh ann 'ch' a fhuaimniú mar 'K' agus amhlaidh leis an seimhiú féin a fágadh ar lár sa chaint go minic ... b'iomaí uair sna bliantaí ina dhiaidh sin a chaith gaeilgeoirí líofa ón taobh amuigh anuas ar iarchimí mar gheall ar na meancóga seo ach ní dhearna seo cothrom na féinne do na coinníollacha inár fhoghlaim cuid mhór againn an teanga ... Ní raibh fáil againn éisteacht le Gaeilge ar an raidió agus bhí daoine ag foghlaim Gaeilge ó dhaoine nach raibh Gaeilge ar bith acu sula ndeachaigh siad isteach. Bhí fuaimeanna aisteacha againn ach bhí áis chumarsáide éifeachtach againn ag an am céanna ... bhí sí an-cumhachtach mar ghléas ardú consiasa ag na leaids, agus smaoinigh mise fán teanga ar an dóigh seo, mar bhonn néamhspléachas intinne, cineál ar nós Steve Biko agus 'Black Consciousness'.

(At the start, all we had was the holy cross, which we could wear around our necks, to write lessons on the cell walls, but later on, we stole toothpaste that screws had left outside the doors, when they were showing visitors in the NIO that we wouldn't wash, etc. ... so we stole them and made pencils out of the part at the bottom of the toothpaste ... as time went on, we got grammar lessons brought in from the cages through the priests when we started attending Mass on a Sunday; we never left the cell apart from then and for one visit a month; this helped us smuggle extra teaching material in, which could be sent around through the pipes at the bottom of the cell ... practically speaking, the teaching of the language developed in a pyramid system; people with moderate Irish taught those with little Irish and those with little Irish taught those who had no Irish at all and this is how it spread even though there was only a small batch at the top who had fluent Irish. Everyone became a teacher ...

Even though is was an effective system of learning, it spread a lot of grammatical errors and bad phonetic habits ... for example, there was a tendency to sound 'ch' like a 'k' and the same with the aspiration which was often left out of spoken Irish ... over the years after that, many fluent Irish speakers on the outside criticised the Irish of ex-prisoners because of these mistakes but this didn't take into account the conditions in which a lot of us learned the language ... we never had a chance to listen to Irish on the radio and people were learning Irish from people who had no Irish at all before they came in. We had a lot of weird sounds but nevertheless had an effective means for communication at the same time ... it was very powerful as a means to raise consciousness and that is the way I thought of the language, as a way of gaining mental emancipation, kind of like Steve Biko and 'Black Consciousness'.) (Interview with Breathnach, 23 July 2003)

The impact of this means of communication on a prison community struggling to survive in a deeply hostile environment 'where the basic human needs of physical and mental health were denied to them' (Coogan 1980: 159) is articulated by Donncha Mac Niallais:

De gnáth rinne muid na ranganna Gaeilge nuair nach raibh na bairdéirí ann le bheith saor ó chuir isteach ... sin ag am lóin, am dinneára agus san oíche, bhí muid ábalta léachtaí, scéalaíocht agus roinnt rudaí eile a dhéanamh ag an am sin ... Ní raibh sé deacair daoine a spreagadh Gaeilge a fhoghlaim ... bhí muid faoi ghlas an t-am ar fad mar sin chuir a lán daoine suim sna ranganna leis an t-am a líonadh, bheadh daoine ag imeacht as a meabhair gan é ar bhealach ... chomh maith leis sin, bhí an Ghaeilge mar áis teagmhála ar na scíathán agus ar an dóigh sin, bhí sé a bheag nó a mhór riachtanach go mbeidh Gaeilge agat ó thaobh cúrsaí slándála agus rudaí praiticiúla ... agus d'fhoghlaim daoine Gaeilge le cinntiú go raibh an scéal iomlán acu ón cheannfort nó ón taobh amuigh srl ... bhí daoine ag caint Gaeilge i rith an ama fríd na doirsí agus fuinneoga agus i ndiaidh tamaill thóg daoine é fiú muna raibh siad ag glacadh páirte i rang foirmeálta, d'foghlaim siad ar bhonn nadúrtha í. Bhí 46 duine i sciathán s'againn agus bhí Gaeilge líofa ag 90% acu agus thiocfadh le hachan duine eile í a thuiscint go maith ... chuir muid le seo fosta fríd cúrsaí siamsaíochta, reachtáil muid deireadh seachtaine na Gaeilge nuair nár labhair tú ach Gaeilge, oícheanta seanchais agus ceolchoirmeacha agus eile chun spraoi a chuir ann chomh maith.

(We usually never had the classes until the screws were off the wing, to be free from interference ... that was at lunch time, dinner time and at night, we could do lectures, storytelling and all sorts of stuff then ... it wasn't difficult to inspire people to learn Irish ... we were locked up the entire time, which meant that a lot of people showed an interest in it to fill their time, in a way people

would have been going insane without it ... as well as that, Irish
was the means of communication on the wings and in that way, it
was more or less essential that you had Irish for security reasons
and for practical things ... people also learned Irish to ensure that
they got all the news of the OC or from the outside ... people
spoke constantly out the doors and windows and after a while
people picked it up even if they were not taking part in formal
classes ... they picked it up naturally. There were 46 people on
our wing and 90 per cent were completely fluent in Irish and the
rest could understand it well ... we added to this as well through
entertainment; we organised Irish-language weekends where you
only spoke Irish and storytelling nights and concerts and so on
to add an enjoyment factor to it as well.) (Interview with Mac
Niallais, 15 March 2005)

However, the atmosphere of learning and solidarity activities
engaged in by republican prisoners on the blanket protest was
counterposed with an increase in prison warden brutality against
them (McKeown, Campbell and O'Hagan 1994, McEvoy 2001).
As Garaí Mac Roibeáird attests, Irish classes were also targeted in
this process:

D'ardaigh imeaglú de réir a chéile; níor ligeadh dúinn an phluid
a chaitheamh ag fágail an chillín fá choinne níocháin. B'éigean
dúinn a ghabháil lomnocht; iarracht chun muid a náiriú a bhí
ann. Rinneadh ionsaí i gcónaí ar mhúinteoirí Gaeilge ... Is cuimhin
liom lá amháin ag scairteadh ranga amach ag inse an dorais agus
shleamhnaigh bairdéir síos agus chaith sé uisce te fríd an doras
ar m'aghaidh. Tugadh greadadh dom go minic fosta ach leanadh
múinteoir eile ar aghaidh leis an rang dá ndéanadh na bairdéirí
ionsaithe tae nó dá dtugadh siad greadadh don mhúinteoir i rith
rang Gaeilge ... sa deireadh, ar mhaithe le cúrsaí foghlamtha,
shocraigh muid na ranganna a dhéanamh nuair nach raibh siad
ann ... ach ghríosaigh fuath s'acu muid ós rud é gur thaispeáin
seo uilig dúinn go raibh fuath acu dár dteanga dhúchais; rud a
thug tuilleadh inspreagadh dúinn.

(Intimidation steadily grew; we weren't allowed to wear the
blanket when leaving the cell to wash. We were made to go
naked which was purely to humiliate us. Irish teachers were
also attacked ... I remember one day, shouting a class out at the
hinge of the door when a screw slid in and threw hot water over

my face. I was also beaten on numerous occasions, but another teacher would step in if a screw attacked with hot water or gave a beating to a teacher ... in the end, for learning purposes, we decided to do the classes when the screws were not there ... but their hatred really inspired us because it showed us that they despised our native language, which gave us extra motivation.) (Interview with Mac Roibeáird, 30 June 2003)

In the wake of such brutality, the situation in the protesting H-Blocks[2] deteriorated drastically, culminating in early 1978 with republican prisoners embarking on the 'no-wash' protest (McKeown, Campbell and O'Hagan 1994). This meant that prisoners would not leave their cells to wash or 'slop out', thereby forcing them to smear their excrement on the walls to nullify its smell (ibid.). The prisoners' protest and appalling living conditions were publicised in a controversial statement released by Cardinal Tomás Ó Fiaich following his visit in July 1978:

> Having spent the whole of Sunday in the prison I was shocked at the inhumane conditions prevailing in H-Blocks 3, 4, and 5 where over 300 prisoners are incarcerated. One would hardly allow an animal to remain in such conditions, let alone a human being. The nearest approach to it that I have seen was the spectacle of hundreds of homeless people living in the sewer pipes in the slums of Calcutta. (Coogan 1980: 158)

In the aftermath of prisoners being subjected 'to harsh beatings, scaldings and humiliations', McEvoy (2001: 243) argues that this protest served to further dehumanise them in the eyes of prison staff, who felt that it 'resonated with sectarian anti-Catholic discourses concerning dirtiness and immorality' (ibid.: 245). This sectarian prejudice would manifest itself in 'the cleaning operations, wing shift, and mirror searches, all of which encouraged a depersonalised attitude to the prisoners' (ibid.).

The dramatic increase in the number of beatings taking place during this period corresponded with this attempt to defeat the protest using the three-layered offensive of 'wing shifts, mirror searches [and] forced washes' (McKeown, Campbell and O'Hagan 1994: 49). The prisoners were moved to different wings every few weeks to disrupt their command structure and solidarity.[3] They were forcibly washed with a scrubbing brush and also subjected to frequent internal bodily searches (ibid.). Coogan describes one of these searches:

> A metal detector is used to inspect the anal area and according to the prisoners this comes in handy for beating them in the testicles as well. Other sorts of harassment by warders also exist such as using the same finger to explore a prisoner's mouth as has been just used to investigate his rectum. (Coogan 1980: 9)

In the words of another prisoner, 'it was no less than sexual assault ... For months after, I bled every time I excreted'[4] (McKeown, Campbell and O'Hagan 1994: 50–1). Ironically, it was during this most challenging period of the protest that the Irish language was most extensively utilised amongst the prisoners. As Mac Siacais highlights:

> Tháinig méadú suntasach ar líon na ngreadtaí ag deireadh '78, chéas na bairdéirí muid ar mhórán bealaí ar feadh na bliana, fliuchadh ár dtochtanna le díghalrán, chaith siad sneachta tríd na fuinneoga anuas orainn i rith an gheimhridh olc an bhliain sin agus bhí muid iomlán síoctha..i rith an ama, thug siad leathbhéilí fuar dúinn don dinnéar rud a chiallaigh go raibh ocras an domhain orainn i gcónaí ... ach sa tréimhse seo a rinneadh an dul chun cinn is mó ó thaobh na Gaeilge de ar bhonn athghiniúna, idir '78 agus '80 sna coinníollacha uafasacha ... Dá mhéad na constaicí inár n-éadan, is amhlaidh is mó diongbháilteacht a thaispeáin muid ... choinnigh muid bloc cearnógach glan ó chacamas ag bun an chillín ar mhaithe le nótaí Gaeilge.

> (The number of beatings increased at the end of '78, the screws tortured us in lots of different ways throughout the year, they soaked our mattresses with disinfectant and threw snow through the windows on top of us during the terrible winter that year and we were totally freezing ... throughout this period, they gave us cold half-dinners which meant we were always starving ... but it was during this period that the Irish language made the most progress in a regenerative capacity, between '78 and '80 in those horrible conditions ... the more obstacles in our way, the greater determination we seemed to show ... we kept a square block at the bottom of the cell wall free from excrement for our Irish notes.) (Interview with Mac Siacais, 18 July 2003)

Paradoxically, forced prison 'wing shifts' could benefit the language classes, as Eoghan Mac Cormaic posits: 'bheadh sé úsáideach nuair a bhogadh muid go sciathán eile mar bheadh na ceachtanna Gaeilge fágtha ar na ballaí dúinn agus d'fhág daoine dánta agus amhráin agus eile chomh maith' (it was useful when we were moved to a different wing because the Irish lessons would be left on the walls for us and people often left poems and songs, etc. as well) (interview with Mac Cormaic, 10 June 2006). However, prison cleaning operations only left a short window of opportunity for prisoners to take advantage of their new cell, as is pointed out by Ciarán Dawson: 'Ní raibh d'ábhar scríofa againn ach na ballaí agus b'eigeán dúinn an deis a thapú go gasta mar ba ghnách iad sin a ghlanadh gach naoi lá' (We had no material to write on but the walls and we would have to grasp the opportunity because they were usually cleaned every nine days) (interview with Dawson, 22 October 2005). He also refers to the increased significance of the language in this period: 'Bhí an teanga lárnach sa tréimhse seo, bhí níos mó daoine á nascadh go dlúth leis na cúiseanna a raibh muid ansin. Thug sí dóchas dúinn' (The language was central in this period as more people were linking it with the reasons we were there in the first place. It gave us hope) (ibid.).

This point is expanded by Máirtín Ó Maolmhuaidh, who also explains his personal motivation to learn the language while on the blanket protest:

Tá míthuiscint amuigh ansin gur ghlac Gluaiseacht na Poblachta cinneadh straitéiseach na cimí pluide a chur ag foghlaim na teanga mar sórt gléas cogaidh rúnda agus muid i ngéibheann ... bíonn fáthanna difriúla ag daoine eagsúla an teanga a fhoghlaim ... I gcás s'agamsa, thuig mé nach Sasanach mé, agus ó tharla gur Éireannach a bhí ionam, rinne mé iarracht mo theanga dhúchais féin a fhoghlaim. Mar sin de, níos mó ná rud ar bith eile, ba é an t-ábhar a spreag mé leis an Ghaeilge ná féiniúlacht agus bród i mo cheantar, i bpobal an cheantair. Thapaigh mé an déis ar agóid na pluide nach bhfuair mé ar an taobh amuigh mar gheall ar chíréibí sráide agus eile ... ach is cinnte sná tréimhsí deacra ar an phluid gur fheidhmigh an Ghaeilge mar sórt armlóin dúinn in éadan an chórais ... mar ghléas spreagtha chun cur in aghaidh an chórás stáit taobh istigh den phríosún mar a chuir muid ar an taobh amuigh ... fuair a lán daoine spreagadh ar an bhonn seo.

(There is a misconception out there that the republican movement took a strategic decision to instruct the blanket prisoners to learn the language as a secret weapon of war while incarcerated ... different people have various reasons to learn the language ... in my case, I understood that I was not English, and because I happened to be Irish, I tried to learn my native language. So then, more than anything else, what inspired me with the language was my identity and pride in my own area, and the community in that area ... I grasped the chance on the blanket that I had not previously had on the outside because of the street rioting and so on ... but there is no doubt that in the difficult times on the blanket, that the language functioned as a weapon against the system ... as an inspirational tool to oppose the state from inside prison as we had opposed it on the outside ... a lot of people were inspired in this way.) (Interview with Ó Maolmhuaidh, 25 June 2005)

Thus it is clear that in the period 1978–80 the prisoners became more acutely aware of the potential of the Irish language to function as a means of resistance in often unbearable prison conditions in which they were being subjected to brutality by the prison wardens. Peadar Whelan underlines this fact:

Learning and speaking Irish became a crucial part of our struggle against criminality and helped form our identity. We had to fight to learn and speaking it was a form of resistance. Every time we spoke Irish, we were telling our enemy that we were Irish republicans, protesting and struggling. We weren't going to let them silence us ... Irish was a weapon we used against the screws, leaving them feeling totally frustrated and excluded. Our expression of identity left them feeling totally powerless. Knowledge is power and ignorance diminished their sense of power and control. (O'Hagan 1991: 4)

The centrality of the language was clear to any new prisoners joining the protest at this stage, as is evident in the account of Pilib Ó Ruanaí, who recounts his own personal development:

Nuair a bhain mise na blocanna amach i '79, bhí an Ghaeilge iomlán beo mar theanga chumarsáide ag an am agus iomlán riachtanach do dhuine ar bith a bhí ag iarraidh páirt iomlán a imirt i gcúrsaí saoil an phríosúin. Thuig achan duine í mar chuid don phoblachtánachas agus an Éireannachas, go háirithe agus muidne mar mhionlach sa tuaisceart. Ghríosaigh seo mé ar ndóigh agus mhéadaigh mo shuim de réir mar a d'fhoghlaim mé í ... bhí an-tionchar ar fad ag cuid do na daoine ionspioráideach i mbloic s'againne, H3 orm ... daoine as an choitiantacht ar fad ... daoine ar nós Bobby [Sands] a bheadh ag dul don úrscéal stairiúil *Trinity* ó bharr a chloigeann achan oíche chomh maith le léachtaí polaitiúla fána Sandinistas i Nicaragua agus cúrsaí polaitíochta fud fad an domhain ... daoine eile cosúil le Tommy McKearney a thug léachtaí staire achan tseachtain ar stair na hÉireann le cúpla míle bliain ... Jake Mac Siacias a rinne amhlaidh trí mheán na Gaeilge chomh maith le hoícheanta scéalaíochta agus eile ... áit iontach a bhí ann agus fuair mise oideachais don scoth óna daoine seo a bhí lán chomh cumasach le duine ar bith eile ar bhuail mé leo bliantaí ina dhiaidh sin ar an ollscoil.

(When I reached the Blocks in '79, the Irish language was alive as the language of communication at the time and completely essential for anyone who wanted to play a complete role in prison life. Everyone understood it as part of their republicanism and their Irishness, especially as we were a minority in the north. This motivated me of course and my interest in the language increased as I learned it ... I was deeply influenced by some of the inspirational people in our block, H3 ... totally extraordinary people ... people like Bobby [Sands] who would recite the history novel *Trinity* off the top of his head every night as well as giving political lectures on the Sandinistas in Nicaragua and political issues from around the world ... others like Tommy McKearney, who gave history lectures every week on Irish history going back thousands of years ... Jake Mac Siacais who did the same in Irish as well as storytelling nights and so on ... it was an amazing place and I got a great education from people who were just as capable as anyone I met years after that at university.) (Interview with Ó Ruanaí, 20 October 2007)

However, after four years of intense protest, the prisoners decided that hunger strike, as the traditional tactic used many times in the history of political imprisonment in Ireland, was their last option in their battle against criminalisation (O'Hearn 2006). Considering that the tactic of hunger striking had had recent success in obtaining special category status in 1972, and in forcing a number of transfers of republican prisoners from Britain to Ireland in 1974,[5]

McKeown (2001: 74) argues that this decision was understandable. In November 1980, seven prisoners in the H-Blocks embarked on a hunger strike which peaked in December, having been joined by female prisoners in Armagh prison.[6] The H-Block hunger strike was called off after seven weeks, with prisoners believing they had reached an agreement with the prison authorities in relation to wearing their own clothing; in actuality, a British government document revealed that they would only be allowed to wear prison-issue clothing (Beresford 1987; O'Hearn 2006).

Therefore a second hunger strike, under the leadership of Bobby Sands, began on 1 March 1981, exactly five years after the beginning of the criminalisation policy (McKeown, Campbell and O'Hagan 1994). The actual dates when participants began their strike was staggered this time to ensure a longer build-up and maintenance of political pressure (ibid.). Despite strong opposition from the leadership of the republican movement outside the prison, Sands was determined to see his strike through to the death (O'Hearn 2006), while conceptualising the prison protest within the wider context of the republican struggle:

> I believe I am another of those wretched Irishmen born of a risen generation with a deeply rooted and unquenchable desire for freedom. I am dying not just to attempt to end the barbarity of H-Block, or to gain the rightful recognition of a political prisoner, but primarily because what is lost in here is lost for the Republic and those wretched oppressed whom I am deeply proud to know as the risen people. (Sands 1998: 219)

Publicity was central to the strike and involved intensive letter-writing campaigns by the prisoners in an attempt to rally support for their campaign for political status. This campaign made appeals to a wide variety of groups and organisations, including the Irish-language movement, as Mac Siacais highlights:

> Bhí an-obair déanta ag na Relatives' Action Committees thar chúpla bliain ag ardú feachtas s'againn ar son stádas polaitiúil fud fad na hÉireann so ar ndóigh rinne muidne iarracht cuir leis an phoiblíocht agus feachtasaíocht lenár gcuid litreacha féin a smugláil muid amach fríd na cuairteanna ... d'eascair a lán grúpaí óna hiarrachtaí seo, CLG in éadan na mblocanna, múinteoirí in éadan na mblocanna, ceardchumainn in éadan na mblocanna agus ar ndóigh; Gaeil in éadan na mblocanna. Mheall muid a

lán tacaíocht óna Gaeil go háirithe mar gur chuir muid an méid béim sin ar an teanga taobh istigh ... bhí nuachtán ag an am 'Preas an Phobail' agus foilsíodh a lán dár gcuid litreacha Gaeilge ann a scaip an scéal fá ról na teanga sna blocanna agus an agóid s'againn ar son stadas srl.

(The Relatives' Action Committees did great work over a few years raising our campaign for political status throughout Ireland, so of course we added to this publicity and campaigning with our own letters that were smuggled out through the visits ... a lot of groups sprang from all these efforts, GAA against H-Blocks, teachers against H-Blocks, Trade Unions against H-Blocks and of course, Gaels against H-Blocks. We attracted a lot of support from Irish speakers especially, because we put so much emphasis on the language in the prison ... there was a newspaper at the time, 'Préas an Phobail', which published a lot of our letters in Irish that spread the word about the role of the language in the prison and our protest for status, etc.) (Interview with Mac Siacais, 18 July 2003)

Prisoner letter writing also involved writing personal appeals to individuals, including Irish-language activists, as is evidenced in the extract below from a letter written by Mac Siacais in March 1981 to prominent Irish-language activist Jack Brady. Brady, who was also known as 'Moscow Jack' (the letter refers to him by his Irish Christian name, Eoghan), was a former internee in Crumlin Road Jail in the 1940s, where he had been central to Irish-language development (see the Appendix for a copy of the original):

Is cimí cogaidh sinn, tuillimid céimíocht polaitiúil – Tá rang agat Eoghan agus mar sin tá tionchar agat. Iarraim ort feidhm a bhaint as an tionchar sin chun Gaeilgeoirí Baile Mac Andair a fháil amach ar na sráideanna ar son na gcimí anseo. Ba chóir go mbeadh buíon ar a laghad le 'Banner' amháin ag gach léirsiú áitiúil. Caithfidh gach aon duine a pháirt a imirt má táimid chun saol na gcimí atá páirteach sa chéalachán a shábháil.

(We are political prisoners and we deserve political status – You have a class Eoghan and therefore you have influence. I ask you to use that influence to get Andersonstown Irish speakers out on the streets in support of these prisoners. There should be at least one company with a 'banner' at every local protest. Everyone will have to play their part if we are to save the lives of these prisoners on hunger strike.) [This letter was received courtesy of Jack Brady's daughter Eibhlín Collins (née Brady).] (Mac Siacais 1981)

Nevertheless, despite huge national and international support for the prisoners' demand for political status, ten H-Block prisoners would subsequently die on hunger strike: Bobby Sands, Francis Hughes, Raymond McCreesh, Patsy O'Hara, Joe McDonnell, Martin Hurson, Kevin Lynch, Kieran Doherty, Tom McElwee and Mickey Devine (Beresford 1987). The very fact that three of the hunger strikers were elected during this campaign – Bobby Sands as MP for Fermanagh–South Tyrone in the north and both Kieran Doherty and Paddy Agnew as TDs in the south for the constituencies of Cavan–Monaghan and Louth respectively – arguably exposed the erroneous nature of the 'criminalisation' tag that prisoners had been labelled with (McKeown 2001). The massive international reaction to the deaths of elected members of parliament on hunger strike, which severely embarrassed the British government, as well as the resulting intense politicisation of nationalist and republican communities in the six counties, lends additional weight to this view (O'Hearn 2006: 376–8).

## THE AFTERMATH

In the aftermath of the hunger strikes, the blanket protest ended, with the only key prisoner demand that had been immediately met being the right to wear their own clothes (McKeown 2001). However, though this meant that they got out of their cells and had access to the library, exercise in the yard and weekly visits, their continued refusal to do prison work lost them remission and other privileges, such as access to the gym, football pitches and shop facilities (ibid.). In this new situation, the role of the Irish language in prison life thus changed immeasurably, as Lawrence McKeown emphasises:

Following the end of the hunger strike, we were obviously all completely devastated that ten of our comrades had died ... but the camp staff embarked on a new, longer-term strategy to achieve our goals and deserve immense credit for that, because political status was achieved within a few years; this involved coming out of our cells and taking a proactive approach from within the prison system[7] ... however, this had a major impact on the language, which began to dwindle as the spoken language of the Blocks ... when people came face-to-face they tended to speak the language they were most comfortable with, which was English; we also had lots of distractions, you could go for a run around the yard, watch the TV, listen to the radio, read newspapers and books, and all these would have been English because Irish books were banned ... this was after the guts of five years locked in your cell ... there were also a lot of new guys coming into the jail from outside and the conforming blocks who had no Irish at all ... so naturally, all this had a big effect on the status of Irish as the spoken language in the jail. (Interview with McKeown, 22 July 2003)

The prisoner camp staff had become aware of this reality and began to implement various measures to counteract it, as Eoghan Mac Cormaic indicates:

Rinne muid iarracht an taoide Béarla a stopadh. Bhunaigh foireann an champa post oifigeach cultúrtha agus ceapadh Donncha Mac Niallais. Rinneadh iarracht struchtúir na ranganna a bhí difriúil ó áit go háit a stiúradh. Bhí muid ag iarraidh curriculum a chruthú nó thuig muid go mbeadh orainn an Ghaeilge a thabhairt don chéad 'ghlúin' eile go gasta agus comh maith leis sin go mbeadh orainn struchtúir a ullmhú a ligfeadh do chimí an Ghaeilge chéanna a fhoghlaim is cuma cén áit ina raibh siad sa champa.

(We tried to stop the tide of English. The camp staff created a cultural officer position and Donncha Mac Niallais was appointed. There was an attempt to standardise the classes, which were different from place to place. We were trying to devise a curriculum, as we knew we would have to quickly provide Irish for the next generation, and in conjunction systematise a structure which would allow prisoners to learn the same Irish, irrespective of their location within the camp.) (Interview with Mac Cormaic, 10 June 2006)

Following consultation with cultural officers in each block and each wing, Mac Niallais drew up a draft cultural policy document which made a wide range of proposals in relation to Irish-language development in the prison. These included ensuring there were systematically structured language classes available at all levels in each wing; encouraging families outside to learn the language and support Irish schools; using Irish at every opportunity in workshops and visits; making and selling handicrafts to raise funds for Irish schools; and actively publicising the cultural discrimination of the prison authorities regarding the banning of Irish books and materials. Mac Niallais himself describes this process:

> D'athraigh saol an phríosúin thar oíche agus bhí orainn déileáil leis sin ... chinntigh muid gur sheas an Ghaeilge amach ónar ngnáthchláracha oideachais mar rud le tábhacht ar leith mar gheall ar an phluid ... Bhrúigh muid an Ghaeilge labhartha mar gheall ar an taithí s'againn ón tréimhse sin ... rinne muid iarracht Gaeilgeoirí a chuir i gcilliní le daoine úrá gan Gaeilge agus iad a chuir i mbun teagaisc ... fuair na cimí a lán spreagadh nuair a chuaigh muid isteach i gcóras oideachais an phríosúin in 1983, thug seo sprioc agus fócas daofa arís agus d'éirigh thar barr ar fad leo, rinne 86 duine an O Level Irish i 1983 agus sílim go bhfuair 84 acu pass agus fuair 90% grád A sa scrúdú ... thug seo a lán féinmhúinín do dhaoine nach raibh cáilíochtaí acu roimhe seo agus ghríosaigh seo iad chun leanúint leis an streachailt cultúrtha ar an taobh amuigh, thuig siad anois nach le gunnaí amháin a thiocfadh leo an streachailt a chuir chun cinn ach ó thaobh an teanga chomh maith i bpobail s'acu féin.

> (Prison life changed completely overnight and we had to deal with it ... we ensured that Irish was independent of our usual education programmes, because it retained a special importance because of the blanket ... we promoted the spoken Irish because of our experience of that period ... we tried to put Irish speakers in cells with new people who had no Irish and get them to teach them ... the prisoners gained great inspiration when we entered the prison education system in 1983; this gave them an objective and a focus again and they did brilliantly, 86 people did the O level Irish in 1983 and I think 84 passed with around 90 per cent achieving an A grade in the exam ... this gave a lot of confidence to people who had no qualifications before this and motivated them to continue with the cultural struggle on the outside; they understood now that it wasn't only with guns that they could develop the struggle, but through the language as well in their own communities.)
> (Interview with Mac Niallais, 15 March 2005)

One of the first prisoners to come through the formal prison education process in 1983, Antóin de Brún, puts his experiences in context:

Sílim gur shíl údárais an phríosúin gur briseadh muid de bhrí gur ghlac muid leis an oideachais foirmeálta ... sin an t-aon fáth a raibh siad sásta múinteoirí Gaeilge a fháil isteach ón taobh amuigh nuair a chuir siad cosc ar gach rud eile gaelach ... níor thuig siad gur cinneadh stráitéiseach fad-téarmach a bhí déanta againn chun muid féin a fhorbairt, chun an ceann is fearr a fháil ar chóras s'acu cibé ... ag an tús, tháinig cupla chancers isteach againn mar mhúinteoirí; fear amháin, ní raibh mórán Gaeilge aige ar chor ar bith, seans gur theagasc sé é ar mheánscoil Béarla éigin agus go bhfaca sé an fógra sa pháipéar, ach tháinig sé isteach sa rang agus bhí muidne ar fad ag suí ag labhairt i nGaeilge; scanraigh muid é, ghabh sé a leithscéal agus d'imigh sé! ... ach de réir a chéile, fuair muid múinteoirí maithe Gaeilge isteach a chuidigh go mór linn, leithéidí Pat O'Neill agus Jim Herron ... fuair muid ár bpríomhoideachas ó chláracha neamhfhoirmeálta s'againn féin, ní raibh sa stuif foirmeálta ach ullmhú do scrúduithe ... thug na scrúduithe múinín dúinn agus tuiscint nach raibh muid bómanta ó thaobh na hacadúlachta ... tá tú ag caint ar dhaoine óga bunaicmeacha anseo nach raibh meas madaí acu ar fhoghlaim foirmeálta agus thug na cáilaíochtaí brod millteanach daofa.

(I think the prison authorities felt we were broken because we accepted formal education ... that is the only reason they were happy to let Irish teachers in when they banned everything else Irish ... they didn't understand that we had taken a long-term strategic decision to develop ourselves to overcome their system in the long run ... at the beginning, a couple of chancers came in as teachers; one guy, who had not got much Irish at all, he must have been an Irish teacher in an English secondary school or something and read the advertisement in the paper; but he came in to the class and we were all sitting speaking in Irish; we scared him, he apologised and left! ... after a while, we got good Irish teachers in who helped us a great deal, like Pat O'Neill and Jim Herron ... but we got our main education from our own informal programmes, the formal stuff was only really preparation for exams ... these exams gave us confidence and belief that we were not stupid in academic terms ... you are talking of young working-class people here who did not have much regard for formal learning, and the qualifications gave them immense pride.) (Interview with De Brún, 15 March 2005)

This idea that interprets the prisoners' educational processes as part of the continuous development of their overall political objectives both inside and outside the prison is emphasised by Jim Herron, one of the outside teachers who taught the prisoners Irish within the formal education process and later also contributed to their many informal language programmes. He recounts his experiences below, giving a general assessment of the function of the Irish language amongst the republican prisoner community in the H-Blocks of Long Kesh:

Theagasc mise Gaeilge sa Cheis Fhada ó lár na n-ochtóidí agus bhain me níos mó sult as na mar a bhain mé as teagasc ar bith eile rinne mé ariamh ... ní amháin gur dhaoine fásta iad a bhí an-díograiseach ó thaobh na teanga ach bhí dearcadh difriúl ar fad acu ar chúrsaí oideachais, d'fhoghlaim mise a lán uathu, ba ghnáth leo mise a ghlacadh isteach sa rang agus shuífeadh muid thart i gciorcal ag plé agus ag cur ceisteanna agus ag foglaim le chéile, ní raibh údáras bréise ag an mhúinteoir, bhí seisean ann chun iad a spreagadh, mar sórt éascaitheoir, bhí seo bainte le meon agus fealsúnacht pholaitiúil s'acu ... d'éirigh mise iontach mór leo de réir a chéile agus chuidigh mé leo le cupla tioncsnamh oideachais dá gcuid féin ... chuir muid scrúdaithe an fháinne le chéile, d'fhorbair muid cupla dianchúrsaí Gaeilge a bhí an-éifeachtach agus bunaithe ar shaol s'acu sa phríosúin agus an stair s'aici agus eile ... bhí an teanga i bhfad níos tábhachtaí acu ná ábhar oideachais, dlúthchuid don pholaitíocht s'acu a bhí ann, d'úsáid siad í chun spiorad na gcimí a thógáil ... bhí siad iontach dáiríre agus fad-téarmach faoi ... nuair a chuaigh mise isteach ar dtús, ní raibh cead acu leabhair Ghaeilge a thabhairt isteach ná fáinní a chaitheamh ach bhris siad seo síos de réir a chéile, thar na bliantaí, agus sa deireadh, bhunaigh siad sciatháin Gaeltachta i ndiaidh domsa imeacht sna lár-nochaidí ... gníomhaithe polaitiúla a bhí iontu agus d'amharc siad ar an phictiúir mór i gcónaí, bhí fís acu fán teanga agus spreag siad daoine sa phobal leis an fhís sin.

(I taught Irish in Long Kesh from the mid-eighties and enjoyed it more than any other teaching experience I ever had ... not only were they adults and diligent in terms of the language, but they had a completely different view on education in general; I learned a lot from them, they used to take me into the class and we would have sat around in a circle, discussing and asking questions and learning together; the teacher had no extra authority, he was there to motivate them as a sort of facilitator, this method was linked to their political attitudes and philosophies ... I became very friendly with them and ended up helping them with some of their educational projects; we put fáinne exams together and developed a couple of intensive Irish-language courses that were very effective and based on their prison life and its history and so on ... the language was much more important to them than merely an educational subject, it was central to their politics and they used it to lift the spirits of the prisoners ... they were very serious and long-term about it ... when I first went in, they were not allowed Irish books in or allowed to wear the fáinne but they broke all this down over the years and in the end they set up Gaeltacht wings after I had left in the mid-nineties ... they were political activists who always looked at the big picture ... they had a vision for the language and they inspired people in the community with that vision.) (Interview with Herron, 9 July 2007)

# 7
# 'Bringing the Language to the People':
# Revival

In the H-Blocks with no books, no paper, no pens, no professional teacher, young Irish men living in filthy conditions, frequently beaten, stripped naked ... but unbowed, taught each other Irish by shouting the lessons from cell to cell. And as one hunger strike was followed by the other, the people outside heard those lessons too and they determined to carry on the cultural struggle – each one from where he/she was.

Pádraig Ó Maolchraoibhe (1986: 9)

This chapter focuses on the post-hunger strike Irish-language revival outside the prison walls in the north of Ireland. Its findings are based primarily on personal narrator reflections – in this case, of the prominent Irish-language activists of that particular era. Concurrently, it also includes the accounts of ex-prisoners who played an integral role in these revivalist activities upon their release from prison.

The accounts specifically relate to the upsurge in interest in the Irish language within the wider community, as evidenced in the significant increase in the number of children attending Irish-medium education schools. They also refer to the subsequent radicalisation of the Irish-language movement through its proactive creation of widespread additional language classes, the formation of additional Irish-language nursery schools and an Irish-language newspaper, and campaigning on language rights issues such as Irish-language street names. Some cognisance will also be taken of related internal tensions within the language movement that stemmed from this revival as well as the British government response to it.

## RECONQUEST

Central to these revivalist developments in the nationalist and republican community was the substantial impact of republican prison protests in Long Kesh and Armagh prisons. As a young Irish-language activist at the time, Eoghan Ó Néill describes his recollection of these transformative events:

D'athraigh an stailc ocrais achan rud ... roimhe seo, bhí sciar don phobal náisiúnach a bhí i bhfách leis an Ghaeilge ariamh ach bhí sciar measartha mór eile nach raibh goite leis ar dhóigh ar bith ... ach thosaigh na scéaltaí fá'n Cheis ag teacht amach agus á scaipeadh fríd daoine ag dul suas ar chuairt fá'n dóigh ar fhoghlaim na cimí an Ghaeilge agus aighneas na mbáirdéirí dá bharr, mhothaigh daoine comhbhá leo cibé ach más rud é go raibh suim agat sa teanga, is amhlaidh is tréise an comhbhá sin ar ndóigh ... bhí mé féin agus a lán Gaeil óga eile ag an am páirteach sna Gaeil in aghaidh H-Bloic agus Ard Mhacha, bhí muid feiceálach ag na céadtaí mórshiúltaí san fheachtas in aghaidh na Ceise Fada, bheadh banners agus póstaeir Gaeilge againn agus muid ag scairteadh manaí Gaeilge os ord ... thóg seo an móthú féiniúlachta a chothaigh agóid na pluide agus an stailc ocrais. Bhí clú ar na cimí a fuair bás mar ghaeil líofa ... d'aistrigh seo dearcaí daoine nár smaoinigh ar an Ghaeilge ar bhealach streachailte ariamh ... bhí bá ann i gcónaí don teanga ach thosaigh daoine ag iarraidh rud éigin a dhéanamh fá'n bhá sin.

(The hunger strike changed everything ... before this there was a section of the nationalist community that was always in favour of the language, but there was another fairly big section that was not interested in it at all ... stories about the Kesh began coming out and spreading through people going up on visits about the way the prisoners learned Irish and the hostility they received from the screws because of this, people were sympathetic to them anyway, but if you were interested in the language, this inevitably increased your sympathy for them ... I was involved along with a lot of other young Irish speakers in the Gaels against the H-Blocks and Armagh, we were visible at hundreds of marches in the campaign against Long Kesh, we would have Irish banners and posters and shout Irish slogans aloud ... this raised the feeling of identity created by the blanket protest and the hunger strike ... the prisoners who died were known as fluent Irish speakers ... this transformed the views of people who had never thought of the Irish language as a means of struggle before ... there was always sympathy for the language but now people wanted to do something about that sympathy.) (Interview with Ó Néill, 29 September 2006)

A similar view is articulated by Seamás Mac Seáin, who, as a founder member of the Shaw's Road Gaeltacht community, explains the reasons for the increased interest in language activism in this period and how it underpinned their early revivalist work:

Bhí síol na hathbheochana leagtha againn agus muid ag treabhadh ár ngort féin, ag treabhadh tionscnamh neamhpleáchais agus ag treabhadh gort ceartais ó thaobh na Gaeilge de ach go bhí muid lag go fóill i dtéarmaí ginearálta, fuair muid a lán tacaíochta airgeadais ón phobal ach níor ghlac siad páirt ghníomhach inár dtioncsnamh go dtí i ndiaidh an stailc ocrais, d'oscail muid doirse na bunscoile don mhórphobal i '78 ach ní go dtí an stailc ocrais gur fhás an t-aeráid neamhpleáchais ... ní gach duine atá ag iarraidh bheith pairteach i bhforéigean nó cogaíocht ach ní challaíonn sin nach raibh siad consíosach ar chúiseanna na streachailte a bhí ag dul ar aghaidh ... chonaic daoine go raibh muidinne ag brú dóigh fhiúntach eile chun ról a imirt ar dhóigh neamhfhoréigeanach ach ag cur na gcuspóirí céanna chun cinn ... sin an fáth ar dhlúthaigh a lán don phobal leis an athbheochan agus an ghaelscolaíocht go ginearálta.

(We had planted the seed of revival and were ploughing our own furrow, ploughing the furrow of independence and ploughing the furrow of rights in relation to the Irish language, but we remained weak, generally speaking. We got a lot of financial help from the community, but they had not played an active role in our project until after the hunger strike, we opened the doors of the Irish school to the wider community in '78, but it was not until the hunger strike that the climate of independence really grew ... not everyone wants to be part of violence or warfare, but that does not mean that they were not conscious of the causes of the struggle that was going on ... people realised that we were pushing another worthwhile means to play a role in a non-violent way yet progress the same objectives ... that was why a lot of people connected with the revival and Irish-medium education in general.) (Interview with Mac Seáin, 26 July 2006)

Concurrently, it is noteworthy that many activists in this era also refer to a lack of interest or understanding amongst the wider republican movement in the values or importance of the language revival prior to the republican prison protests. This point is exemplified by republican activist Féilim Ó hAdhmaill in his analysis of the wider dynamics of the period:

Bhí na stailceoirí ocrais agus cimí na pluide mar splanc mhisnigh ag an phobal seo. Dúirt daoine 'má tá siadsan ábalta fulaingt leis an teanga a fhoghlaim, thig linne é a dhéanamh le múinteoirí, áiseanna agus timpeallacht cheart' ... d' ardaigh na cimí tuiscint fán Ghaeilge i ngluaiseacht na poblachta chomh maith, mar shampla, is cuimhin liomsa sna mall seachtóidí ag dul thart ag iarraidh sínithe a bhailiú do shuirbhe fá'n Ghaeilge a bhain le cláracha Gaeilge ar an ráidió agus bhí cúpla ceannnaire de chuid Sinn Féin ag an am a dhiúltaigh é a shíniú agus dúirt siad nach raibh aon bhaint aicí leis an réabhlóid mar gur iarsma don sean-nationalism nó hibernianism a bhí ann agus gur 'daoine ardnósach amháin a labhair Gaeilge' ...

Roimhe seo, dhírigh an ghluaiseacht isteach ar an fheachtas míleata amháin agus bhí barúil ann gur cur amú ama é an Ghaeilge agus an feachtas príosúin chomh maith mar gur diversions iad ón chogadh féin ... d'athraigh an stailc ocrais an tuairim seo is chothaigh sé tuiscint níos leithne ar an pholaitíocht féin ... ach, ó thaobh na teanga de, bhí dream gaeilgeoirí nach raibh sásta leis an Ghaeilge mar ábhar polaitiúil, shéan siad an nasc sin, rud a bhí amaideach ar fad, dar liomsa, mar tá gach rud bainte leis an pholaitíocht go háirithe tionchair agus fachtóirí sóisialta, eacnamaíochta agus cultúrtha ... sa tréimhse seo, mhothaigh daoine faoi chois agus d'amharc siad ar an Ghaeilge mar áis le taispeáint gur Éireannaigh a bhí iontu, nuair a bhí gach duine eile ag rá nach raibh seo amhlaidh.

(The hunger strikers and blanketmen were a spark of courage for this community. They inspired people to learn Irish, especially when people heard about the terrible conditions, the brutality, and the lack of resources. People said, 'if they are able to suffer to learn the language, we can do it with teachers, resources and a proper environment' ... the prisoners also raised an awareness of the language amongst the republican movement as well, for example, I remember in the late seventies going around collecting signatures for a survey in relation to Irish programmes on the radio and there were a couple of Sinn Féin leaders at the time who refused to sign it and said that the Irish language had nothing to do with the revolution because it was a remnant of old nationalism or Hibernianism and that only 'stuck-up people spoke Irish' ...

Before then, the movement only focused on the military campaign and there was a perception that the Irish language and even the prison campaigns were a waste of time as they were diversions from the war itself ... the hunger strike changed this view and created a wider understanding of politics itself ... but, in relation to the language, there were a group of Irish speakers who were not happy about it being a political matter, they denied this link, which was ridiculous in my view, because everything is connected with politics, especially social, economic and cultural influences and factors ... in this period, people felt oppressed and saw the language as a means to express their Irishness when everybody else was denying them that.) (Interview with Ó hAdhmaill, 22 August 2003)

During this era of immense politicisation and popular mobilisation in nationalist and republican areas in the six counties, the Irish language took on an added relevance amongst many ordinary working-class people who had not previously been associated with it. A significant factor in this was the formation in 1982 of Sinn Féin's Roinn an Chultúir (Cultural Department), which would oversee the organisation of scores of additional language classes throughout Belfast and a controversial campaign to create bilingual street signs, which remained illegal from the 1948 Stormont Public Health and Local Council Act (Ó hAdhmaill 1985).[1] One of the founders of Roinn an Chultúir, Terry Enright, explains the context of its formation and the rationale behind its revivalist work:

The Cultural Department was not part of a grand republican leadership strategy, who at this stage were consumed with the armed struggle and political plans to contests seats and elections, etc. ... like many such transforming events, this had a dynamic of its own, stemming from the prisons and the many young Irish-language activists being attracted to the movement after the hunger strike ... not everyone of this influx could join active service units and shoot at Brits and plant bombs, etc. ... at a grassroots level, it was decided to find useful, relevant and political outlets in which to channel these new found energies ... in implementing the Bobby Sands dictum about everyone having their own part to play, and so on. This coincided with the reinvigorating impact of scores of released prisoners from Long Kesh who were fluent Irish speakers and motivated around the language and more than willing to commit their time ...

Our plan was to bring the language to working-class people who had no confidence to go to the likes of the Cluain Ard to learn it. Therefore, we recruited people who could go in to the various working-class areas and take classes where people were comfortable, whether it be in their own living room or the local community centre ... the key was to utilise it to break their alienation in a time of immense poverty, oppression and degradation, etc.; also to create community solidarity by encouraging people to leave their homes and stop watching popular soaps at the time, like *Dallas*, etc. We saw it as a great opportunity to promote a liberating education amongst ordinary people and build confidence and self-worth in people who usually had very little. You had energetic and fresh young language activists like Bairbre [de Brún], Máirtín [Ó Muilleoir] and Paddy Dubh [Ó Donnchadh] going around the city to lots of different areas and asking people did they want to learn Irish and explaining our motivation behind providing them with the free opportunity to do just that. We encouraged people to set up their own classes and find teachers to take them. This would eventually draw on scores of voluntary language activists, including many ex-prisoners, and even saw some old hands coming back into the fold, like former internees from the forties like Pat McCotter and Gene Thornbury, who were only too delighted at the new enthusiasm for the language ...

The first proper campaign was the Irish street names, which was of course illegal ... money was raised from door-to-door throughout many areas and thousands of street names were made which still exist today ... actually erecting the signs was not the main part of the project, it was actually engaging with people on the doors and asking them whether they wanted this or not and engaging them at this level ... a gentle in-your-face way, if you like, of raising the question of identity at the base level with ordinary people. I can remember some Irish-language activists really fearing the project and assuming that it would not work, and of course it did in the end. (Interview with Enright, 30 March 2007)

One of the activists who played a pivotal role in these early developments, Bairbre De Brún, describes her experiences:

Nuair a ghlac Roinn an Chultúir na ranganna Gaeilge ar fud na gceantar, nasc muid iad le stair fhada an choilíneachais in Éirinn agus polasaithe naimhdeacha Rialtas na Breataine dá réir. Rinne muid iarracht daoine a speagadh fríd teagasc na Gaeilge a chur sa chomhthéacs stairiúil agus polaitiúil. D'éirigh go geal leis an chur chuige seo agus na ranganna i gcoitinne; is cuimhin liom go raibh níos mó na tríocha rang Gaeilge á reachtáil againn ar fud fad Bhéal Feirste ag am amháin sna luath ochtóidí. Bhog an cleachtas seo chuig áiteanna eile chomh maith le díograiseoirí poblachtánacha ag cuir tuilleadh ranganna ar siúl i nDoire agus Ard Mhacha srl ... b'amhlaidh an scéal leis an fheachtas sráidainmneacha a scaip amach chuig na háiteanna seo i ndiaidh dúinn tús a chuir leis i mBéal Feirste ...

Bhí cumhachtú iontach ag baint leis an fheachtas seo sa chaoi go ndearna muid an t-suirbhe, gur bhailigh muid an t-airgead chun iad a dhéanamh, ansin go ndearna duine cruthaitheach inár measc ár gcuid comharthaí féin le go gcuirfeadh muid in airde iad. Bhí contúirtí ag baint leis seo ar ndóigh agus é mídhleathach. Bheadh plé iontach suimiúil ag na doirsí chomh maith le cuid daoine a rá go raibh eagla orthu go ngearrfar tuilleadh idirdhealú orthu i gcúrsaí fostaíochta dá mba rud é go raibh seoladh s'acu i nGaeilge srl. Lena chois sin, fuair muid neart ábhair dhíospóireachta stairiúila fá'n bhealach a fuair sráideanna áirithe a gcuid ainmneacha ar nós Cavendish Street i mBéal Feirste a ainmníodh i ndiaidh Ard-Rúnaí na Breataine in Éirinn, Lord Frederick Charles Cavendish a mharaigh na Invincibles i bpáirc Phoenix i 1882. San iomlán, bhí tacaíocht iontach ann do na sráidainmneacha agus thug daoine nach raibh pingin rua acu, go fial fláithiúil chun tacú linn.

(When the Cultural Department took classes throughout the areas, we linked it to the history of colonialism in Ireland and the policies of the hostile British government accordingly. We tried to motivate people by putting the teaching of Irish in the historical and political context. This approach was very successful, as were the classes themselves; I remember that we were running over 30 classes across Belfast at one point in the early eighties. This practice also moved to other places, as republican activists provided additional classes in Derry and Armagh, etc. ... it was the same with the street name campaign, which spread to these places after we started them in Belfast ...

This campaign was very empowering, in that we carried out the survey, collected the money to make them and then one of the more enterprising amongst us actually manufactured them in order for us to erect them. This could be dangerous of course, because it was illegal. There would also be interesting discussions on the doors, with some fearing they would suffer further discrimination in employment if the address was in Irish. As well as that, we had plenty of sources for historical debate as to how some of our streets got their names, such as Cavendish Street; named after the British chief secretary for Ireland Lord Frederick Charles Cavendish, who was assassinated in the Phoenix Park in 1882 by the Invincibles. On the whole, there was great support for the street names and people who had not got a penny gave generously to support us.) (Interview with De Brún, 4 September 2003)

The Irish-language street name project developed successfully across Belfast in accordance with the willingness of working-class communities to give generously to the fundraising activities that paid for them. For example, in one particular area, Twinbrook, where the unemployment rate was over 70 per cent, local Irish-language activists made and erected over 160 Irish street signs, raising in the region of £1,500 in the area itself to pay for them (Naíonra na Fuiseoige 1988: 15). However, those engaged in the campaign were often challenged by the coercive apparatus of the British state in the six counties, as Ó hAdhmaill (1985: 7) attests: 'many of the organisers were arrested, and many of the signs removed by the RUC and British Army'. Despite the inherent dangers in the street sign campaign, its main strength, according to one of its key activists, Máirtín Ó Muilleoir, was its capacity to unite language activists of disparate political viewpoints in the promotion of an ostensibly radical pursuit:

An rud is fearr fá dtaobh den obair chultúrtha a bhí ar siúl againn sa tréimhse seo, cuirim i gcás na ranganna agus an feachtas sráidainmneacha, ná gur chothaigh sé spiorád comhoibrithe ó réimse iomlán éagsúil de dhíograiseoirí ó ghrúpaí difriúla ar nós, Chonradh na Gaeilge, Ghlór na nGael, Chumann Chluain Ard agus Ghaeltacht Bhóthar Seoighe. Is cinnte nár aontaigh achan duine a bhí páirteach ann le polaitíocht Shinn Féin nó an streachailt armtha ag an am ach bhí siad sásta dícheall s'acu a chuir san obair ar mhaithe le hathbheochan na Gaeilge de ... Thóg muid gréasáin de ghaeil in achan cheantar a bhí i ndan cuidiú leis an athbheochan ar bhonn praiticiúil agus d'imir na cimí a bhí ag teacht amach as na príosúin ról ríthábhachtach sa phróiseas seo, don chuid is mó ag glacadh ranganna ina gceantracha áitiúla féin agus ag spreagadh daoine le scéaltaí rathúla foghlamtha s'acu féin!

(The best thing about the cultural work in this period, if you take for example the classes and the street name campaign, is that they created a spirit of co-operation from a whole different range of activists from different groupings like Conradh na Gaeilge, Glór na nGael, Cumann Chluain Ard and the Shaw's Road Gaeltacht. There is no doubt that not everyone who took part agreed with the politics of Sinn Féin or the armed struggle at the time, but they were willing to commit to the work for the sake of the Irish-language revival ... We built a network of Irish speakers in every area that was able to help the revival on a practical basis, and the prisoners who were coming out of the jails played a vitally important role in this process, for the most part taking classes in their own local areas, inspiring people with their own successful language-learning stories!) (Interview with Ó Muilleoir, 2 September 2003)

In the context of this upsurge in interest in the Irish language, a small number of young language activists took the decision to establish the Irish-language newspaper *LÁ* in 1984. One of its founders, Ó Néill, describes the initiative:

Bhí gach duine againn a bhí bainte leis an tionscnamh ar an dól ag an am agus in inmhe ár gcuid ama uilig a chaitheamh isteach ann. Bunsmaoineamh Ghéaróid Uí Chairealláin a bhí ann chun freastal ar Ghaeilgeoirí i mBéal Feirste agus go príomha ar Phobal Bhóthar Seoighe ach ar ndóigh bhí an líon seo ag méadú agus sciar níos mó ag dul don Ghaeilge agus ag tacú léi. Chiallaigh seo go raibh níos mó rath ar an pháipéar agus muid ag freastal ar phobal níos leithne i ndiaidh splanc na stailce ocrais. Togra an-pholaitiúil ar fad a bhí ann ach ní páirtí polaitiúil, bhí muid ar son Gaelú na tíre agus ar son aontú na tíre agus ar son na mbunchuspóirí a bhí ag achan náisiúntóir is poblachtóir anseo sa tuaisceart ach cheangail muid dearcadh s'againn ar an tír fríd an Ghaeilge féin.

(Everyone connected with the project was on the dole at the time and able to commit our time to it. It was Géaróid Ó Cairealláin's basic idea to serve Irish speakers in Belfast, primarily the Shaw's Road community, which of course was growing with more people learning the language and supporting it. This meant that the paper was more successful now that we were providing for a broader community following the spark of the hunger strike. It was a very political project, though not party political; we were for the Gaelicisation of the country and the unification of the country and the basic objectives of every nationalist and republican here in the north, but we connected our views of the country through the language itself.) (Interview with Ó Néill, 29 September 2006)

The above combination of sociopolitical and sociocultural factors had, according to a research study carried out by Féilim Ó hAdhmaill in 1985 for Irish-language community organisation Glór na nGael, put 'the Irish language on a platform where previously it had not existed to any great degree' (Ó hAdhmaill 1985: 37). One expression of this shift in popularity referred to in Ó hAdhmaill's research is the significant growth of Bunscoil Phobal Feirste, the north's first Irish-medium primary school, in the 'climate of independence' created by the hunger strikes. He highlights this by focusing on enrolment figures for the primary one class in the school from 1976 to 1982.

In addition, Ó hAdhmaill's research included a survey amongst Irish learners to ascertain what motivated their efforts to learn the language. As a result of the number (said to be in the region of 60) and extensive spread of Irish classes in Belfast at the time of the research in 1985, 223 students were interviewed in 36 classes in 14 separate centres in west Belfast. Interestingly, the results of the 1985 findings showed that 87 per cent of those interviewed decided to learn the language between 1981 and 1984; 86 per cent were motivated by the aspiration to 'to strengthen my Irish identity' and 70 per cent were influenced by 'Bobby Sands and the H-Block protests' (ibid.: 35). Ó hAdhmaill concluded the research by linking the revival to the alienation of nationalist working-class areas from the British state:

[W]hereas in the past reactions from nationalists in West Belfast ranged from calls for power-sharing to armed insurrection, at the present time another vehicle exists – the Irish-language movement – through which some of the reaction to Government policy is being channelled. (Ibid.: 38)

Nevertheless, it is worth noting that this sustained period of growth for the Irish language was accompanied by increased tensions and internal divisions within the language movement, as some activists feared the link being established between the language and the republican movement. This viewpoint is encapsulated in the views of Aodán Mac Póilín, who spent time as chairperson of Bunscoil Phobal Feirste in this period:

Phléasc uimhreacha na scoile in 1982 agus tháinig b'fhéidir trí-ceathrú de na páistí ó chlanna poblachtánaigh ... tá idirdhealú le déanamh idir na cineálacha daoine a chuir páistí s'acu chuig an scoil; ar dtús, bhí daoine a chuir spéis sa Ghaeilge ann féin, ansin, bhí daoine eile le spéis sa Ghaeilge de thairbhe na polaitíochta agus ansin poblachtánaigh a thug úsáid don Ghaeilge mar ghléas earcaíochta ... ghlac mise an dearcadh céanna leo agus a ghlac mé leis an Eaglais Chaitliceach, nach mbeadh seilbh ag dream amháin ar an Ghaeilge, chonaic mise an dochar a rinne seo sa stair; bíonn tionchar fiúntach gearrthéarmach ann ach go fad-téarmach, cailleann an Ghaeilge amach don pholaitíocht, so chonaic mé ról s'agamsa iad a stopadh. Mar shampla, bhí tionchar an-deimhneach ag an nasc poblachtánach ó thaobh uimhreacha ach chuir sé bac cúpla bliain ar an deontas don scoil ... bhí mise ag iarraidh cuma mheasúil a chur ar an scoil agus bhí daoine eile á bhaint ...

Mar shampla, mhol mise Pádraig Ó Maolchraoibhe mar chathaoirleach ar an Bhunscoil, bhí a fhios agam gur phoblachtánach é ... ach shíl mé gur thuig sé go raibh áit ann d'ide-eolaíochtaí eile agus ansin chuaigh sé mar chomhairleoir de chuid Sinn Féin, rud a chuir leis an íomhá a bhí ag an scoil ... agus bhí sé ag rá rudaí poiblí chomh maith mar chuid de pholaitiú s'acu ar nós an ráiteas clúiteach, 'Every word of Irish is another bullet in the freedom struggle'. Rinne an abairt sin an-dochar ar fad; chuir sé le híomha na n-aontachtóirí gur teanga Sinn Féin í an Ghaeilge agus thug sé tuilleadh leithscéaltaí do Rialtas na Breataine cur i gcoinne na teanga.

(The school numbers exploded in 1982 and around three-quarters of the children came from republican families ... there is a distinction to be made between the different kinds of people who sent their children to the school; firstly, there were those who were interested in the language for its own sake, then, there were others who were interested in the language because of politics, and then there were republicans who used the language as a recruitment mechanism ... I took the same view of them as I did of the Catholic Church, that no one group will have ownership of the language, I saw the damage it had done in history; there is a useful short-term effect, but in the long term, the language loses out to politics, so I saw that my role was to stop them. For example, the republican link had a very positive aspect as regards numbers, but held back the funding for a few years ... I was trying to give the school a respectable look, and others were taking this away ...

For example, I proposed Pádraig Ó Maolchraoibhe as chair of the school; I knew he was a republican, but thought he understood that there was space for other ideologies, and then he went and became a Sinn Féin councillor, which added to the image of the school ... he was also saying things publicly as part of their politicisation like the famous statement, 'Every word of Irish is another bullet in the freedom struggle'. This sentence did terrible damage, it added to the unionist conception that Irish was a Sinn Féin language and gave the British government further excuses to oppose the language.) (Interview with Mac Póilin, 6 October 2006)

Other language activists, like Seamás Mac Seáin, though initially wary of significantly increased republican involvement in the language movement, take a less critical view than Mac Póilin:

Bhí teannas an ag an tús agus Sinn Féin ag teacht chun cinn agus bhí mé féin amhrasach go raibh polaitíocht oscailte ag dul gluaiseacht oscailte s'againne a scrios ach bhí daoine eile i bhfad níos binbí agus don bharúil go raibh poblachtánaigh ag déanamh hijacking mar leas ar dheáoibre s'againne ... ach sa deireadh thiar thall, níor tharla a leithéid agus chuir siad leis an obair, thacaigh siad linn agus chomhoibrigh siad linn ... fuair muid an-chuid airgid óna chimí poblachtánacha thar na blianta, ba ghnách leo agus a chuid teaghlaigh airgead a bhailiú dúinn fríd rásanna urraithe a dhéanamh sná príosúin.

(There was tension in the beginning with Sinn Féin coming to the fore. I was wary that an overt form of politics was going to destroy our open movement ... but others were more bitter and of the opinion that republicans were hijacking the benefits of our good work ... but this never happened in the end and they added to the work, they supported us and worked along with us ... we got a lot of money from the republican prisoners over the years, both they and their families used to raise money for us through doing sponsored runs in the prisons.) (Interview with Mac Seáin, 26 July 2006)

The view that republican language activists in this period had taken a narrow and self-serving interest in the Irish-language revival to further their own party political agenda is strongly refuted by Pádraig Ó Maolchraoibhe. He contextualises their political analysis of the revivalist work they were engaged in, including his own often-cited militant statement, within the post-hunger strike era:

Bhí féiniúlacht náisiúnta an phobail múscailte i ndiaidh an stailc ocrais. Mar shampla, bhí an scoil Ghaelach trí bliana déag gan mhaoiniú agus fá'n am a bhfuair muid an t-airgead i 1984, bhí seacht múinteoir againn. Bhí seacht bpáistí ann i 1971 agus seacht múinteoir i 1984. D'eascair seo uilig ón streachailt phoblachtánach gan aon amhras. Ach bhí cuid daoine bainte leis an scoil ag iarraidh an Ghaeilge a scoilt ón phoblachtánachas agus ag iarraidh poblachtánaigh a choinneáil amach ach thuig muid ag an am an chumhacht a bhí againn mar thuismitheoirí agus rinneadh cathaoirleach domsa cuirim i gcás i 1984. Bhí cuid daoine feargach nuair a toghadh mé mar chomhairleoir Shinn Féin ag an am céanna agus ag maíomh go ndearna mé polaitiú ar an scoil ach Rialtas na Breataine a rinne an 'polaitiú' sin nuair a dhiúltaigh siad an maoiniú a bhí tuillte ag an scoil a thabhairt di … poblachtánach bródúil atá ionam agus ní raibh mé chun m'aitheantas polaitiúil a shéanadh do dhuine ar bith go háirithe nuair a bhí an stát ag séanadh sin orm …

Bhí muid gníomhach ar an teanga, ag glacadh ranganna, ag feachtasaíocht, ag traenáil múinteoirí, ag bunú scoileanna nó ag bunú craobhacha de Chonradh na Gaeilge mar Ghaeilgeoirí agus mar phoblachtánaigh agus bhí muid iontach soiléir faoi sin. Seo an rud nach dtuigeann siad siúd a labhraíonn ar 'hijacking' agus eile; polaitíocht na teanga. Bhraith mise ariamh gur cheist pholaitiúil ceist na teanga agus tá sin fíor go dtí an lá inniu. Cén fáth faoin spéir a mbeadh muid ag iarraidh an Ghaeilge a chur amach faoin phobal ach go bé go mbaineann sé le stair na tíre, an coincheap agus an fhealsúnacht atá againn? Tá se mar a chéile leis na Bascaigh nach bhfuil ag rá, 'Hold on we speak a pre indo-European language here'; d'fhoghlaim siad í mar gheall ar an pholaitíocht. Bhí muid ag iarraidh go mbeadh an Ghaeilge go loighiciúil dúinn mar chuid den phléchúrsa ar son na saoirse … is léir sin ón ráiteas a dúirt mé agus seasaim leis go hiomlán go háirithe sa chomhthéacs inar dúradh é. Bhí atmaisféar ar leith sa tír ag an am sin. Bhí na stailceoirí ocrais i ndiaidh bás a fháil, bhí an pobal náisiúnach tógtha faoi cheisteanna a bhain le cad is rud a bheith Gaelach ann, den chéad uair ag go leor acu. Bhí pobal s'agamsa faoi chois i ngléic fíochmhar agus dearcadh frithnaisiúnach i mbarr a réime sna meáin chumarsáide, thuaidh agus theas ... bhí mise ag iarraidh an pobal seo a spreagadh chun an teanga a aithint mar ghléas díchoilínithe ... cinnte, is trua gur baineadh mí-úsáid as mo chuid focal ach má amharcaimid ar cé hiad is mó a bhain an mhí-úsáid seo, is na haontachtóirí céanna a chuir agus a chuireann cos-ar-bholg ar an chultúr s'againn so ní ábhar iontais é sin!

Chuir muid fealsúnacht pholaitiúil s'againn chun cinn leis an obair chultúrtha ach ní raibh muid ag rá go raibh bealach amháin chun an Ghaeilge a chur chun cinn agus go deimhin bhí muid sásta nuair a bhí daoine eile gníomhach ó thaobh na Gaeilge de. Bhí muid dairíre faoin Ghaeilge, sin an difear. Bhí daoine meánaicmeacha ann agus caitheamh aimsire a bhí ann daofa agus bhí siad den bharúil gur tharraing muidne drochchlú ar an chaitheamh aimsire s'acu. Ach, lean muidne sampla bunaitheoirí Ghaeltacht Bhóthair Seoighe, ba phoblachtánaigh le 'p' beag iad uilig beagnach agus de bhunadh lucht oibre ... ghlac poblachtánaigh le dearcadh s'acu, 'ná habair é, dean é!

(The national identity of the people was awakened after the hunger strike. For example, the Irish school was 13 years without funding, and by the time that we got the funding in 1984 we had seven teachers. We had seven children in 1971 and seven teachers in 1984. Without doubt, this sprang from the republican struggle. But some people involved with the school were trying to split the Irish language from republicanism and trying to keep republicans out, but we understood the power that we had as parents and I was made chairperson, for example, in 1984. Some people were angry that I was elected as a Sinn Féin councillor at the same time and suggested that I had politicised the school, but it was the British government who politicised the school by refusing to give the school the funding it was entitled to ... I'm a proud republican and was not got going to deny my political identity for anyone especially when the state was already denying me that ...

We were active on the language, taking classes and campaigning, training teachers, forming schools or forming branches of the Gaelic League as Irish speakers and as republicans, and we were very clear about that. This is what those who speak of 'hijacking', etc. don't understand: the politics of the language. I've always thought that the language question was a political question and that remains true to this day. Why else in the world would we be trying to promote the language out amongst the community if it was not linked with the history of our country, our concepts and philosophies? It is the same with the Basques, who are not saying, 'Hold on, we speak a pre-Indo-European language here'; they learned it because of politics. We wanted the language to logically form part of the discourse for Irish freedom ... this is clear from the statement that I made, which I stand over, especially in the context in which it was said. The hunger strikers had just died, the nationalist community was inspired with questions concerning what it meant to be Irish, for the first time for many of them. My community were being suppressed in a ferocious struggle and an anti-nationalist agenda was in the ascendancy in the media, both north and south ... I was trying to inspire this community to recognise the language as a decolonising tool ... of course, it's a pity that my words were misused, but if we look at who was mostly responsible for this misuse, it is the same unionists who suppressed and continue to suppress our culture, so it is no surprise!

We promoted our political philosophy through our cultural work, but we were not saying that there was only one way to promote the language, and we were certainly happy when other people were active regarding the Irish language. We were serious about the language, and that is the difference. There were middle-class people who had it as a hobby, and they were of the opinion that we tarnished their hobby with a bad reputation. But we followed the example of the founders of the Shaw's Road Gaeltacht, who were almost all republicans with a small 'r' and from working-class stock ... we accepted their approach, 'Don't say it, do it'.) (Interview with Ó Maolchraoibhe, 16 June 2006)

In the process of following this revivalist approach, republican language activists organised a number of education seminars which brought together learners, teachers and activists and discussed topics such as 'reasons for learning Irish', 'Irish in the community', 'difficulties in learning Irish', and its links to the wider 'national struggle'. These seminars, which led to a publication, were introduced by Ó Maolchraoibhe who summarised the ideological rationale for their project of 'reconquest' in classic decolonisation rhetoric:

Given the all-pervasiveness of the Anglo-American culture ... the Coca-Cola culture, I don't think we can exist as a separate people without our language. Now every phrase you learn is a bullet in the freedom struggle. Every phrase you use is a brick in a great building, a rebuilding of the Irish nation ... and that is what we are aiming at ... the ending of the feeling alienation produces by having in our mouths the language imposed on us by imperialism. The process of decolonisation will have stopped half-way if, the day we succeed in driving the English from our shores, what is left behind is an Irish people possessed of the language, culture and values of the English. To be completely free we must not only remove the British presence but also reject the materialism, individualism and opportunism of the capitalist system which has been imposed on us. (Ó Maolchraoibhe 1985: 3–6)

## PROVIDING FOR THE 'NEXT GENERATION'

The most novel and audacious form of language activism to be promoted and developed in this period was the formation of Irish-language nursery schools in various areas, thus bringing Irish-medium education provision to certain communities for the first time. Language activists and, most notably, newly released republican prisoners would play a significant role in these developments. Pilib Ó Ruanaí describes developments in the Short Strand area:

Chuaigh mé ar ollscoil nuair a scaoileadh saor mé agus thosaigh mé ag teagasc ranganna Gaeilge agus mé ar choiste na naíscoile sa Trá Ghearr. Ghlac mé dhá mhaidin sa seachtain iad le tuismitheoirí ar feadh dhá bhliain. Máithreacha a bhí ann don chuid is mó, deirim i gcónaí gur seo an dream ba dhíograisí san athbheochan, go minic, bíonn smaointe maithe ag na fir ach níl siad toilteanach ualach na ndualgaisí a iompar mar atá na mná! Murach an dícheall s'acu, is ar éigean a bheadh aon Ghaelscoil ann ... Bhunaigh beirt iarchime eile, Christy Keenan agus Daithí de Paor, an naíscoil sa cheantar ag deireadh '81/ tús '82 agus iad gníomhach le Cumann Gaelach an Tine Bheo ... tháinig an Naíscoil faoi ionsaithe polaitiúla ag deireadh na n-ochtóidí nuair a baineadh siar an deontas ón Naíscoil. Chuaigh muid i mbun feachtasaíochta agus bhailigh muid a lán airgid chun maireachtáil ... d'ullmhaigh muid na páistí don Bhunscoil ar Bhóthar Seoighe ag an tréimhse seo agus bhí se de sprioc fad-téarmach againn ár mbunscoil féin a bheith againn ... b'éigean dúinn bogadh chuig an Mhargadh ag pointe áirithe mar go raibh suíomh níos fearr acu agus chríochnaigh muid sa Droichead ar Bhóthar Ormeau, áit a bhfuil scoil bhreá againn anois agus ionad cultúrtha lán-aimseartha ... i rith an ama seo, bhí mise iomlán tiománta go mbeadh Gaeilge ag ár bpáistí, bhí an Ghaelscolaíocht do mo spreagadh go hiomlán mar fhís ag an am, cineál múscailt consiasa a bhí ionam chun an streachailt a chur ar aghaidh ar bhealaí eile.

(I went to university when I was released and also began teaching Irish classes while on the committee of the nursery school. I took them two mornings a week with parents for two years. It was mostly mothers, I always say that this is the most committed group in the revival; men often have good ideas but are not willing to carry the weight of the responsibilities like the women are. Without their commitment, I doubt there would be one Irish school ... Two ex-prisoners, Christy Keenan and Daithí de Paor, founded the nursery school in the area at the end of '81/early '82 while they were active in the Tine Bheo Gaelic society ... the nursery school came under political attack at the end of the eighties when its grant was removed. We started campaigning and raised a lot of money in order to survive ... we prepared the children for the primary school on the Shaw's Road in this period, but it was our long-term aim to have our own primary school ... we had to move to the Markets at one point as they had a better site and we ended up in An Droichead on the Ormeau Road, where we now have a fine primary school and a full-time cultural centre ... throughout this period, I was completely determined that our children would have Irish, Irish-medium education really inspiring me as a vision ... it was almost like an awakening of consciousness that made me realise the importance of other ways to take forward the struggle.) (Interview with Ó Ruanaí, 20 October 2007)

Similar developments were taking place in north Belfast, where a high concentration of republican prisoners played an active role in Irish educational developments. Seán Mag Uidhir explains the outworkings of these new dynamics in the Ardoyne area:

Scaoileadh saor mé in '84 agus bhí dearcadh iomlán difriúl agam ar an teanga sa dóigh go bhfaca mé mar rud beo í agus mar dhlúthchuid de mo chuid polaitíochta ... tamall gearr ina dhiaidh seo, d'fhreastail mé féin agus tuilleadh iarchimí eile ar chruinniú a d'eagraigh Máirtín Ó Muilleoir faoi bhunadh naíscoile in Ard Eoin agus bhí mé an-tógtha faoi seo. D'eagraigh muid cruinniú le tuismitheoirí le seans a thabhairt dúinn eolas a roinnt leo faoin

Ghaeloideachas. Bhí an ceantar thar a bheith báúil don Ghaeilge, go háirithe i ndiaidh na stailce. Chuir muid coiste le chéile agus ba iarchimí bunús na ndaoine ar an choiste. Bhailigh muid airgead, d'eagraigh muid discos don aos óg agus thuig siad ar fad go raibh an t-airgead ar fad ag dul chuig an naíscoil agus chuidigh sin linn daoine eile a fháil ar bórd agus an scéal a scaipeadh. Chuidigh sé linn teagmháil a dhéanamh athuair leis an aos óg sa cheantar ... Thosaigh muid ag dul do na ranganna chomh maith agus an feachtas sráidainmneacha, bhunaigh muid craobhacha de chuid Chonradh na Gaeilge leis an obair sin a dhéanamh agus bhí muid sásta comhoibriú le achan duine, ba chuma faoina dhearcadh polaitiúil, a fhad is go raibh siad báúil don teanga. Fuair muid cúig déag leanbh le toiseacht ar an naíscoil agus fuair muid bothán i gceantar Mhachaire Botháin leis an naíscoil a lonnú. Phéinteáil muid é agus bhí muid lán brí, mar a bhí an ceantar ar fad ó thaobh cúrsaí Gaeilge. Bhí na seanGhaeilgeoirí aitheanta sásta an bealach a fhágáil dúinn ár gcuid oibre a dhéanamh ... bhí teannas san iarthar le roinnt den sean ghlúin nach raibh sásta le 'hijacking' na teanga mar a dúradh ... ach níor tharla sin linne i dtuaisceart na cathrach.

(I was released in '84 and had a totally different view of the Irish language in that I knew it was a living language and central to my politics ... a short while after this, I attended a meeting along with several other ex-prisoners organised by Martín Ó Muilleoir about forming a nursery school in Ardoyne and I was really motivated about this. We organised a meeting with parents to give us a chance to share information with them about Irish-medium education. The area was extremely sympathetic to the language, particularly after the hunger strike. We put a committee together and most of those on it were ex-prisoners. We collected money, we organised youth discos and they all understood that all the money was going towards the nursery school and this helped us get people on board and to spread the word ... we also started Irish classes as well as the street name campaign, and we formed branches of the Gaelic League to carry out this work and we were happy to work with everyone, regardless of their political opinions, as long as they were sympathetic to the language. We got 15 toddlers to start in the nursery school and got a Portakabin on the Bone area to locate the nursery school. We painted it and were very enthusiastic as was the entire area at the time regarding Irish-language developments. The older, recognised language activists in the area were willing to leave us to our work ... there was tension in the west with some of the old hands unhappy about so-called 'hijacking' and so on, but that never happened with us in the north of the city.) (Interview with Mag Uidhir, 17 February 2005)

This new atmosphere of revivalist activity in Ardoyne is accurately depicted by Michael Liggott, who had also been involved in Irish-language activity in the area prior to the hunger strike:

I was very active with my Da in Conradh na Gaeilge in the late seventies. He had learned his Irish in the Ardscoil and had been interned in the fifties and was a real traditional Anglophone. There were a handful of us who took classes which were always well enough attended and did collections for the language on St Patrick's Day which also did well ... I brought my experience of teaching into the Crum with me and taught lads basic Irish to prepare them for reaching the Blocks ...

When I got out of jail, the boom in Ardoyne as regards the language was unreal; everybody from the RA [IRA] who weren't about when I got caught in 1980 were now released and they all had Irish, whereas none of them had it when we were younger, nor any interest in it for that matter! ... we then started the Irish *naíscoil* and went around the doors doing collections and there were teams of 30 and 40 of us compared to a handful of us in the late seventies; St Patrick's Day collections were now massive events as the boom in activity and activists was amazing ... this was fantastic in my eyes and I can remember thinking to myself when we took the street names down and put bilingual signs up, this is it, the revolution in full flow. I mightn't have had the balls to join the RA or anything anymore, but I realised there were many other ways of developing this struggle ... it was all about demanding our rights ...

People in the area were unbelievably sympathetic and gave whatever they had to spare ... we then got the second *naíscoil* in the New Lodge and this really began to justify all the work and the collections in people's eyes, as they saw the results staring them back in the face. This would justify our first *bunscoil* [primary school], and now we have two of course. Ex-prisoners were central to all this ... the organisational skills and commitment that the ex-prisoners in Ardoyne brought to the revival was second to none, everything was approached with a never-say-die attitude

... whether we'd no building, no funding or no money to pay the teachers, we still dug in and always seemed to pull through in the end. This was really important because it brought a permanency to the revival, especially in that it involved the next generation. (Interview with Liggott, 25 March 2005)

The prevalent form of language activism amongst republican ex-prisoners in this period seemingly involved acting decisively, rather than engaging in protracted long-term planning in emulation of the classic Shaw's Road approach. Jim McCann's account of Irish-medium education development in Ballymurphy in west Belfast illustrates this:

After my release from prison I was heavily involved in political work, including language work. I knew the language and I knew the politics of it and I was good working with people. Around this time we were involved in a campaign to bilingualise the street signs in Ballymurphy. We were doing door to door collections. This was around 1983/84, the views on the streets was 100 per cent in favour, although this was one of the most deprived communities in Europe. On the back of this, a number of people on the doors asked us about when Ballymurphy would get an Irish school and after this we sort of just thought, come on we'll give it a go ...

We started the school about three weeks later with about three or four kids! I then took the job in the *naíonra* [preschool] because the guy who was teaching got arrested for political offences and they asked me would I do it! After the first year we had one child, Seamus O'Neill, who was the first one who left and we sent him to Gaelscoil na bhFál.[2] Once we achieved this, it really motivated us and as we thought: well that's one! You have to remember that there was no real preschool provision in the area, so we were being initially used as a babysitting service, but then we made it compulsory that one of the parents had to also learn the language.

After a few years Gaelscoil na bhFál couldn't take no more of our kids as we were consistently meeting the quota, so we then had to eventually open a primary school. And the first *naíscoil* was opened on the grounds of the local primary school (St Aidan's). However, after a while the local Christian brothers became a bit hostile and they began asking us for rent, but to be honest we couldn't have got by without the school's initial support. Ironically, now our local *bunscoil* is the greatest threat to the future of St Aidan's and their numbers have dramatically dropped over the last number of years as a direct result of the existence of the local *bunscoil*; this of course is very gratifying now! (Interview with McCann, 12 March 2005)

It is worth noting that these organic educational developments were not specific to Belfast: Irish-medium education spread to various counties in the north of Ireland including Down, Tyrone, Derry, Armagh and Fermanagh, in the form of both nursery and primary school facilities. Antoin De Brún sheds some light on developments in Derry City:

D'athraigh mo mheon go hiomlán nuair a d'fhág mé an príosún in '88. Ba dhuine muiníneach mé agus nasc mé seo leis an Ghaeilge, thuig mé gur theanga s'agamsa í agus gur theanga ghalánta í. Lena chois sin, thuig mé gur dhualagas s'agamsa mar phoblachtánach í a chuir chun cinn. Ach, níos tábhachtaí ná aon rud eile ná gur chreid mé go raibh sé furasta í a fhoghlaim dá mba mhian leat iarracht cheart a dhéanamh ... thuig me anois go dtiocfadh leat pobal Gaeilge a chruthú chomh maith ... chruthaigh muid í sna blocanna agus bhí mise don bharúil ar theacht amach as an phríosúin dom go dtiocfadh amhlaidh a dhéanamh sna pobail féin ...

Bhí an-mhuinín agus dea-thaithí ag muintir na mblocanna ag teacht amach sna ceantracha s'againne i nDoire ... thuig muid an deathionchar a d'fhéadfadh bheith ag an teanga agus bhí muid tiomanta chun í a scaipeadh agus an mhuinín chéanna agus an meon deimhneach céanna sin a scaipeadh leis ... Bhunaigh muid an scoil [Gaelscoil Éadáin Mhóir] seo seacht mbliana ó shin agus an chéad seisear páistí a bhí againne, ba pháistí iarchimí uilig iad agus de bhunadh poblachtánach ar fad. Iad siúd a thacaigh linn agus a choinnigh ag dul muid ... fuair muid aitheantas trí bliana ó shin. Tá muid ag dul ó neart go neart. Is cuid lárnach muid anois de phobal Cluain an Bhogaidh.

(My mentality had completely transformed when I left the prison in '88. I was a confident person and linked this to the language; I understood that it was my language and a beautiful language at that. As well as that, I understood that it was my duty as a republican to promote the language. But, more importantly than anything else, I believed that is was easy to learn the language if you wanted to make a proper effort at it ... I understood now that it was possible to build an Irish-speaking community as well ... we proved this in the Blocks and I was of the opinion once I was released that we could do the same thing on the outside in our own communities ...

Ex-prisoners from the Blocks had a lot of confidence and good experience when coming out into the areas in Derry ... we understood the worthwhile effect that the language could have and we were determined to spread it along with that same confidence and positive mentality ... we founded this school seven years ago and the first six children that we had were the children of ex-prisoners and all from republican stock. They were the ones who supported us and kept us going ... we received recognition three years ago and are going from strength to strength. We are now a central part of the Bogside community.) (Interview with De Brún, 15 March 2005)

A similar direct link with personal prison experience and the development of Irish-medium education on the outside is made by Seán Ó Loingsigh from Fermanagh:

By the time the mid nineties had come about, we had turned the prison full circle with ourselves in control of our own affairs. The Gaeltacht wings had sprang out of this process and perhaps even initiated it. They had a massive knock-on effect on the development of the language throughout the prison and I grasped the opportunity to spend some time there when I was given the chance ... it brought my level of Irish on in a big way and also brought my attention to issues such as the revival on the outside ...

I remember having a conversation with a friend of mine from Fermanagh in H6 and committing to try and set up an Irish school in the county when we were released, because Fermanagh was one of the only counties in Ireland that never had a *gaelscoil* [Irish school] at the time ... we organised a meeting about three days after I was released in 1998 and people were saying to me, 'What the hell are you doing here, you are only out after doing 12 and a half years!' ... it took us a while to get it up and going, there were a few ex-prisoners involved in the project along with me, including my brother. In the first year, we set up Naíscoil an Traonaigh in the local GAA ground and there were six in the class, in the second year we got a piece of ground off them and we are now in our fifth year, and have a *bunscoil* which has been officially recognised. (Interview with Ó Loingsigh, 3 June 2005)

The pivotal role played by the families of republican prisoners is noteworthy. Having initially taken an interest in the Irish language under the influence of imprisoned family members, many relatives of ex-prisoners would take the lead in revivalist activity, as Ó Maolmhuaidh attests:

Ó 1988 go 1993, scríobh mé na céadta litreacha ón phríosún agus chuir mé gearrtháin nuachtáin den *Andersonstown News* chuig Gaeilgeoirí ar an tSrath Bán, mo dheirfiúr ina measc, ag moladh dóibh naíscoil a chur ar bun ar an tSrath Bán agus bunaíodh Naíscoil an tSratha Báin sa bhliain 1994. Osclaíodh Gaelscoil Uí Dhochartaigh dhá bhliain ina dhiaidh sin agus tá breis agus 130 daltaí scoile againn sa Ghaelscoil anois. Thosaigh mo dheirfiúr amach mar bhall de Chonradh na Gaeilge a bhunaigh an Naíscoil. Chaith sí cúpla bliain mar Cheannaire sa Naíscoil agus tá sí ag obair go fóill mar chúntóir ranga ar riachtanais speisialta sa Ghaelscoil. Tá a hiníon féin ag teagasc mar mhúinteoir cáilithe sa Ghaelscoil agus chuidigh trí dheirfiúracha eile leis an naíscoil agus an ghaelscoil mar bhaill na gcoistí nó mar chúntóirí ranga in amanna agus, ar ndóigh, tá ceathrar dá bpáistí ag freastal ar an Ghaelscoil. Is amhlaidh atá an scéal le teaghlaigh na bpríosúnach poblachtánaí fud fad na Sé Chontae; i bPort an Dúnáin ar an Lorgáin, i mBéal Feirste, in Iúr Cinn Trá, i Lios na Scéithe agus go leor áiteanna eile.

(From 1988 to 1993, I wrote hundreds of letters from the jail and sent newspaper cuttings from the *Andersonstown News* to Irish speakers in Strabane, including my sister, recommending to them that they start an Irish nursery school in Strabane, and Naíscoil an tSratha Báin was founded in 1994. Gaelscoil Uí Dhochartaigh was formed two years later and has over 13 pupils in the school now. My sister started out as a member of the Gaelic League, which started the nursery school. She spent a couple of years as a leader in the nursery school and still works as a Special Needs Classroom Assistant in the primary school. Her own daughter is teaching as a qualified teacher in the primary school and three other sisters helped with the nursery school and the primary school as either committee members or assistants at times, and of course four of their children now attend the primary school. It is the same with the families of republican prisoners throughout the six counties; in Portadown, in Lurgan, in Belfast, in Newry, in Linaskea and plenty of other places.) (Interview with Ó Maolmhuaidh, 25 June 2005)

## 'DIVIDE AND CONQUER': BRITISH GOVERNMENT RESPONSE TO THE REVIVAL

The post-hunger strike rise of republicanism as a political force saw British prime minister Margaret Thatcher and Irish Taoiseach Garret Fitzgerald develop the 1985 Hillsborough Agreement in order to consolidate the constitutional nationalist position in the six counties (McKeown, Campbell and O'Hagan 1994). British policy during this period, which involved denying official recognition to Irish-medium schools, had the additional implications that both aspirations of Irishness and the nationalist community in general were subversive and illegitimate (Ó hAdhmaill 1985). The community-inspired Irish-language revival in this period was also a source of concern for the British government, which adopted a divisive strategy of attempting to incorporate the language into the discourse of the 'two traditions in Northern Ireland' by consciously isolating radical language initiatives (Kachuk 1993). Mac Seáin explains the political rationale behind the decision to fund Bunscoil Phobal Feirste after 13 years without funding:

> Bogadh polaitiúil ar fad a bhí ann ón aire oideachais ag an am Nicholas Scott nuair a fuair muid an maoiniú in '84 i ndiaidh bliantaí fada de naimhdeas. Bhí na Sasanaigh ag iarraidh cinntiú nach bhfuair Sinn Féin gréim iomlán ar an athbheochan agus bhrúigh siad an SDLP chun tosaigh go mór de bhrí go raibh siad buartha go raibh siad ag cailleadh smachta ar an phobal náisiúnach ó thuaidh, thug siad maoiniú do Lagan College, an coláiste imeascaithe, ar an lá céanna.

> (It was a completely political move by the education minister Nicholas Scott when we got the funding in '84 after years of hostility. The British were trying to ensure that Sinn Féin did not get complete control of the revival and they promoted the SDLP as they were worried that they were losing control in the nationalist community in the North; they gave funding to Lagan College, the integrated college on the same day.) (Interview with Mac Seáin, 26 July 2006)

However, these attempts to isolate republican involvement in the language revival through selective funding would also entail coercive attacks on many community-based initiatives, in the form of blatant discrimination. Ó Néill links this government hostility to the greater cognisance of rights-based demands amongst the language community as it grew following the hunger strike:

Bhí na húdárais ag déanamh neamháirde orainn go dtí gur fhás muid agus ansin ár n-ionsaí agus iad ag polaitiú achan rud ó mhaoiniú bunscoileanna agus naíscoileanna go dtí Glór na nGael agus eile … d'amharc na Sasanaigh ar gach rud fá'n Ghaeilge mar rud a bhí le haisíoc óna náisiúnaithe chun iad a cheannacht arshiúl ó Shinn Féin nó cibé … d'amharc siad air mar chuid den dreach tíre naimhdeach ina n-éadan. D'ardaigh seo ar ndóigh nuair a d'ardaigh líon na ngaeilgeoirí … thiar sa lá, bhí muintir Bhóthar Seoighe agus iad róghnóthach ag cuir rudaí ar siúil le bheith buartha fán stát … lean muidinne seo leis an pháipear agus níor éiligh muid deontas ag an tús, ach thosaigh seo ag athrú i ndiaidh na stailce agus tháinig an focal cearta i bhfád níos coitianta sa chomhréir is thosaigh daoine ag caint ar cheartaí teanga … bhí cás na bpríosúnach bainte go dlúth leis seo agus an t-idirdheálú a ghearradh orthu sa phríosúin maidir leis an teanga, thug muid ardán daofa sa pháipeár ach bhí na húdárais binbeach ina n-éadan, bhí cás s'acu frithchaiteach don stát ar fad, bhí déistín agus doicheall roimh an Ghaeilge agus achan doras sa stát druidte do Ghaeil.

(The authorities were ignoring us until we grew, then attacking as they politicised everything from Irish primary and nursery school to the funding of Glór na nGael, etc. … the Brits looked at everything about the Irish language as something to be repaid by the nationalists in order to buy them away from Sinn Féin or whomever … they looked at it as part of the hostile landscape against them. This increased of course with the amount of Irish speakers; before that, the people in the Shaw's Road and that were too busy setting things up to worry about the state … we followed this with the paper and never asked for a grant at the start, but this began to change after the hunger strike and the term 'rights' became much more common in the syntax and people began speaking about language rights … the prisoners' case was centrally involved in this and the discrimination they suffered in the prison as regards the language, their case was reflective of the entire state, where there was hostility and churlishness towards the language and every door in the state closed to Irish speakers.) (Interview with Ó Néill, 29 September 2006)

However, this overt hostility and discrimination directed towards language revivalist activities in nationalist and republican areas was tempered by the British government's attempt to strategically divide the language movement by providing financial assistance to a cross-community Irish-language initiative. This came in the form of the Ultach Trust, set up in 1989 after the groundwork had been laid by the Cultural Traditions Group (O'Reilly 1999). As the first time in the history of the Northern Ireland state that the British government had given financial assistance to Irish-language development, Bairbre De Brún described it as 'beartaíocht ciniciúil chun airgead a thabhairt do "dheá-ghaeilgeoirí" seachas eagraíochtaí athbheochana' (a cynical tactic to give money to 'respectable Irish speakers' rather than revivalist organisations) (interview with De Brún, 4 September 2003). As a Sinn Féin councillor at the time, Máirtín Ó Muilleoir wrote numerous articles pointing out that no nationalist politicians were on the the new group's board of trustees, which included unionist politicians such as Chris McGimpsey, who at the time was supporting the policy banning the Irish language in Belfast City Hall (Ó Croidheáin 2006: 258). Therefore many language activists accused the government of deliberately designing a policy to portray the Irish revival movement as sectarian and, by association, to blame state discriminatory practices against the movement on its links with nationalism and republicanism (O'Reilly 1999: 108–9).

Such suspicions among language activists were confirmed in August 1990 when the west Belfast Irish-language community organisation, Glór na nGael, had its funding withdrawn under the NIO policy of 'political vetting'. The decision was based on the 1985 Douglas Hurd principles that dictated that groups that 'have the effect of improving the standing and furthering the aims of a paramilitary organisation, whether directly or indirectly' would be denied funding (O'Reilly 1999: 115). This decision would not only impact on community development, but also remove funding from seven of the eight Irish nursery schools in Belfast. The Irish-language community immediately began campaigning nationally and inter-nationally to have the decision overturned. The Irish-language newspaper *LÁ* accused the British government of a policy of 'divide and conquer', while the *Andersonstown News* responded in an equally angry manner:

> We are being asked to act as our own worst enemy – turning our backs on our neighbours because the Government decrees that they are unacceptable and unclean. We are to serve as a vetting body, screening our own community. Thus we can appear on the radio as long as we agree to the censorship of our neighbours. We can receive grant-aid for community projects as long as we agree to use government buzzwords and adopt as Gospel government policy. (O'Reilly 1999: 116–17)

The effect of the political vetting is described by Mícheal Mac Giolla Ghunna, who worked for Glór na nGael at the time:

> In Iarthar Bhéal Feirste, bhí poblachtánaigh ag obair le beagnach achan ghrúpa pobail ... in amanna, d'oibir siad go hoscailte mar phoblachtánaigh ach in amanna eile díreach mar bhaill den phobal féin. Bhain siad airgead ó roinnt grúpaí, mar shampla ionad pobail ar nós Conway Mill ... chruthaigh seo eagla i measc grúpaí go gcaillfeadh siad airgead dá gcáinfeadh siad an stát nó dá mbeadh baint acu ar bhealach ar bith le cúrsaí polaitiúla. Bhí an Ghaeilge istigh sa suíomh polaitiúil sin ar an ábhar gur bhain sí leis an chultúr náisiúnach a raibh faoi ionsaí ag an stát agus dá bharr sin, baineadh maoiniú Ghlór na nGael arshiúl. Bhí gréasán grúpaí pobail in iarthar Bhéal Feirste, a bhí poblachtánaigh bainte leis agus ní thiocfadh leis an Rialtas na Breataine sin a bhriseadh ach go bé fríd airgead a tharraing siar. Ach, bhí siad fite fuaite fríd an phobal agus ní thiocfadh leo ionsaí a dhéanamh orthu gan ionsaí a dhéanamh ar an phobal féin, rud a chothaigh níos mó naimhdeas don stát.

(In west Belfast, republicans were working with almost every community group ... at times openly as republicans, but in other times as members of the community itself. They removed funding from a lot of groups, for example community centres like Conway Mill ... this created a fear amongst groups that they would lose money if they criticised the state or became involved in politics. The Irish language was within this political framework, because it was linked with the nationalist culture that was being attacked by the state and, as a result, Glór na nGael had its funding removed. There was a community network in west Belfast that republicans were linked to and the only way the British government could break that was through removing funding. But they were ingrained in the community and could not be attacked without attacking the community itself, which created more hostility to the state.) (Interview with Mac Giolla Ghunna, 4 April 2005)

Similarly, Ó Maolchraoibhe gives his view on the reasoning behind the British goverment approach:

Níl na Sasanaigh i bhfách leis an Ghaeilge agus ní bheidh ariamh ach bhí straitéis acu chun comhoibriú le roinnt Gaeilgeoirí 'measúla' chun muidinne a imeallú agus dúirt an t-Aire Stáit Mawhinney seo ag an am, agus é ag tabhairt airgid d'Iontaobhas Ultach, go raibh sé ag 'baint na teanga arshiúil ón pholaitíocht' ... Bhí an Ghaeilge mar chuid lárnach de ghléic s'againn agus níl aon dabht go raibh Rialtas na Breataine i n-éadan na gléice sin agus i n-éadan na Gaeilge go ginearálta. Rinne siad iarracht créidiúnt a bhaint dúinn agus bhí siad sásta daoine eile, leithéid [Aodán] Mhic Póilin, a cheapadh mar stiúrthóir ar Iontabhas Ultach, a úsáid leis sin a dhéanamh. Ach, níor éirigh leis seo, mar gur bhaill don phobal muid agus athbheochan pobal a bhí san athbheochan teanga féin.

(The Brits are not in favour of the language and they never will be, but they had a strategy to co-operate with 'respectable' Irish speakers in order to marginalise us, and the state minister at the time, Mawhinney, said this when he gave the funding to the Ultach Trust, that he was 'taking the Irish language out of politics' ... The language was a central part of our struggle and there's no doubt that the British government was against that struggle and against the language in general. They tried to take credibility away from us and were happy to use others like [Aodán] Mac Póilin, who was employed as the director of the Ultach Trust, to do this. But this did not succeed because we were members of the community and the language revival itself was a community revival.) (Interview with Ó Maolchraoibhe, 16 June 2006)

Mac Póilin, on the other hand, points out that he viewed the Ultach Trust as a worthwhile means to gain government funding for the Irish language, while also highlighting the extremely high internal tensions of the period:

Bhí an Rialtas ag iarraidh airgead a thabhairt don Ghaeilge agus bhí leithéidí Ruairí de Bléine agus Séamas de Napier ag obair leis an Cultural Traditions Group ar feadh deich mblian agus tháinig an t-Iontaobhas ó seo. Cineál 'toe in the water' a bhí ann don Ghaeilge ó thaobh airgid de. Chuaigh mise isteach don phost agus fuair mé é ... Thig leat seasamh taobh amuigh an t-am ar fad ach tá brú ar an taobh istigh de dhíth fosta ... ag an am, ní raibh aon bhealach eile ann. Rinneadh ionsaithe pearsanta fíochmhara ormsa dá bharr agus scaipeadh bréaga go raibh muidinne taobh thiar den deontas ar baineadh de Ghlór na nGael, raiméis a bhí ann, thacaigh muid leo agus chaill muid airgead bliana mar gheall air!

(The government wanted to give money to the Irish language and the likes of Ruairí de Bléine and Seamas de Napier; we were working with the Cultural Traditions Group for ten years and the Trust came out of this. It was a kind of 'toe in the water' for the Irish language regarding funding. I went for the job and got it ... you can stand outside the entire time, but pressure from the inside is required as well ... at the time, there was no other way to go. There were a lot of vicious attacks on me because of it and lies were spread that we were behind Glór na nGael losing their grant; this was rubbish, we supported them and lost a year's funding because of it!) (Interview with Mac Póilin, 6 October 2006)

A similar point about the genuine aspirations of those behind the Ultach Trust initiative is made by Mac Seáin, who nevertheless relates his own personal reasons for feeling unable to attach himself to such a project in the context of the hostile political and military conflict in the six counties:

Tá meas agam ar Iontaobhas Ultach agus meas ar leith agamsa ar Shéamas de Napier agus Ruairí de Bléine a bhí taobh thiar de – thuig siadsan gur deis a bhí ann chun airgead a fháil don Ghaeilge. Ach go pearsanta, ní raibh mise sásta mé féin a cheangal leo [rialtas na Breataine] agus an pobal thart orm faoi chois acu agus ag troid chomh fíochmhar sin ina n-éadan.

(I have respect for the Ultach Trust and in particular, I respect Séamus de Napier and Ruairí de Bléine who were behind it – they realised it was an opportunity to get money for the Irish language. But personally, I was not willing to associate myself with them [the British government] while the community around me was being oppressed by them and fighting so ferociously against them.) (Interview with Mac Seáin, 26 July 2006)

Following an 18-month national campaign, which also included international support, Glór na nGael eventually succeeded in having its funding restored (O'Reilly 1999: 122). Although the 'political vetting' fiasco had deeply divisive repercussions for the Irish-language movement, it nonetheless raised the profile of the language revival in the north and consolidated a language rights methodology. As Ó Néill posits:

Meancóg ollmhór a bhí ann do na Sasanaigh, thug siad ardán dúinn ... tharraing sé aird ar leatrom na Gaeilge ar bhonn uile-oileánda agus chuir sé ceist na Gaeilge fán mhicreascóip. D'éirigh daoine iontach consiasach fá'n leatrom seo, bíodh seo sa sochaí nó sa phríosúin, bhí daoine corraithe faoi.

(It was a major mistake by the British, it gave us a platform ... it drew attention to the inequality of the language on an all-island basis and it put the issue of the language under the microscope. People became very conscious of this inequality, whether this was in society or in the prison, people were very angry about it.) (Interview with Ó Néill, 29 September 2006)

Another example of a language rights issue that became a campaigning focus for Irish-language activists in this period was the 'cultural discrimination' on the part of the Long Kesh prison authorities, who effectively banned the Irish language from open use in the prison. Having first come to the fore during the hunger strike in 1981, Irish-language organisations such as the Gaelic League had been lobbying consistently on behalf of the prisoners, as evidenced in one of their increasingly militant press statements:

This denial of the right to communicate in the national language of the country must be unique in the long history of imperialism. The prisoners in Long Kesh and especially those in the H-Blocks have derived great inspiration and strength from the Irish language. They have used it as a shield to ward off the callous attempts by the authorities to rob them of their Irishness. Deprived of even the basic necessities for a dignified existence, they were forced back on their own resources, and it is quite evident from letters smuggled out of the H-Blocks, that the Irish language became, to quote Terence McSwiney, 'the standard behind which they, as Irishmen, could defy the taunts of the warders and deprivation of everyday life' ...

Conradh (The Gaelic League) will be lobbying the government in the 26 counties and other governments in Western Europe to fight this denial of fundamental human rights, and we will not rule out the possibility of taking this as far as Strasbourg if necessary. The prisoners cannot be denied their Irishness. It is the duty of Conradh na Gaeilge and all true lovers of freedom to ensure that they are given their rights. (Conradh na Gaeilge 2008)

This campaign culminated in June 1989, when two republican prisoners, Eoghan Mac Cormaic and John Pickering, brought a court case against the NIO and the prison authorities citing discrimination arising from:

1. a ban on correspondence in Irish;
2. a ban on wearing the fáinne;
3. a ban on speaking Irish during visits;
4. the non-recognition of Irish name forms;
5. undue delay in publications other than those in English passing through the censor; and
6. a ban on playing Gaelic games. (O'Hagan 1991: 17)

Having initially had their claims dismissed in the Belfast County Court, the prisoners took their case to the High Court and had public backing in the court from prominent members of the Gaelic League and the GAA, including Seán Mac Mathúna and Íte Ní Chionnaith (Ó Néill 1990). However, the reputation of the Ultach Trust was further damaged in the Irish-language community by their unwillingness to lend public support to the campaign or any campaign that could be perceived as anti-state (Kachuk 1993).

Although the prisoners' case of cultural discrimination was lost, the prison authorities had already begun easing their ban on the Irish language during the case itself, 'in a deliberate attempt to avoid an embarrassing verdict in court' (Ó Néill 1990: 2). According to Mac Cormaic, the case publicly highlighted the issue of cultural discrimination in the six counties:

Bhí mise i mo oifigeach cultúrtha sa champa nuair a chuir muid an plean le chéile chun cás cúirte a eagrú mar chuid de straitéis cheannaireacht an champa ... bhuaigh muid cuid den chás agus chaill muid cuid den chás fosta ach cuimhním ar an chás mar bhua mór morálta dúinn. Bhí a fhios againn go mbeadh 'slándáil' mar chosaint acu [NIO] ach rinne argóintí s'againn a bheag den chosaint sin agus thaispeáin muid go poiblí go raibh idirdhealú cultúrtha i bhfeidhm acu agus sa stát ó thuaidh i gcoitinne.

(I was a cultural officer in the camp when the plan for a court case was initiated, as part of the camp leadership's strategy ... we both won and lost aspects of the case, but I remember the case as a massive moral victory. We knew they [NIO] would use 'security' in their defence, but our arguments made little of this defence and showed publicly that they were practising cultural discrimination, as was the state in the north in general.) (Interview with Mac Cormaic, 10 June 2006)

Thus, the community-led, post-hunger strike language revival in the six counties, which formed part of the intense politicisation of the republican and nationalist community in this period, had reignited the classic British colonial perception that the Irish language represented a threat to its cultural hegemony in the north, and by extension to its own strategic political objectives. However, as Bairbre De Brún underlines, their own policies designed to deal with this 'threat' often accentuated rather than nullified this perception:

Is iad polasaithe idirdhealuithe agus frithGhaelacha Rialtas na Breataine a rinne ceist pholaitiúil den Ghaeilge agus a chruthaigh stádas di mar 'cheist achrannach' nó mar 'cheist chonspóideach'. Bhain said deontais de Ghlór na nGael; cruthaíodh ceist pholaitiúil. Dhiúltaigh siad aitheantas airgeadais a thabhairt do Mheánscoil Feirste [an chéad mheánscoil lanGhaeilge i dtuaisceart na hÉireann]; cruthaíodh ceist pholaitiúil. Chuir said cearta cultúrtha na gcimí faoi chosc; cruthaíodh ceist pholaitiúil ... . Níor réitigh siad ceist na Gaeilge fós de thairbhe go mbaineann sí le Gaeil, Éireannaigh agus féiniúlacht i stát atá fós mar dhéantús de stair fhada an coilíneachais.

(It is the discriminatory and anti-Gaelic policies of the British government that has made the Irish language into a political issue and they created a status for it as a 'contentious issue' or a 'controversial issue'. They removed grants from Glór na nGael; a political issue was created. They refused to give financial recognition to Meánscoil Feirste [the first Irish-medium secondary school in the north of Ireland]; a political issue was created. They trampled on the prisoners' cultural rights; a political issue was created ... They haven't solved the Irish-language issue because it involves Gaels, Irish people, and identity in a state that is still a product of the long history of colonialism.) (Interview with De Brún, 4 September 2003)

# Conclusion

[H]istory is important for understanding the present and ... reclaiming history is a critical and essential aspect of decolonisation.

Linda Tuhiwai Smith (1999: 29)

This conclusion acknowledges the key contributions of the narrators as sources of history, whose experiences of contemporary historical events shape this book. While its analysis draws from a wider decolonising framework and broader 'determining contexts', this book prioritises oral history in a manner that both recognises and celebrates the role of 'social beings' and human agency. Therefore, while recognising that republican prisoners and Irish-language activists 'made their own history', it is also vital to note that they did not make it 'under circumstances chosen by themselves' (Marx 1979: 103). Thus the various forms of resistance and activism recounted above are valuable, because they illuminate 'facets of power relations which are easily overlooked because the actions in which relatively powerless people engage are different from the dramatic confrontations that attract the attentions of historians and journalists' (Gledhill 2000: 70).

## RESEARCH FINDINGS IN CONTEXT

In assessing the ideological dynamics of the Irish-language revival in the north of Ireland through focusing on the transformational impact of the republican Long Kesh prison struggle, this book has drawn on the defining processes of colonialism and its contemporary variants of neocolonialism and neoliberal globalisation. The historical decline of the Irish language, it has been argued, was dictated by the politico-economic and cultural necessities of British imperialism in Ireland. Through comparative analysis, this process has been framed into a wider international understanding of cultural shift in colonial and neocolonial contexts. Likewise, colonisation in Ireland can be seen to have inspired an ideology of decolonisation and resistance that has practically manifested itself in the revival or reinvention of indigenous cultures, claiming continuity with the 'historic past'. By exploring both the practical and ideological motivations of activists involved in this revival, this book argues that Fanon's concept of 'hegemonic mirroring' as a necessary strategy for survival and resistance has defined successful participatory forms of Irish cultural revival.

Such forms of cultural revival arguably provided the inspiration for the Irish political independence movement at the beginning of the twentieth century. Similarly, their derived ideological foundations, which have formed the basis of popular constructions such as national identities, can also be interpreted as key motivating factors for Irish republican prisoners and, by extension, the contemporary Irish-language revival movement in the north of Ireland. The survival and development of this movement in the north, in spite of the often recalcitrant policies of the six-county unionist regime, has been presented as a practical example of resistance-based language activism. As a collective and organised 'hidden Ulster' of revivalism, these forms of activism gave rise to a committed cohort of young Belfast language activists in the late 1950s. Their radical decision to break ranks with traditional revivalist activities and develop their own urban 'Gaeltacht' and Irish-medium school laid the practical foundation for the decolonising language revival that would emerge in the highly volatile post-hunger strike context.

The ideological continuum that defines the militant republican definition of decolonisation as a form of 'cultural reconquest' often found expression in Irish prisons amongst successive generations of republican prisoners who both learned and utilised the Irish language as a 'language of struggle' while incarcerated. This is evident in the views of narrators from the 1940s and 1950s prison campaigns. These activists attest that the language formed an integral part of their political education programmes as both a collective prisoner coping strategy that maintained morale and collective organisation and a representation of continued political activism while imprisoned.

The very fact that imprisonment in the 1970s, as described in narrator accounts, indicates almost identical prisoner rationalisation for Irish-language learning, and often some of the same activists promoting a longstanding, traditionally structured teaching methodology, underlines a historical continuity in the education of imprisoned republican activists. However, the actual success or predominance of Irish-language development amongst republican prisoners, as is clear in accounts from the Long Kesh internment camp, depended largely on the conditions of their incarceration and their capacity to organise and sustain educational development in unfavourable circumstances. The difficulties facing the interned prison community in educational development have a number of explanations: the impermanence of the interned community; a generational divergence amongst activists; and an incongruent organisational structure, in which a significant number of those imprisoned were not members of the IRA and thus were not under the strict remit of the prison command structures.

The importance of these conditions is highlighted when they are contrasted with the educational developments within the sentenced prison community in the cages of Long Kesh. A traditional, hierarchical and overtly militaristic system, with its emphasis on rigorous discipline and compulsory military lectures, was eventually contested by younger activists who promoted a more egalitarian organisational structure prioritising political education and debate (McKeown 2001). In the highly politicised enthusiasm that permeated cage 11 in the mid 1970s, the Irish language became integral to the individual ideological advancement of activists like Breathnach, who referred to the political inspiration that prisoners were drawing from African and Latin American anti-colonial struggles.

This idealistic commitment to the Irish language as a component of their overall political vision is articulated by activists like McCann, whose observation that 'we recognised the lengths the imperialists went to destroy the language and from this reasoned that it must be important' (interview with McCann, 12 March 2005) perfectly illustrates the Fanonian decolonising model. These prisoners began to benefit from reflective and liberating educational processes in which, as McCann posited, 'not only did I learn the language but I learned why I had went to jail and what was keeping me in jail and more importantly we learned how to begin breaking all these things down' (ibid.). This educational process treated them as 'knowing subjects' and not 'as recipients' and helped them achieve 'a deepening awareness both of the sociocultural reality which shapes their lives and the capacity to transform that reality' (Freire 1972b: 51).

While other cages in the sentenced end of the camp retained a more rigid organisational structure, the primacy of political and personal development in Cage 11 is epitomised in the personal accounts depicting the impact of the Gaeltacht huts on the prison community at both individual and collective levels. Prisoners frequently refer to an increase in confidence and self-esteem in accordance with an increase in fluency levels or a general interest in Irish-language development. These developments were consolidated through a highly empowering and participatory teaching methodology, in which all learners took up teaching responsibility after they had achieved a certain level of fluency and in which the 'teacher-of-the-students and the students-of-the-teacher cease[d] to exist' as everyone became essentially 'responsible for a process in which all grow' (Freire 1972a: 61).

In the context of their imprisonment and involvement in what they perceived as a popular 'war of liberation', the language helped fundamentally shape an oppositional identity. Hence colonial history could be appropriated and alternative versions asserted as a means of challenging or subverting the all-pervasive reality of their subordinate structural position. This tendency was heightened not only by developments in the Irish-language revival outside the prison walls, but primarily by the 'blanket protest' in the H-Blocks of Long Kesh, where the Irish language became a central plank in resistance to 'criminalisation'. This elevated the role of the language amongst prisoners in the cages as a practical means to provide solidarity and support to their fellow prisoners suffering in extreme conditions of hardship. Prisoner accounts also suggest that the effect of the intermittent prison regime attacks upon the Gaeltacht hut was in fact counterproductive – thus increasing the hut's status within the prison community. As the outworkings of the British criminalisation policy stagnated the number of 'special category' prisoners in the cages, their focus shifted to a specific emphasis on political and academic education 'as a building block in the theory and practice of resistance' (Buntman 2003: 251).

The importance of educational and ideological development amongst republican prisoners in the cages to the role the language subsequently played in the prison protests of the H-Blocks is emphasised by a wide range of narrators. These activists attest to the key organisational and educational role played by fluent Irish speakers and ex-cages prisoners. The role played by these activists arguably corresponds with Gramsci's conception of the 'organic intellectual', who performs organising roles for particular social groups by giving 'symbolic expression to the collective identity of the groups they represent', and using their own political awareness to 'elaborate, modify and disseminate' its 'conception of the world' in the economic, political, social and cultural fields (Jones 2006: 84).

By ideologising the Irish language as both a practical and a political means of resistance, and simultaneously replicating the cages' language-learning model of informal education, which saw the 'pupil' become the 'teacher' after arriving at a particular level of fluency, these activists inspired truly phenomenal educational development in exceptional and often unbearable conditions. While their primary resistance may have been a refusal to wear a uniform and accept the label of criminalisation, they also demonstrated an extraordinary capacity to transform their sacrificial circumstances into a transformative arena that educated them and politicised their defiant acts of resistance. The daily struggle on the blanket protest, which has been described as the 'great leveller' that forged more participatory and horizontal forms of prison leadership and organisational structure, also saw the republican prisoner acquire 'his revolutionary consciousness through interpreting his struggle as he simultaneously physically waged that struggle' (McKeown 1998: 329–30).

Moreover, prisoner accounts indicate that widespread use of the Irish language was most powerful during periods of the protest when there was an intensification of prison warder brutality, a fact that contributes compellingly to aforementioned concepts of resistance. Concurrently, an analysis of prisoner rationale and motivations in this respect reveals a remarkable similarity with Buntman's (2003: 54) resistance categorisations: resistance as survival; resistance as dignity and self-consciousness; resistance as open challenge; resistance as reducing state power or defeating the ends of the oppressor or dominator; and resistance as the appropriation of power or at least the attempt to acquire power. However, it is notable that the role of the Irish language as a form of resistance during the blanket protest took on a multifaceted significance that simultaneously incorporated and often transcended all these categories. According to Máirtín Ó Maolmhuaidh:

Chuidigh an Ghaeilge liom féin go pearsanta … neartaigh sí féiniúlacht chuile dhuine a d'fhoghlaim a theanga dhúchais i ngéibheann. Mar sin féin, nuair a bhaintear chuile shórt díot agus nuair nach bhfuil fágtha agat ach pluid shalach agus do chuid smaointí féin, bíonn ort dul go domhain isteach i do mheon agus i do chroí chun cloí leis an phearsa atá ionat féin. Mar a dúirt duine de Thír na mBascach, 'Our language is the only free space we hold', agus sin mar a bhí muid ar Agóid na Pluide agus i ngéibheann go ginearálta. Poblachtánaigh, Gaeil agus Éireannaigh a bhí ionainn ach in amanna ba í an Ghaeilge an t-aon ábhar amháin a bhí againn a d'fheidhmigh mar bhia na hintinne agus a chothaigh ár spioraid dúinn mar chimí polaitiúla. Go bunúsach, choinnigh sí an inchinn beo agus an spiorad slán do chuid mhaith againn. Tá cineál comrádaíochta ar leith ann go fóill i measc na gcimí a bhí le chéile ar Agóid na Pluide agus tá an Ghaeilge ina gné thábhachtach den tréimhse stairiúil sin ...

Gan Agóid na Pluide agus gach aon duine a chaith an phluid, gan na Stailceoirí a fuair bás agus iad nach bhfuair bás, agus gan an Ghaeilge le linn na tréimhse crua sin, ní bheadh mórán cimí ag foghlaim na Gaeilge agus ní thiocfadh an deis le Gaeltacht na Fuiseoige a chur ar bun. Cé go raibh an fonn orm an Ghaeilge a fhoghlaim i bhfad sula ndeachaigh mé isteach i bpríosún níor thuig mé cé chomh tábhachtach, chomh cumhachtach agus chomh lárnach agus a bhí sí i bhféiniúlacht an duine ach go háirithe i mo shaol féin go deireadh na stailceanna ocrais. Mar a dúirt mé cheana féin, creidim gur chuidigh agus gur athraigh an Ghaeilge cách a d'fhoghlaim an teanga i ngéibheann. Chan amháin gur chuir sí lenár bhféiniúlacht mar Ghael, mar Éireannaigh agus mar Phoblachtánigh agus chuidigh sí go mór le forbairt phearsanta agus i múnlú charachtar do chuid mhaith chimí atá gníomhach anois mar ghníomhairí teanga agus gnoimhairí polaitiúla san iliomad tionscnamh fud fad na tíre ... creidim gurbh í eiseamláir na bhFear a d'fhoghlaim a gcuid Gaeilge le linn Agóid na Pluide agus sna Bloic-H ina dhiaidh a thug spreagadh agus misneach don mhuintir náisiúnta go háirithe go gcaithfidís troid in aghaidh chóras na Breataine sna Sé Chontae dá mba mhian leo an Ghaeilge a chur chun cinn mar ba cheart.

(The Irish language helped me personally ... it strengthened the identity of all those who learned their native language while imprisoned. That said, when everything is taken from you and all you have left is a filthy blanket and your own thoughts, you have to delve deeply into your mentality and your heart to remain true to yourself as a person. As someone from the Basque country said, 'Our language is the only free space we hold', and that is how it was on the blanket protest and in prison for republicans in general. We were republicans, Gaels and Irishmen, but at times the Irish language was all that we had as mental stimulation that could build our spirit as political prisoners. It basically kept the mind alive and the spirit safe in many of us. There remains a special comradeship amongst the prisoners who were on the blanket and the Irish language is a central component of that historical period ...

Without the blanket protest and all those who wore the blanket, without the hunger strikers who died and those who didn't, and without the Irish language in that dreadful period, not many prisoners would have learned Irish in the prison thereafter and Gaeltacht na Fuiseoige would never have been formed. Even though I had always wanted to learn the language long before I had ever went into prison, I never understood how important, how powerful and how central it is to the identity of a person and especially in my own life until the end of the hunger strikes. As I said before, I think the language both helped and transformed all those who learned it in prison. Not only did it add to our identities as Gaels, Irishmen and republicans but it also helped the personal development and moulded the characters of many prisoners who are now working as language activists and political activists in a variety of projects throughout the country ... I believe that the example of the men who learned their Irish during the blanket protest gave both inspiration and courage to the nationalist people in particular, that they had to fight against the British system in the six counties if they wanted to develop the Irish language properly.) (Interview with Ó Maolmhuaidh, 25 June 2005)

Thus the use of the Irish language as a means of resistance during the blanket protest had a 'transcendental power' that was 'first and foremost directed at the prison itself' and subsequently transformed 'the cell into a pedagogical space' and an 'act of personalised political appropriation' (Feldman 1991: 216–17). Crucially, however, its more general relevance surpassed the confines of the cell and the immediacy of the prison protest itself.

As a method for developing political consciousness and a sense of community amongst republican prisoners in Long Kesh during this period, the Irish language can also be conceptualised with reference to 'emancipation'. This follows the initial formative phase of resistance, when it is 'not simply about saying no, reacting, refusing, resisting, but also and primarily about social creativity, introducing new values and aims, new forms of co-operation and action' (Buntman 2003: 236). Thus if survival and the maintenance of dignity are the baseline of resistance, powerful outlets like the Irish language clearly contributed to the longer-term construction of critical consciousness or 'conscientisation'. It helped sustain successful 'opposition and resistance to the status quo' having been promoted as part of 'the articulation and development of ideologies and organisations of protest' (ibid.: 250). That this growth in critical consciousness amongst the community of prisoners could resignify and recast resistance methodologies, both overt and covert, both 'categorical' and 'strategic', is expressed in the post-hunger strike narratives, which indicate how prisoner actions often entailed 'strategic acquiescence; the recognition that limited compliance may expand the scope for other strategies of resistance' (ibid.: 252).

The significant overlap between the story of Irish-language development within the republican prisoner community and its subsequent revival beyond the prison walls also reveals a resemblance in resistance approaches. For Eoghan Ó Néill:

Bhí an naimhdeas céanna in éadan na teanga ar an taobh istigh den phríosún agus a bhí ar an taobh amuigh ... bhí na príosúnaigh cliste i gcónaí agus an-seiftiúil is ag smaoineamh ar bhealaí chun an teanga a chur chun cinn go praiticiúil chomh maith le bheith ag tógáil raic fá chearta s'acu agus eile ... rinne siad ranganna agus smuigleáil siad leabhair, ansin throid siad go hoifigiúil ar son tuilleadh leabhair. Achan uair a bhí doicheall sa bhealach orthu, d'aimsigh siad bealach thart air ... Tharla an rud ceannan céanna ar an taobh amuigh ... mar shampla le feachtas Bhunscoil Phobal Feirste, a throid ar son aitheantais ar feadh trí bliana déag; ní raibh streachailt níos faide ag scoil ar bith sa tír gan fiú trácht ar an tuaisceart, lean siad leo ar bhealach an-seiftiúil agus an-ghlic. Cosúil leis an Cheis féin, thosaigh sé b'fhéidir le baicle beag agus ansin spréigh sé amach de réir a chéile mar gheall ar an leatrom agus mar gheall ar an athrú consiasa an phobail náisiúnaigh i gcoitinne. D'athraigh an stailc ocrais achan rud sa chaoi sin tá sé cosúil le 1916 gan aon amhras. D'athraigh dearcadh daoine ar an stát, ar an stair, ar an pholaitíocht ... ar achan rud a bhain leis an sochaí anseo ó thuaidh. D'athraigh an ghluaiseacht teanga maraon leis seo agus achan rud eile.

(The hostility towards the language inside the prison changed as well as on the outside ... prisoners were always clever, very resourceful, and thinking of ways to advance the language practically, as well as raising a storm over issues of rights and that ... they did classes, they smuggled books ... then they fought officially for more books ... every time there was obstruction in their way ... they found a way around it ... the exact same thing happened on the outside ... for example with the campaign for Bunscoil Phobal Feirste, who fought for recognition for 13 years; there was not a school in the country, never mind the north, who had a longer struggle ... they continued, were very resourceful and very clever. It was the same with the Kesh ... it started maybe with a small group and then it spread out gradually as a result of the oppression and because of the transformation in the nationalist community's consciousness in general. The hunger strike changed everything in that way and was like 1916 without a doubt. People's opinion of the state, of history, of politics, it all changed, as did everything to do with society here in the north ... the language movement changed along with this and everything else.) (Interview with Ó Néill, 29 September 2006)

A similar point in relation to the transformative influence of the hunger strikes is made by Terry Enright:

This period had a massive impact and when you actually stand back from it and analyse it in the cold light of day, it probably accelerated and transcended about 80 or 90 years of normal, gradual evolution in terms of the cultural revival. The hunger strikes were the key wake-up and inspirational call to people all over Ireland to put the language back on the agenda. (Interview with Enright, 30 March 2007)

It has been universally recognised by all the above narrators that the 1980–81 hunger strikes provided the 'cultural tipping point' for the expansion of the Irish-language revival in the north of Ireland. While the general comparison with the Easter Rising is undoubtedly apt, in the sense that both events radically refocused popular sentiment on the issue of national sovereignty by harnessing latent anti-British sentiment, their immediate ideological foundations are less congruent. While the early-twentieth-century period was shaped in classical anti-colonial terms by a longer-term 'appropriation of history' and 'recuperation of identity', the contemporary phase in the north was instead defined by a reactive dynamic in which 'less consciously radical forms of resistance' have 'unintended consequences because the state reacts to them in a repressive way' (Keesing, in Gledhill 2000: 93).

Thus in the former, the construction of cultural nationalism formed part of a long-term and consciously disseminated 'derived' ideological construct that effectively paved the way for the revolutionary period; while in the latter, 'inherent' ideas based on cultural identity as a highly politicised concept, which had been passed down from the earlier revolutionary period through popular historical narrative, laid the ground for a newly imbued 'derived' element relating to radical cultural decolonisation to be 'effectively absorbed' in the highly charged political conditions created by the hunger strikes (Rúde, 1980). Essentially, however, the practical methodology by which such a newly energised 'oppositional identity' could manifest itself had also been previously constructed, albeit in a marginal sense, by the decolonising activists of the Shaw's Road Gaeltacht community. In addition, the defining aspect that elevated cultural revivalism as one of the major political outworkings of the hunger strike period was the groundbreaking language-learning activities of republican prisoners in Long Kesh.

In the post-hunger strike phase in the six counties, it's perhaps unsurprising, considering previous historical precedent, that a rejuvenated republican movement would recognise the Irish language as a rational constituent element of the increased politicisation of the nationalist community in the north of Ireland. However, it would be wholly inaccurate to overemphasise the role played by the republican movement or Sinn Féin in the contemporary language revival as being a role of predetermined theoretical or organisational importance, when the accounts of narrators prove the case to be otherwise. These narratives indicate that in the pre-1981 phase, the Irish language was incidental to popular republican discourse, which was primarily concerned with the ostensibly reactive phase of the political and military conflict in the north of Ireland. Equally, it has been recognised that its relevance within the republican movement significantly altered under the transformative influence of the republican prison protests, in which the Irish language and cultural reconquest defined openly political forms of resistance.

In a similar vein, it would be inaccurate and erroneous to suggest, as commentators like O'Reilly (1999) and Nic Craith (2001) have done, that the involvement of the republican movement in the language revival stemmed from a calculated political opportunism to achieve party-political gain. This view ignores the autonomous ideological dynamics of the revivalist period and has arguably led to a misreading of the rationale behind some of the key events that took place. One example of this is Nic Craith's (2001: 79) assumption that 'Irish was also used to define a community and exclude the other', and that Gaelicised street names 'marked Irish territories'. Rather than viewing these developments as part of a narrow, exclusivist 'Catholic communalism' (Andrews 2000), it would make more sense to interpret them within a decolonising framework, in which 'one of the first tasks of the culture of resistance was to reclaim, rename, and reinhabit the land' (Said 1993: 273). The narratives of the key participants in this revivalist activism strongly indicate liberationist nationalism, in which cultural revival was utilised as a means of people-centred decolonisation. This sought to engender 'critical consciousness' amongst structurally oppressed working-class nationalist communities with a view to transforming 'the subject from feelings of hopelessness and inferiority to hope and self-awareness thereby developing his capacity to become an "agent for change"' (Freire 1972a: 75).

Although the revivalist literature and popular rhetoric of republican language activists in this period also included references to 'inherent' nationalistic symbols of identity and anti-Britishness, these views are best understood as an expression of reaction in the post-hunger strike conditions of intensive military occupation. Their ideological motivation, however, was based on an emancipatory definition of decolonisation as a critical form of resistance against what they argued were the regressive consequences of colonialism and 'the materialism, individualism and opportunism of the capitalist system which has been imposed on us' (Ó Maolchraoibhe 1985: 3–6). Furthermore, this analysis and its projection in the post-hunger strike phase rationally utilised Fanon's ideological template, in which the revival of the 'national culture' was integral to the struggle for national self-determination and popular sovereignty.

Activist accounts show that the outworkings of these decolonising processes in campaigning terms saw the emergence of a greater emphasis on rights-based demands. This fact is in keeping with the view that the reinvestment of value in a minoritised language helps minority groups develop 'confidence in their own identity' and 'the knowledge and critical awareness to articulate their rights', thus making them more 'resistant to exploitation at the hands of the dominant group' (Cummins 1995: 160). The tactical and policy nuances of the British government responses to such rights-based demands tended to alternate in accordance with the demands of political expediency. As has demonstrably been the case in previous periods of popular cultural revival, British strategy often varied, ranging from outright coercion and discrimination to divisive policies of strategic incorporation and conciliaton.

The divisions these British government strategies created in the Irish-language community are also evident in some of the narrator conclusions on the impact of this period. In this scenario, activists who played a part in the community language revival often view their contribution in contrast to those who went before, as is clear from Michael Liggott's view: 'The reality is, if the prisoners hadn't have been there when they were and made the impact they did, there would still be a wee hut in the back off the Shaw's Road, because that's all there was in 1978' (interview with Liggott, 25 March 2005). A similar sentiment can be found in the overview of Jim McCann:

> This might be a bit arrogant to those people who had previously been working on the language, but I know I did more in ten years than ten of them could have did in all their lives, I know this. I didn't sit in a club somewhere in Belfast waiting for people to come to the door wanting to learn the language. We went out and made Irish-language classes available to people and started them all over Belfast. If it hadn't had been for Long Kesh it would not have happened ... In this respect Cage 11 had a particularly massive impact throughout the north within working-class community politics. (Interview with McCann, 12 March 2005)

While the retrospective views of Liggott and McCann highlight the undoubtedly central role of the republican prison struggle in the historic development of the Irish-language revival, they admittedly undervalue the pivotal role played by the original founders of the 'hidden' revival in the north, who planted the seeds that would flourish in the 1980s. Conversely, it is worth noting the views of other activists who highlight the disadvantages of the republican activists' involvement in the language revival. As Mac Póilín posits:

> Cé go dtáinig an fuinneamh atá i ngluaiseacht na teanga fá láthair ó ghluaiseacht na poblachta, agus gur thug seo a lán díograiseoirí isteach sa ghluaiseacht nach mbeadh ann murach an nasc seo, tá a lán míbhuntáistí le hardphróifíl s'acu chomh maith. Chuir seo leis an alienation a bhí ag aontachtóirí a shíleann anois gurb ionann rud éigin tugtha don Ghaeilge agus rud éigin a thabhairt do ghluaiseacht na poblachta agus cailleadh a lán díograiseoirí de mo mhachasamhail féin a bhí sásta obair don teanga ann féin ach nár mhothaigh compórdach mar gheall ar an nasc leis an pholaitíocht ... bíonn tionchar an-mhór sa ghearrthéarma ach tá buaireamh ann go fad-téarmach mura bhfuil an Ghaeilge in éadan rud ar bith ... caithfidh an íde-eolaíocht a bheith oibriste amach agus an cultúr agus an Ghaeilge a chuir chun cinn ar mhaithe leo féin agus ní ar bhonn frithiúil.

(Even though the current energy in the Irish-language movement has come from the republican movement, who have also brought a lot of activists into the movement who would not be there only for this link, there are also a lot of disadvantages to their high profile. This added to the alienation of unionists, who now think that something given to the Irish language amounts to something given to the republican movement and saw the loss of a lot of activists like myself who were happy to work for the language for its own sake, but who never felt comfortable due to the link with politics ... this has a big effect in the short term, but there is a worry in the longer term if the Irish language is not against anything ... the ideology has to be worked out and the culture and the language promoted for their own sake and not in an oppositional sense.) (Interview with Mac Póilin, 6 October 2006)

The above summations appear to demarcate between views that convey a highly politicised republican analysis of language revivalist activities and a more moderate culturalist interpretation. It would nonetheless be wholly restrictive to divide an overriding analysis of the contemporary language revival in the six counties into such rigid distinctions. Such a restrictive analytical framework is evident in the work of Kachuk (1993), who proposed an arbitrary division between alternative language activists, who wish to promote the Irish language in the 'Northern Ireland' context, and oppositional language activists, who view it as part of a 'revolutionary struggle for a "free and Irish," 32-county Republic of Ireland'. In assessing the dynamics of the bottom-up forms of language activism in the north of Ireland that impacted significantly in the contemporary period, perhaps a more flexible understanding can be gained through generally conceptualising the politics of decolonisation. Mac Siacais's overview is apt in this regard:

Rith sé linne sa phríosún mar a rith sé le Pádraig Mac Piarais, Ó Cadhain, Freire, Fanon agus eile go raibh ról lárnach ag an chultúr in athghabháil na tíre. Sna cásanna, bhí muid ag léamh go mion ar mheon an chóilíneachais agus ról an fhrithchóilíneachais agus an ról a bhí ag teangacha dúchasacha in san troid ar ais in aghaidh an chóilínigh. Scaip an teanga i measc na príosúnaigh ar an bhonn sin, mar áis streachailte agus bhí an claonadh réabhlóideach seo i measc na gcimí a scaoileadh saor ó thaobh na teanga de ...

Chomh maith leis sin, réabhlóidithe a bhí sna daoine a rinne éacht Bhóthair Seoighe. Gníomhairí radacacha polaitiúla a bhí

iontú a thuig tábhacht na Gaeilge mar ghléas díchoilínithe agus
an chumhacht a bhí aici mar ghléas streachailte. Fuair siadsan
a gcuid inspioráide ó ghluaiseacht na gcearta teangan agus
cearta sibhialta in san ghaeltacht, leithéidí Ó Cadhain agus iad.
Bhunaigh siad cur chuige s'acu ar an ghníomh. Baicle beag a
bhí iontu nach ndeachaigh i bhfeidhm ar an mhórphobal Béarla
go dtí aimsir na stailce ocrais ... an phríomhchosúlacht idir an
dá dhream seo ná gur daoine misniúla iad a chreid sa ghníomh
athbheochana ... díríonn daoine isteach barraíocht ar ghrúpaí
agus eagraíochtaí agus brúann siad daoine isteach i mboscaí.
An phríomhaidhm a bhí agus atá ag gníomhairí misniúla ná
athbheochan agus díchoiliniú a chothú agus a neartú. Is minic
go dtapaíonn gníomh deis agus mar a dúirt Fintan Lalor, 'níl aon
rud ina mhórcheist go dtí go ndéanann duine cinneadh mórchéist
a dhéanamh de'.

(We realised in the prison, as did Pádraig Mac Piarais, Ó Cadhain,
Freire, Fanon, etc., about the central role of culture in the
reconquest of a country. In the cages, we were reading in depth
about the mentality of colonisation and the role of anti-colo-
nialism and the role that native languages have in the fight back
against the coloniser. The language spread amongst the prisoners
on that basis, as a means of struggle, and this revolutionary
tendency in terms of the language was also evident in the prisoners
who were released ...

Similarly, those who created the Shaw's Road project were revolutionaries. They were radical political activists who understood
the importance of the Irish language as a means of decolonisation
and its power as a means of struggle. They got their inspiration
from the language and civil rights movement in the Gaeltacht,
with the likes of Ó Cadhain. They based their approach on action.
They were a small group who never really impacted on the wider
English-speaking community until the hunger strike period ...
the main similarity between the two groups of activists is that
they were courageous people who believed in revivalist action ...
people get overly focused on groups and organisations and push
people into certain categories and boxes. The primary aim of
courageous activists was and is to build and strengthen revival
and decolonisation. Action often forges opportunities, and as
Fintan Lalor says, 'nothing becomes a major issue until someone
decides to make a major issue of it'.) (Interview with Mac Siacais,
18 July 2003)

Mac Siacais's point on the arbitrary categorisation of language activists into 'boxes' is highly pertinent when analysing some of the more prominent interpretations of the Irish-language movement in the north of Ireland – for example, the social–anthropological reading of Camille O'Reilly (1999). She summarises the revival within the confines of three discourses: 'decolonising discourse', which she links to republicanism, nationalism and party politics; 'cultural discourse', in which the language should be kept separate from politics; and 'rights discourse', in which campaigning for the language as a human right attempts to solve the political–apolitical dichotomy. However, her analysis, both historic and contemporary, fails to fully grasp the overarching defining context of colonisation and the extent to which it conditions all responses to it, including the complex machinations of decolonisation.[1] Within the context of colonisation, the narrative evidence in this book has shown that forms of cultural revival, across a wide range of approaches, including language rights and identity building, amount to highly political manifestations of decolonisation.

In a similar vein, the rationale behind purely 'culturalist' activity, whereby minoritised languages are promoted for their 'own sake', within the confines of notions such as antiquarianism or linguistic beauty, is also shaped, both past and present, by the processes of colonialism. This point is made by Said (1993: 234):

> Exactly as in its triumphant period imperialism tended to license only a cultural discourse that was formulated from within it, today post-imperialism has permitted mainly a cultural discourse of suspicion on the part of formerly colonised peoples and of theoretical avoidance at most on the part of metropolitan intellectuals.

This point was made more explicitly by Fanon (1961: 179–80) in his call for radical decolonisation: 'You will never make colonialism blush for shame by spreading out little-known cultural treasures under its eyes.' Concurrently, writers and commentators like Ngugi Wa Thiong'o (1997) and Alexander (2003) provide ample practical evidence that the question of language in colonial and neocolonial contexts cannot be separated from fundamental problems such as social inequality, national sovereignty, political discrimination, and democratic or human rights.

In the Irish context, 'culturalist arguments of the Irish language which assert the primacy of language over political issues' have ultimately 'failed to return the language to its former position of mass popular use in day-to-day situations' (Ó Croidheáin 2006: 18). However, it is also worth noting that allowing language revival to be subsumed by a reductively nationalist state ideological project, as arguably happened in the neocolonial Free State, can also function to its detriment, by effectively emptying it of its decolonising or emancipatory content (ibid.: 161). A 'thoroughgoing decolonisation [as] envisaged by Memmi or Ó Cadhain', necessitating a bottom-up projection of a 'truly decolonised identity' (Mac Síomóin 1994: 69), would be a fitting legacy for the contributors to this book.

# Epilogue

For the colonised just as for the coloniser, there is no way out other than a complete end to colonisation. The refusal of the colonised cannot be anything but absolute, that is, not only revolt, but a revolution.

Albert Memmi (1965: 194)

The development of the language movement in the north witnessed a corresponding growth in self-reliance and self-respect amongst active groups and individuals, in which the bottom-up approach to community revivalism represented an 'autonomist space' creating 'a new level of confidence and self-awareness that propels people to organise and become agents of change' (Harris 2007: 14). The powerful social dimension to these new structures also created an empowering sense of identity. Furthermore, the Irish-medium educational movement represented a counter-hegemonic 'education for emancipation', a popular system whereby power remained in the community, offering a cultural and linguistic alternative to the dominant societal model.

The British government obstructed these developments through denying official recognition to Irish-medium schools and promoting the notion of the language and 'Irishness' as illegitimate, thereby further alienating those involved from the state. This created a pattern of intransigence met by resistance that fuels radical Irish-language activism to this day. One of the younger generation of activists, Ciarán Mac Giolla Bhéin, describes how Meánscoil Feirste's high-profile campaign for state recognition led to his personal radicalisation as a pupil:

Bhí rud ar leith fá'n mheánscoil. Bhí muidinne ag glanadh na scoile agus ár dtuismitheoirí ag bailiú airgid i rith na hoíche sna chlubanna éagsúla ar an bhóthar. Bhí achan duine tiomanta don tionscnamh agus ag eagrú rothaíochta urraithe agus siúlóidí sléibhe srl ar ár son, agus ar mhaithe le hoideachas s'againne. Bíodh is gur thuig muid gur streachailt a bhí i gceist, thug an tacaíocht seo iomlán muiníne dúinn go n-éireodh linn, rud a tharla sa deireadh. So [mar sin] nuair a d'fhág mise an scoil, mhothaigh mise go raibh dualgas ormsa rud éigin a chur ar ais isteach sa streachailt.

(There was something exceptional about the Meánscoil. We, as pupils, cleaned the school and our parents went out at nights collecting money in the local clubs on the road. Everyone was totally committed to the project and organising sponsored cycles and sponsored mountain walks, etc. on our behalf and for the sake of our education. Although we knew that we were involved in a struggle, this help gave us the confidence that we would succeed, and that's exactly what happened in the end. Therefore, when I eventually left school, I felt it my duty to put something back into the struggle. (Interview with Mac Giolla Bhéin, 23 October 2007)

Meánscoil Feirste eventually succeeded in 1996, following an international campaign, when it became an issue of 'parity of esteem' during the peace process (O'Reilly 1999: 132–3). However, the British government, as at the beginning of the twentieth century, arguably only acceded to demands when the pressure became so great that to do otherwise appeared detrimentally intransigent.

This peace process culminated in the 1998 Good Friday Agreement, which promised a 'New Era', wherein the language would be 'encouraged and facilitated in public and private life' (Muller 2010: 70). However, no sooner was the ink dry on the GFA, than, in time-honoured colonial fashion, a senior civil servant, Tony Canavan, highlighted the ambiguity of this commitment in an internal policy document.[1] 'What these worthy sentiments might mean in practice is a matter of interpretation and we could argue that our interpretation is as valid as anyone else's' (ibid.: 71). In addition, the Irish language's development suffered further impediment, with its statutory promotion linked to that of Ulster Scots.[2] This permitted unionism to mimic nationalist arguments of 'parity of esteem', thereby frustrating proportionate allocation of resources. In effect, the British government formulated a policy of 'minimalism in the protection, promotion, or development of the Irish language, and disproportional generosity in the promotion of Ulster Scots' (ibid.: 230).

More recently, the British have adhered to this policy regarding the long-standing demand for an Irish Language Act, which would grant similar legal protection to that enjoyed by Irish speakers in the south of Ireland, and Welsh and Scottish Gaelic speakers. Having agreed to enact legislation at Westminster, following the 2006 St Andrews Agreement,[3] the British government then delayed public consultation, before announcing a second consultation process that extended until after the restoration of devolution at Stormont, thereby granting Ulster unionism a veto over any future Irish Language Act.[4] This continued unionist intransigence towards Irish has its roots in the age-old settler–colonial psyche, as articulated in the DUP's (Democratic Unionist Party – the foremost unionist party in the north of Ireland) submission to the consultation process, which stated:

> The Irish language serves no communicative purpose in Northern Ireland, but simply the promotion of a political cause. An Irish Language Act is divisive, would alienate the majority population in Northern Ireland and would be a complete waste of money. (DUP Party submission; see DCAL 2007)

A similar attitude was evident in submissions from more hard-line elements in the Orange Order:

> It is plain silly and wrong to give precedence to a minority language that nobody really speaks as part of a political concession to Sinn Féin/IRA. We would earnestly ask the government to reconsider this unwanted legislation, which is discriminatory and not applicable to over 90 per cent of the population. (Armagh Orange Lodge submission; see DCAL 2007)

The Irish-speaking community counters such assertions with rights-based arguments. A leading language legislation expert, Fernand de Varennes, argues that minority speakers should have the opportunity to use their languages, as

> the respect of the language principles of individuals ... flows from a fundamental right and is not some special concession or privileged treatment. Simply put, it is the right to be treated equally without discrimination, to which everyone is entitled. (Ibid.)

Nonetheless, the British government consistently rejects the compelling logic of an Irish Language Act, thereby reinforcing unionist intransigence.

Indeed, the British government DCAL (Department for Culture, Arts and Leisure) document on the proposed Irish Language Act ignored the role of planned cultural colonisation in language decline, which occurred, in their view, 'due to the dominant growth of English in the fields of industry and trade' (DCAL 2007). Additionally, the introduction defined Irish as 'controversial' because unionists held 'genuine fears and concerns' about 'the erosion of their British identity' (ibid.). Thus, in colonial vein, the British excuse discriminatory views as 'genuine fears', thereby denying rights to Irish speakers. Furthermore, the British position epitomises the counter-argument of monolinguals and speakers of the 'powerful languages' internationally, who disingenuously portray minority rights as a threat to the majority. Arguably, it is not the demand for rights but rather the continued denial of those rights that renders minoritised languages 'controversial' (May 2002: 312).

Internationally, such obstructionism stems from a highly politicised neoliberal consensus, representing a modern extension of imperialism and neocolonisation. Thus, these processes of neoliberal globalisation have created unprecedented 'linguacide' based firmly on political and socio-economic inequality. Nevertheless, minority languages will 'continue so patently to play a significant (even central) part in many of the political disputes in the world today' (May 2002: 316) as neoliberalism meets with opposition from people who completely 'resent the erosion of their cultural identities, the loss of control over their lives, over their governments, over their countries, and ultimately, over the fate of the earth' (Castells 1997: 69).

Indeed, echoing Castells, Gaeilgeoirí like Mac Siacais define their continued activism as resisting and challenging neoliberal hegemony:

Le domhandú, tá iarracht ag dul ar aghaidh ár gcultúir ar fad a shlogadh isteach in aon chultúr Meiriceánach, Sasanach amháin, is nua-impiriúlachas é a shíolraíonn ó sheanmheon na himpireachta ... Ach, mar sin féin, tá pobail dhúchasacha ann fud fad an domhain atá réidh le troid ar ais ar son an rud atá le cailliúint againn.

(With globalisation, there is a concerted effort being made to subsume all our cultures into the one Anglo-American culture; its simple neo-imperialism that derives from the same old aspirations of empire ... However, minority communities and native peoples throughout the world are ready and willing to fight back for all that is being lost.) (Interview with Mac Siacais, 24 October 2007)

These views conform to an ideology of decolonisation, which positioned the language in the wider fusion of progressive forms of nationalism and socialism, playing a pivotal role in the early-twentieth-century Irish revolution, and continuing to motivate many current activists (Ó Tuathaigh 2011: 104). That ideology ultimately directed a people-centred decolonisation as evident in transformational activism, such as the *gaelscoileanna* founded on emancipatory voluntary endeavour.

Nonetheless, bottom-up community activism has benefited from state support post-GFA, with the Education Order (NI) placing a statutory duty upon the Department of Education to encourage and facilitate Irish-medium education, resulting in the formation of Comhairle na Gaelscolaíochta in 2000 and Iontaobhas na Gael-scolaíochta (Irish-Medium Trust Fund) in 2001 to provide financial support and expand Irish-medium provision (Muller 2010: 51). Over 4,000 children in the north are currently educated through Irish in 81 schools, from preschool to post-primary level. However, despite the noteworthy achievements in the intervening years, the establishment, development and long-term sustainability of Irish-medium schools still largely depend on bottom-up voluntary endeavour. Consequently, many activists criticise statutory organisations like Comhairle na Gaelscolaíochta, stating that a more proactive developmental approach would bear greater fruit.[5]

Nevertheless, as with any popular grassroots movement, rapid growth and success have brought the inevitable dangers of institutionalisation, assimilation and manipulation by the state or by conservative elites intent on maintaining the status quo (Ó Croidheáin 2006: 315). This is particularly pertinent in processes of conflict resolution, which often yield greater avenues of state recognition and funding. On this note, Rudé (1980: 36) asks the question, 'What happens to this new popular ideology, forged in the fire of revolution, when the "popular" phase ... is over or when the counter-revolution sets in?' Theorists of institutionalisation point to 'a loss of radical impetus within a social movement without the achievement of real gains' (Hourigan 2006: 127). In these processes, 'popular organisations always face the danger of becoming an appendage of state clientelism as mass participation withers' and 'are often incorporated into the state as local mediators with a power to distribute resources' (Harris 2007: 14).

This usually occurs when 'political elites' use 'social capital to divide and conquer a movement network and marginalize dissent within the public sphere' (Hourigan 2006: 138). In essence, 'the structures created by the dominant strata to implement their hegemony' consume oppositional ideologies (Gledhill 2000: 92). Indeed, 'elites may even be able to manipulate such reactive oppositional discourses to their own advantage' (ibid.). In a more general analysis of the capacity of the advanced capitalist and neocolonial state to carry out this function, Stuart Hall points to the 'purposeful construction and manipulation of popular consent' that neutralises opposing forces and incorporates 'some strategic elements of popular opinion into its own hegemonic project' (Scraton 2007: 226).

As Ó Maolchluiche speculated:

Sa lá atá inniu ann, tá a lán contúirtí os comhair na hathbheochana, bíodh is go bhfuil muid ag dul chun cinn i rith an ama ... de bhrí gur chruthaigh muid a lán fostaíochta, is rud nádúrtha ar bhealach go bhfaighidh muid daoine úra atá ag obair san earnáil s'againn ar mhaithe le careers s'acu féin ... titeann caighdeán na ngníomhaithe ar an bhealach seo agus is cinnte nach bhfuil daoine ann chomh tiomanta ó thaobh na Gaeilge agus a bhí fiche nó tríocha bliain ó shin.

(Notwithstanding the considerable progress that has been made, there are still dangers in terms of the cultural revival ... because a lot of employment was created I suppose it's inevitable that we are getting some people working in the Irish-language sector to promote their own careers ... this lowers the standard of the activism and there is no doubt that there is not the same degree of commitment amongst people as there was 20 or 30 years ago.) (Interview with Ó Maolchuiche, 28 July 2003)

While such trends may appear inevitable following the financial mainstreaming of the Irish-language sector post-GFA, they nevertheless highlight the danger of 'rule by quango', or over-reliance on the state playing the role of a 'benign benefactor' (Williams 2000: 17). Eoghan Ó Néill also identified the potential for polarisation between 'respectable' and 'radical' activists:

Má amharcann tú ar an Bhreatain Bheag, d'fhás dhá ghluaiseacht teanga éagsúla de réir mar a d'fhorbair an athbheochan. Anois tá taobh measúil ann agus taobh radacach ann. I bpobal na Gaeilge inniu tá cuid mhaith don taobh measúil againn ... ach níl mé chomh cinnte go bhfuil an taobh radacach chomh flúirseach agus a bhí fiche bliain ó shin. Caithfear béim a chur ar an ghlúin úr atá ag teacht fríd na Gaelscoileanna agus tuilleadh díograiseoirí radacacha a chothú.

(If you look at Wales, two separate movements developed the more the revival grew. Now they have a respectable side and a radical side. In the Irish-language community today, there is a lot of the respectable side, but I'm not so sure that the radical side is as abundant as it was 20 years ago. The emphasis must be put on the new generation coming through the Irish schools to create additional radical activists.) (Interview with Ó Néill, 29 September 2006)

Despite the differing circumstances of more overt and proactive state support, the Welsh example provides an interesting comparison in institutionalisation, where Williams (Muller 2010: 59) identifies a 'deep ambiguity ... about the dominance of government in language revitalisation because of the tendency of institutionalisation to create dependency, severing control of language promotion from the community'. Notwithstanding the merit of such comparisons, the existing minimalism and outright hostility towards the Irish language in the north undermines too direct a comparison with Wales.

McCoy (2001: 213) clearly overestimates the degree of change in the north of Ireland, when he argues that the Irish-language movement has 'undergone a rapid transformation from counter-culture to officialdom' during the peace process, due to a 'radical transformation' from 'reactive' to 'proactive' attitudes among British officialdom (ibid.: 216). These conclusions on 'proactive' British policy are arguably unfounded, considering the patterns in neocolonial methodology whereby overtly discriminatory practices become more veiled and sophisticated, as recently demonstrable in the Irish Language Act campaign. Thus 'moves by powerful states to appear more liberal and fair towards minority languages are merely symbolic moves in the power game' (Rahman 2001: 65).

Whether through close links between the language movement and grassroots communities or the continued structural manifestations of neocolonialism within the northern state, the language issue retains potency in heightening sociocultural and political awareness amongst younger activists such as Mac Giolla Bhéin:

Mothaím go bhfuil mé ag leanúint leis an íde-eolaíocht radacach teanga a d'fhorbair Mac Piarais, Ó Cadhain agus Ó Seachnasaigh atá mar chuid d'fhealsúnacht pholaitiúil s'agam i leith na tíre seo agus an domhain araon. Ar ndóigh, athraíonn an suíomh catha i gcónaí ... I ndiaidh daichead bliana de streachailt, tá neart rudaí nach bhfuil muid sásta glacadh leis, tá bunlíne againn anois ó thaobh na Gaeilge de agus ardófar seo i gcónaí sa todhchaí chun cinntiú go leanann an réabhlóid s'againne ag dul ó neart go neart.

(I feel that I'm continuing with the radical decolonising ideology that was promoted by Pearse, Ó Cadhain and Sands as part of my overall political philosophy regarding this country and the entire world for that matter. Of course, the battleground continually evolves ... After 40 years of struggle, there are many things that we are not prepared to accept; we have a bottom line now regarding the Irish language that we will continue to raise in the future to ensure that our revolution goes from strength to strength.) (Interview with Mac Giolla Bhéin, 23 October 2007)

Within this rationale, Irish-language activism and the numerous bottom-up community empowerment projects and self-sustaining school communities can still be defined as a transformative expression of 'cultural resistance' and a form of 'counter-consciousness' (Freire 1972b: 68–9). However, to simplify the nature of this 'resistance' in the north's contemporary 'new dispensation', post-St Andrew's 2006, would be to underplay the political complexities of new conditions forged under the emerging status quo.

From the hour the Stormont Assembly commenced, unionism continued their discriminatory agenda by taking the DCAL ministry and effectively vetoing the fundamental demand for an Irish Language Act.[6] Evidence of the DUP's successful strategy of obstructionism is provided by former DCAL minister Edwin Poots, who pointed to the failure of the Irish Language Act and proceeded to increase funding for Ulster Scots (Muller 2010: 132). His party colleague Gregory Campbell, who assumed ministerial responsibility in April 2008, promised to develop a single strategy for Irish and Ulster Scots 'that narrows or eliminates the disparity' between the two.[7] Campbell's successor in June 2009, Nelson McCausland, further exacerbated the sense of alienation felt by Irish speakers towards the new power-sharing arrangements by his flagrant intransigence towards the language.

Frustration with marginalisation in the 'new dispensation' has led to activists publicly criticising the nationalist political parties and long-term allies of the language. The editorials of *LÁ Nua* consistently highlighted an absence of resources and rights for the Irish-speaking community. In January 2008, Eoghan Ó Néill questioned Sinn Féin and the SDLP's avoidance of the DCAL ministerial brief, asking, 'Was it ... because they have their own agenda ... and that the welfare of the Irish language would have to wait?' He concluded that 'the six Nationalist ministers are failing to show leadership and the Irish-language community will pay the price' (Ó Néill 2008). When Foras na Gaeilge stopped the paper's funding in 2008, with eight jobs lost, the editor labelled *LÁ Nua* as a 'victim of power-sharing', because it 'gave voice to criticism from many in the Irish-language community who were disappointed at the way the Irish language was being treated in the "new dispensation" between Sinn Féin and the DUP' (*AN* 2008).

Within neocolonialism, leading social actors from the subordinate community gain limited state autonomy in a skilful strategic framework that absolves the powerful of direct responsibility, thereby casting 'local mediators' as 'instruments of suppression on behalf of the neo-colonialists' (Nkrumah 1964: 101). In the six counties, this phenomenon has fostered internal divisions, disunity and confusion within republican and nationalist civil society. Ironically, therefore, minoritised language communities often find that they 'had it better when the iron fist was still in fashion', when the 'source of their misfortunes' was more tangible and they were wholly self-sufficient rather than dependent on state support (Fishman 2005: 9). Muller (2010: 132) argues that this reflects the 'double bind in which many minoritised language communities find themselves. How far can they go in criticising the parties most likely to act in a positive manner on their behalf?' This very conundrum emerged regarding Irish-medium education when Sinn Féin's minister, Caitríona Ruane, held the education portfolio in the reconvened power-sharing executive of 2007.

As a proactive Irish speaker, Ruane took immediate action by approving development proposals for three Irish-medium schools, including Gaelscoil Éanna, which British direct rule minister Maria Eagle had rebuked in late 2006. However, her department's 'Review of Irish-Medium Education' (December 2008) contentiously proposed that post-primary IME (Irish Medium Education) should be developed through units and streams in English-medium schools rather than by following the independent free-standing model favoured by language revivalists. This precipitated the refusal of two proposals for a small freestanding post-primary school in County Tyrone, Coláiste Spéirín, which closed in August 2009 amid bitter recriminations amongst its founders and supporters.[8]

In February 2011, the inherent contradictions in the consensus politics of the 'New Northern Ireland' led Coláiste Feirste, Belfast's Irish-medium post-primary, to take a judicial review against the department because of its continued refusal to provide transport services. Despite the provision of over 2,020 dedicated buses to post-primary schools across the north, with some grammar schools allocated ten such buses, DE refused to provide transport to the Falls Road school, thus forcing pupils from Downpatrick to travel upwards of 5 hours a day on public transport (AN 2011). The chairperson of the school's board of governors, Seán Mistéil, stated that 'the Department's withholding of bus services is an outrage ... an injury inflicted on children on many levels', claiming that 'discriminatory treatment of Coláiste Feirste students will cripple the growth of the IM sector, in direct violation of Article 89 of the Education Order 1998' (ibid.).

However, amidst widespread bemusement, Ruane's department stated that the refusal was 'practical', as its statutory duty to 'encourage and facilitate IME' was non-enforceable under the merely 'aspirational' GFA (ibid.). Nevertheless, in his landmark ruling of 25 October 2011, Judge Seamus Treacy announced that 'DE has failed to give proper weight and consideration' to its statutory obligations, which are 'intended to have practical consequences and legislative significance' (Gaelscéal 2011). Treacy's dismissal of the DE argument that the 'proper discharge of this duty' would 'set a precedent in respect of other education sectors to whom this statutory duty is not owed' has opened the door for additional rights-based campaigning for the Irish-language movement (Mac Ionnrachtaigh 2011d).

These divisions within republican civil society were perhaps unavoidable under a peace process which often imposes consensus politics over the rights of those on the downside of power relations. In this context, post-agreement ideological jargon elevates new agendas such as 'good relations' and 'shared future' in a manner that entrenches 'cross-sectarian social relations' that derive their power 'from an alliance between cross-sectarian political entrepreneurs, a new cross-sectarian middle-class, civil service, and bureaucratic elite' (McKearney 2011: 17). Thus a peace-process orthodoxy has emerged from Stormont that embodies a 'new social and institutional ossification of sectarianism', under which progressive, oppositional activists must choose to 'generally remain silent or to become apolitical' (ibid.: 18). The assimilationist orthodoxy of the 'New Northern Ireland' arguably seeks to impose the state's terms of reference at all costs, while obscuring unequal power relations.

Indeed, DCAL's launch of the 'Líofa 2015' ('Fluent 2015') initiative, in September 2011, demonstrates that the language movement has not escaped this all-pervasive discourse. The Sinn Féin minister, Caral Ní Chuilín, an ardent supporter of Irish and republican ex-prisoner, announced the commendable aim of encouraging '1,000 people from all walks of life across the north to sign up to be fluent in Irish by 2015' (*Irish News* 2011). Nonetheless, the media essentially commandeered the project's launch to promote the assimilationist discourse, a move encapsulated in Ní Chuilín's own stated intention to introduce 'measures aimed at de-politicising the Irish language and returning it to a status where it can be practised and enjoyed by people of all backgrounds and traditions' (ibid.). This remark eerily echoed the relentless NIO discourse of 'depoliticisation', such as when, in 1990, the then secretary of state, Brian Mawhinney, sought to 'take the Irish language out of politics'. Indeed, this aim conformed to the policy of 'political vetting', which removed funding from community organisations like Glór na nGael and many Irish nursery schools due to perceived 'links with republicanism'. This 'depolicisation' agenda portrays the Irish-language movement as sectarian, thus incongruously blaming discriminatory state policy on links with nationalism and republicanism.

Unsurprisingly, this sparked intense debate within the Irish-language community, with some critically engaged activists viewing Líofa as 'merely a symbolic, yet highly political move'[9] and 'the latest example of the New Northern Ireland trying to "hijack" our language movement by imposing its own terms of reference on how we promote the language' (Mac Ionnrachtaigh 2011b). This critical analysis provoked concerted responses from Sinn Féin activists, one of which described such critics as 'elitist Gaeilgoiristas' (Kearney, in *AN*, 24 September 2011). Clearly, as Muller (2010: 230–1) argues, 'former advocates of independence, now seemingly supporting institutions which reinforce interlocking relations may experience unease and insecurity', ultimately leading to 'defensive/aggressive action to stifle criticism in the media and in the community; to vilify analytical commentators as "negative"; to sideline particular NGOs; to withdraw funding and so on'.

Indeed, the inherent consolidation of an all-pervasive state hegemony, typical within conflict resolution processes, makes a culture of critique a prerequisite for any meaningful transformational change. For example, Feilim Ó hAdhmaill promotes a more nuanced understanding of the dialectical relationship between the state and civil society in the protracted struggle for social change: 'If we cannot have challenge, critique, rational debate, and indeed, disagreement, without feeling threatened with abuse and marginalisation we simply reinforce a culture of quiet, unquestioning acceptance, within our communities, stunting even further the potential for change and progress' (Ó hAdhmaill 2011). In arguing for the independence of the language movement, Ó hAdhmaill indicates that this 'democratic dialectic' (Harris 2007: 17) should provide a complementary rather than conflictive dynamic: 'We shouldn't be careless with our allies but then neither should we allow our vision, our needs, our demands, to be constrained by them. A healthy society allows campaigning and lobbying and critique to flourish; through that we get change' (Ó hAdhmaill 2011).

The relationship between activists exercising limited forms of state power and those civil-society organisations and movements campaigning for structural change is similar the world over. In contextualising the new revolutionary movements in South America, for example, Jerry Harris outlines the issues at hand:

These different strategies for social change, focused on either the state or civil society, naturally create tensions and, at times, bitter disagreements. On the one hand, activists in civil society often label those involved in the electoral arena as untrustworthy reformists or, worse, as traitors to the mass democratic project. On the other, party militants trying to get the vote out see autonomists as unwilling to confront the real problems of power and responsibility ... The tension between the two strategies, state power versus autonomous civil society and what can be accomplished in either political realm, will and should continue to be a contradiction within any truly dynamic democratic society. Establishing counter-hegemonic positions within the state and society are both necessary, with both having their strengths and dangers of co-option and corruption. Sometimes, they will complement and strengthen each other; sometimes their interaction will reflect different needs, perspectives, pressures and strategies. (Harris 2007: 17)

Yet, radical social change through this 'democratic dialectic' requires 'considerable skills in analysis, negotiation and power brokering, and the ability to distinguish that which is illusory' (Muller 2010: 10). The absence of such issue-based alliance building and an inability to maintain a counter-hegemonic ideological fervour amongst activists could ultimately lead to the consolidation of hegemonic power structures and the assimilation of the Irish-language movement.

In periods of stagnation, institutionalisation can cultivate the aforementioned disunity and disillusion, gifting the initiative to the state. Currently, funding for the Irish-language community and voluntary sector is under the threat of a 'rationalisation' process stemming from the decision from the North–South Ministerial Council to reconfigure Foras na Gaeilge's support for Irish-language NGOs (Muller 2010: 135).[10] Precipitated by the spectacular collapse of the Celtic Tiger in 2008, Eamon Ó Cuív, then minister for Gaeltacht and rural affairs, promised to make 'significant savings' by 'collapsing' and 'merging' Irish-language organisations as part of savage government spending cuts (Mac Ionnrachtaigh 2011c).[11] Foras na Gaeilge's intention to introduce 'scheme-based' funding prioritises 'a top-down trend towards competitive tendering, which can force funding below subsistence levels, disempower and divide' (Muller 2010: 135). Consequently, the implementation of this divisive state 'rationalisation' methodology could 'result in growing isolation and competition over social resources based solely on each organisation's immediate needs', which 'makes it easy for the state to incorporate some and attack others, controlling certain social movements to strengthen its own hold over civil society' (Harris 2007: 14).

The greatest impediment to the assimilationist designs of both states in Ireland, however, is the historic capacity of the Irish-language community to maintain its independence through radical campaigning and a willingness to organise from below amongst communities (Mac Ionnrachtaigh 2011b). The enduring legacy of the six-county revival proves that such activism creates 'a critical theory of knowledge' (Freire: 1972a: 68–9) promoting active participation, empowerment and purposeful action. This encourages a radical perspective through which individuals can critically examine their culture and politics in local, national and global contexts. Such activism easily conforms to an ideology of decolonisation that 'can continue to imbue the language movement with that radical edge that provides succour from the dangers of complacency and institutionalisation' (Mac Ionnrachtaigh 2011a: 153). Thus, as an emancipatory, participatory vehicle for change, this ideology is 'one of the most effective instruments for keeping the revolution from becoming institutionalised and stratified in a counter-revolutionary bureaucracy; for counter-revolution is carried out by revolutionaries who become reactionary' (Freire 1972a: 118). It can help maintain 'a vibrant Irish-language movement ... which is prepared to debate the issues, create its own agenda, challenge the "common sense" views of the world and indeed make its own history' (Ó hAdhmaill 2011).

According to Helen Ó Murchú, this ideology should be defined by a new republicanism, a 'civic republicanism' that encourages 'civic values once again' and 'human freedom' (Walsh 2011a: 98). She argues that this republicanism should represent

> the liberation of people, liberation from the understanding that they are dependent, that things happen to them, that they have control over their own cultural future. It means empowerment of people to the freedom of having the choice, a choice of language; and of having a right, language rights. (Ibid.)

This corresponds with the idealism promoted by the progressive strand of the Irish Ireland movement at the beginning of the last century. This movement promoted concepts of 'civic virtue and political integrity' that 'reflected the enlightenment republicanism of Rousseau', which 'rejected self-interest' in favour of 'self-sacrifice for the common good' (McCluskey 2011: 157). For example, the revolutionary self-help endeavour that initiated the Shaw's Road Urban Gaeltacht community proved that civil-society activism is at its strongest when it develops community self-sufficiency. This also lends weight to Fishman's (2005:10) view that an over-reliance on proactive state support is 'tantamount to succumbing to slow-paced euthanasia rather than to the firing squad'. Likewise, the Shaw's Road initiative demonstrated the central importance of inter-generational language transmission in the sustenance of minoritised language communities (Fishman 1991). Radical ideology will not suffice as a support base for the normalisation of minoritised languages, which must have social use and functionality if they are to survive (ibid.: 396). For instance, one such 'realistic revivalist campaign' envisages channelling the significant existing resources towards the creation of a living community of between 50,000 and 100,000 Irish speakers, based partly on a sophisticated publicity strategy amongst sympathetic members of the English-speaking community (Mac Siomóin (2011: 249–50).

Indeed, the world capitalist crisis has created the potential for ideas of republican civic virtue to take root. The comprehensive collapse of the Celtic Tiger in 2008 exposed the southern state as 'a sheep in wolf's clothing', ill equipped to maintain its precarious status as 'a service industry to a global elite' (Ó Croidheáin 2006: 309). Its insatiable and unregulated economic growth model ignored the concept of 'equitable distribution of income, wealth and opportunities' and oversaw the 'exclusion of a significant segment of the population from participation in the economy' (Bradley and Kennelly 2008: 75). These social consequences only exacerbated the legacy of colonialism and neocolonialism, where a weak sense of identity and underlying inferiority complexes reinforce existing alienation in a 'republic' with one of the highest rates of income inequality, drug and alcohol abuse, unequal access to health services, and poor levels of literacy in the EU (Moane 2002: 110).

Ideologically, the Celtic Tiger imbued contemporary Irish culture with Anglo-American values of materialism and consumption (Mac Siomóin 2011: 244). This neoliberalism promotes crass individualism and selfishness in place of community cohesion and social responsibility (ibid.: 246). Conversely, a contemporary Irish cultural revival can create an alternative discourse, prioritising a 'dynamic, competent, positive, creative' approach towards an 'energetic mentality that breeds a self-respect and self-confidence' through community empowerment (Ó Tuathaigh 2011: 100, my translation). This revival and recovery can herald a new model of 'development' that is 'more holistic and more inclusive of economic, social, cultural, environmental and linguistic aspects of a community's life', leading communities to 'engage more closely with the meaning, process and outcome of development' (Walsh 2011a: 407).

Such a reconceptualised development would recognise the Irish language as a key contributor 'to a more participative process where communities take control of their own development, rather than being guided by an external model inappropriate to their particular circumstances' (ibid.: 407–8). This overlaps with the Bolivarian concept of 'endogenous development', which aims to involve 'the mass of the population that has been excluded from their share of the achievements of modern civilisation' (Lebowitz 2006: 40). This model welds economic to human development, producing a 'democratic, participatory, and protagonistic' society (ibid.: 49). The current worsening economic crisis and associated sociopolitical upheaval provide us with a unique opportunity to begin a debate on what form such a development should take.

Likewise, the limited power and influence exercised by the northern assembly has been exposed by their grudging implementation of savage public-spending cuts administered through Westminster. Thus, the reality of widespread 'social injustice and material deprivation' as 'determining, structural contexts' has challenged the official discourse of a successful 'society in transition' (McAlister, Scraton and Haydon 2009: 156). Additionally, the trans-genera-tional trauma of the political and military conflict has left a residue of marginalised, disadvantaged and under-resourced communities whose collective alienation seems most prevalent amongst the young (ibid.). If a newly energised civic republicanism is to address real and relevant issues, it must draw its support 'from among the more disadvantaged sections of society' and 'demand a fundamental change to the existing status quo' (McKearney 2011: 214). This book demonstrates that the Irish-language community revival is capable of playing a transformational and integral role in this endeavour.

Therefore, a progressive future for the language movement rests on its positioning 'as part of a generalised movement against oppression of all kinds, rather than in splendid isolation' (Ó Cathasaigh 2011: 29). For social movements exclusively wedded to 'specific social sectors often fail to develop lasting social solidarity and a united political strategy' (Harris 2007: 14). If the language movement is to align itself with an emerging counter-hegemonic politics of the left, it must build working alliances with other radical civil society organisations that have emerged from the rubble of economic collapse.[12] Such alliances must be strategically flexible and ultimately conditioned by the specific challenges of building sustainable language revival communities. This will also require alliance building with sectors, organisations, and state institutions of differing political persuasions in order to positively influence unequal power structures and attract additional state resources and wider community support (Ó Tuathaigh 2011: 106).

Accordingly, successful resistance struggles 'may entail strategic acquiescence; the recognition that limited compliance may expand the scope for other strategies of resistance' (Buntman 2003: 252). These strategies must move beyond defeatist rhetorical grandstanding. Resistance is 'not simply about saying no, reacting, refusing, resisting, but also and primarily about social creativity, introducing new values and aims, new forms of co-operation and action' (ibid.: 126). The relationships between the state, civil society and the market are extremely complex and the 'idea that any one theory or strategy can encompass and account for the whole of these complexities assumes a narrow and reductionist approach' (Harris 2007: 23). Therefore, grassroots activism requires an adequate understanding of these relationships, in order to develop strategies appropriate to the existing dialectic (ibid.).

In the twenty-first century, a relevant Irish-language movement will require a radical yet flexible approach, which challenges and influences the state for requisite rights and entitlements, yet does not depend on it for survival. One topical example of a revivalist project epitomising this parallel approach was RITH 2010 and 2012, a biannual nationwide festival involving a continuous sponsored run across Ireland, inspired by the highly successful Basque Korrika.[13] Involving thousands of people in every corner of the island, this project attracted substantial and diverse support, fostered community participation and empowerment and raised much-needed funds for grassroots revivalist projects. In this sense, it represented 'individuals and communities' playing a 'trans-formational ... part in the revolutionary process of changing the general relations of power in Irish society', while simultaneously challenging the current global Anglo-American cultural hegemony (Ó Croidheáin 2006: 18).

The civic republicanism inherent in the commentary of the language activists in this book contributes immeasurably to our collective understanding of culture, community, resistance and revival. By projecting their voices via an oral history, it drew on Nigerian Wole Soyinka's commitment to the 'conscious activity of recovering what has been hidden, lost, repressed, denigrated, or indeed simply denied' (Mac Síomóin 2006: 39–40). By emphasising the historic legacy of colonialism and neocolonialism to the present, this book aims not merely to challenge the dominant mainstream narrative, but to explore alternative conceptions of history from which more liberating future trajectories can arise. The republican prisoners and language activists engaged in this grassroots transformative struggle have provided a lasting legacy for a new generation of language activists, who must now 'make their own history ... under circumstances existing already, given and transmitted from the past' (Marx 1979: 103).

Globally, ordinary people are channelling aspirations for social justice through structural participatory, democratic forms of activism that oppose socio-economic inequality and cultural assimilation. The contemporary Irish-language revival undoubtedly provides a staging post in this wider struggle for a better world. Fittingly then, this book represents a 'history from below' that attempts to make an activist contribution to the wider project of decolonisation. This fits neatly with Maori activist Tuhiwai Smith's definition of the subtext and potential of such contributions: 'The past, our stories local and global, the present, our communities, cultures, languages and social practices – all may be spaces of marginalisation, but they have also become spaces of resistance and hope' (1999: 4).

# Notes

## INTRODUCTION

1. This jurisdiction is known officially as 'Northern Ireland', but is referred to by many who view it as an illegal entity as the 'north of Ireland' or 'the six counties'. This book will alternate between these two descriptions so as to avoid asserting the state view over the claims of a people to the right of national self-determination.
2. Long Kesh prison is situated in Lisburn just ten miles outside Belfast and had both the cages and the H-Blocks at its location. During this research, the common terminology used by the participants and narrators will be used when referring to the prison. Thus, the terms 'Long Kesh', 'cages' and 'H-Blocks' will be used instead of the official names, such as 'the compounds' and 'HMP Maze'.
3. The school moved to new premises behind Beechmount leisure centre on the Falls Road, only a few hundred yards from the Cultúrlann, in 1999 in my seventh school year. The current multi-million pound facility exists on the same site and the school, renamed Coláiste Feirste in 2005, now has over 550 pupils.
4. The cages, or compounds, of Long Kesh were opened in 1971 to house political prisoners, both internees and sentenced prisoners. Prisoners were held in old-style Nissen huts and effectively had political status. Internees were imprisoned in the internment camp and sentenced prisoners were held in the sentenced camp. The cages were closed in 1987, when the remainder of the prisoners were transferred to the H-Blocks (see McKeown 2001).
5. The Ardscoil was founded in 1911 as headquarters of Belfast Gaelic League. It resided in Queen's Street at the centre of language revival activity in the city before moving to Divis Street in 1928, where it continued in the same vein until being accidentally burned down in 1985 (Foras na Gaeilge 2007).
6. Cumann Chluain Ard was set up in 1936, during a period of mass unemployment, by 'two unemployed young men, Seamus Maxwell and Liam Rooney, in an old covered gateway in Kane Street beside Clonard Monastery in west Belfast' (Mac Seáin 2006: 4). It was a focal point for cultural activism thereafter and eventually moved to Hawthorne Street, where it remains as an Irish-language centre today.

## CHAPTER 1

1. For example, Curtis (2003: 323) highlights Britain's malevolent role in Kenya, including the killing by colonial government forces of around 10,000 Africans in the 1950s, while he also provides evidence of Britain's complicity in the deaths of over 1 million Indonesians in 1965 (ibid.: 387).
2. Curtis (2003: 234–5) shows that the current roots of neoliberal globalisation lie in the US and UK post-Second World War plan to take control of the world economy through the 'open door' economic exploitation of key regions such as Africa, Latin America, South-East Asia and the Middle East. He quotes British

Foreign secretary Ernest Bevin in 1948, who aimed 'to develop the African continent and to make its resources available to all', especially the United States, which 'is very barren of essential minerals and in Africa we have them all'.

3. Pilger (2006: 211–13) explains how mass privatisation took place after the end of apartheid, which saw the emergence of a new 'black business class', including many ANC (African National Congress) leaders, in alliance with pre-apartheid wealthy white elites and international corporations, at the expense of the well-being of the majority black population. In addition, Naomi Klein (2007: 198) accounts for the human cost of neo-right 'shock-therapy' economics, which has seen the life expectancy of black South Africans decrease by 13 years since the ANC came to power in 1994, with the country surpassing Brazil as the most unequal country in the world. The same intervening period witnessed the unemployment rate for blacks more than double, from 23 to 48 per cent, while the number of people living on $1 a day doubled to more than 2 million people (ibid.: 215).

4. One example of this was the announcement in January 2008 by the UK prime minister, Gordon Brown, of a new Internet project with the British Council to vastly expand the teaching and learning of English worldwide in 'every continent'. He stated, 'with more teachers, with more courses, more websites and now a deal involving the publishing media and communications industries, we will open up English to new countries and new generations'. He said he hoped to make English the 'world's common language of choice' (BBC 2007).

5. The struggle for linguistic and cultural rights amongst nationalist activists in Quebec culminated in the campaign for independence, organised primarily by members of the Parti Qúebécois (PQ). In the October 1995 referendum on the issue of Quebec's sovereignty, they lost by only 54,288 votes, or 1.6 per cent of the vote (May 2002: 230).

6. Richard Jenkins states that 'the defence and promotion of Welsh culture – symbolised most sharply by the Welsh language – [has been] the dominant item on the nationalist agenda, with some form of devolved self-government coming a poor second' (May 2002: 79).

7. May (2002: 22) quotes from Marx and Engels's description of how *'ethnic trash* always become the fanatical standard bearers of counter-revolution and remain so until their complete extirpation or loss of their national character, just as their whole existence in general is itself a protest against a great historical revolution. Such in Scotland are the Gaels ... in France are the Bretons ... in Spain are the Basques.' Irish commentator Mac Síomóin (2007: 112–15) cites this same quote from Engels before referring to his later views on Ireland, which he argues contradicted this position, in which he mentioned how the 'Irish formed a distinct nationality on their own' despite 'seven centuries of English conquest and oppression', and thus 'their first and most pressing duty as Irishmen was to establish their own national independence' (ibid.: 114). He stresses how these views on the Irish are incompatible with Engels's earlier call for the 'cultural genocide' of their cultural compatriots in Scotland, Brittany and the Basque country – a message which Stalin would later 'bloodily' adhere to in various regions. He argues that this provides evidence of the flawed, undeveloped view of the founders of Marxism on nationalism, which would be belied by the 'democratic and humane principles of socialism' (ibid.: 115).

8. Fukuyama's role as vocal functionary of such 'hegemonic ideology' is underlined by the fact that he actually served in the Reagan–Bush State Department (Chomsky 2004: 29).

## CHAPTER 2

1. See Greene 1966; Ó Murchú 1971; Crystal 1994; Williams 1992.
2. This is conveyed in Cromwell's account of the massacre of Drogheda: 'It hath pleased God to bless our endeavours at Drogheda ... The enemy were about 3,000 strong in the town ... I do not think 30 escaped with their lives. Those that did are in safe custody for the Barbados ... I wish that all honest hearts may give glory of this to God alone, to whom indeed the praise of this mercy belongs ... I am persuaded that this righteous judgment of God upon these barbarous wretches ... will tend to prevent the effusion of blood for the future, which are satisfactory grounds to such actions' (Curtis 1984: 25).
3. Whelan (2005: 149) points out that the GAA is acknowledged by most sports historians as the most speedily and extensively established sporting organisation in the world.
4. Bardon (1992: 421) estimates that the League failed to attract more than 500 Ulster Protestants in its formative years.
5. The Gaelic League became a vehicle for IRB recruitment, as is clear from Seán T. Ó Ceallaigh's description of how he used his position as manager of the League's newspaper *An Claidheamh Soluis* to promote IRB politics from as early as 1903: 'When working with *An Claidheamh Soluis* in the early years I had an opportunity to do a lot for the IRB ... I used to go around the country to *feiseanna* trying to increase sales of the paper, and, of course I met many young people of my own age in the different towns ... and I recruited young men for the IRB in every one of them' (Ó Huallacháin 1994: 62).
6. Hyde would later claim in a memoir written in 1918: 'I am not at all sure that the League did not do the right thing for the language in practically throwing me over – I did not see that at the time, however, for I did not foresee the utter and swift debacle of the IPP, and the apotheosis of Sinn Féin. The only reason I had for keeping politics out, was the desire to offend nobody and to get help from every party, which I did. But when Sinn Féin swallowed up all except the unionists, this was no longer necessary in the same way, because when all the country was one party, and that a friendly one, we could lose nothing by embracing it, except a certain amount of unionist assistance, which did not amount to very much, although it had been so invaluable to us when we were growing. I think we had won over the best of the unionists who were inclined that way, and I doubt that many more would have come in to us' (Ó Huallacháin 1994: 74).
7. These divisions were evidenced during the Treaty debates when language activist and anti-Treaty TD Cathal Brugha 'condescended to speak to his opponents in English, "the language of their masters"' (Laffan 1999: 237).
8. This is reflected in one 1924 newspaper bulletin: 'It would be well for the public to inquire how much the Irish language is used in Free State departments. Gossip is current to the effect that Irish is not welcome in these departments, to the extent that the staffs of the land Commission are strictly forbidden to sign their names in Irish' (A. Ó Snódaigh 2006: 12).

9. This term is widely used by A. Ó Snódaigh (2006), Fennell (1989) and Whelan (2004).
10. Lee (1989b: 132) draws attention to the fact that 'as late as 1932, 93 per cent of children did not proceed beyond primary education'.

## CHAPTER 3

1. Ó Croidheáin (2006: 193) points out that the existence of Gaeltacht or bilingual areas in the six counties was completely dismissed, thus leading to their extinction. 'The census figures of 1851 and 1891 demonstrated the presence of Irish-speakers respectively as follows: Antrim 3,033 (1.2 per cent) and 885 (0.4 per cent); Armagh 13,736 (7.0 per cent) and 3,486 (2.4 per cent); Derry 5,406 (2.8 per cent) and 2,723 (1.8 per cent); Down 1,153 (0.4 per cent) and 590 (0.3 per cent); Fermanagh 2,704 (2.3 per cent) and 561 (0.8 per cent) and Tyrone 12,892 (5.0 per cent) and 6.687 (3.9 per cent). There were minor Gaeltachtaí in Tyrone, the Sperrins (Derry), the Antrim Glens and Rathlin Island that had all but died out by the 1940s.'
2. The significance of this agenda is attested to by Fanon (1961: 169): 'Colonialism is not satisfied merely with holding a people in its grip and emptying the native's brain of all form and content ... it turns to the past of the oppressed people, and distorts, disfigures and destroys it.'
3. The Act itself became a permanent part of the six counties' legal code in 1928. See Rowthorn and Wayne (1988: 35–6) for a list of its provisions.
4. Comhaltas Uladh was formed in 1926 by Fr. Lorcan Ó Muireadhaigh and Seán Mac Maoláin and remained technically within the Gaelic League, while retaining its independence. While the Gaelic League branches in the whole of the six counties stood at only a handful in 1926, this rose to 78 by 1940, peaked at 182 by 1946 and averaged 155 per annum over the next nine years. Comhaltas Uladh also played a hugely significant role in developing the Gaeltacht summer colleges which exposed thousands of younger learners and speakers to the language (Mac Póilin 2006: 124).
5. The LFM were vocal opponents of the Free State language revival in the 1960s (Ó Tuathaigh 2011: 92).

## CHAPTER 4

1. It is noteworthy that O'Donovan Rossa, himself a native Irish speaker, also relates such punishment for the speaking of the Irish language in Pentonville: 'O'Keefe [a fellow prisoner] was a good Irish scholar, I tried to draw him out by giving him a word of Gaelic, which was high treason to the jailers. They prohibited us from speaking in our mother tongue even on the days when we were allowed to talk. They called it slang. I believe it was Thomas Duggen, of Ballincollig, that was severely reprimanded once for speaking Irish and threatened with severe punishment if he repeated the offence' (O'Donovan Rossa 1967: 101).
2. Following the 1916 Easter Rising in Ireland, 3,509 men and women were detained, with 2,519 of this number being transferred to Britain in May and June of 1916 (McGuffin, 1973: 26; O'Mahony, 1987: 20–1). Of these, 159 were tried by military courts, with 90 individuals being sentenced to death,

16 of whom were eventually executed by the British government (McGuffin 1973: 27).

3. Ashe, a native Irish speaker from Kerry and prominent Gaelic Leaguer, was the IRB's supreme commander. His death on hunger strike, via force-feeding, in Mountjoy in August 1917 'released a new outburst of popular feeling' and according to the *Irish Independent* 'made 100,000 Sinn Féiners out of 100,000 parliamentarians' (Rees 1998: 228). Ó Muirthile (1967: 48) points out that only one week after Thomas Ashe's death, Mountjoy's republican prisoners were recognised as political prisoners.

4. MacSwiney died after 74 days on hunger strike in prison in London on 26 October 1920. Over 30,000 people, mainly second and third generation Irish, took to the streets of London in his honour. He would become a political prisoner icon across the world (Ó Briain 1979: 147).

5. The death penalty was applicable in the new Irish Free State regime for possession of weapons and other activities. Between 77 and 85 republicans were executed by Free State forces during this period (Coogan 2002).

6. Following the end of the Irish Civil War, a small number of republicans remained imprisoned in the 26-counties until Fianna Fáil came to power in 1932, including some who were detained in Arbour Hill prison in Dublin. A number of these republicans, including well-known activists like Frank Ryan and George Gilmore, went on a no-work strike in 1931 and refused to wear a prison uniform (Coogan 2002).

7. 'Craobh na Sróine Deirge' translates as 'branch of the red nose'; it was named by Liam Ó Briain, who would later become professor for romance languages at University College, Galway (O'Mahony 1987).

8. These teachers were said to be among many nationalists targeted by 'the specials' for arrest and internment who had good jobs and were subsequently replaced in their jobs by unionists 'inside a fortnight' (Kleinrichert 2001: 278).

9. Irish books were banned by the Derry governor, Captain Stephenson. A later governor, Captain Stewart, dropped the ban and allowed Irish books and writing materials, but only within the solitary cells (Kleinrichert 2001: 148).

10. An estimated 840 republicans were detained, with sentenced prisoners facing significantly worse conditions than those interned (Coogan 2002). One such prisoner, Cahir Healy, who had been elected as an MP for Fermanagh and South Tyrone while interned on the *Argenta* in 1922, was again interned in July 1941 while an elected member of the Stormont parliament (ibid.).

11. In this period nine republicans were executed by the Fianna Fáil regime, six more were shot dead by state police and three would die on hunger strike (MacEoin, 1997).

12. Seán Óg Ó Tuama was president of the Gaelic League when he was imprisoned in the Curragh (MacEoin 1997).

13. For details and accounts from prisoners on both sides of the divide, see MacEoin (1997).

14. 'Terry Wilson' is the English version of 'Tarlach Ó hUid'; Moscow Jack Brady is the father of Eibhlín Collins, an Armagh ex-prisoner and one of the narrators in the research. Liam McGratton is better known as Liam Mac Reachtain, and was a noted Irish literary writer upon his release. He is also credited for his work on Irish-language development in the prison by Paddy Devlin in his autobiography *Straight Left* (1993: 42).

15. William Dawson Bates was the minister for home affairs in the Unionist government for over 20 years (Kleinrichert 2001).

16. It is worth noting that in an earlier autobiography, *Ar Thoir mo Shealbha* (1960), Tarlach Ó hUid retrospectively rejected republicanism and his time in the IRA as a mistake and attempted to dissuade young people from 'following his mistakes'. His book and the views in it were stringently attacked by Mairtín Ó Cadhain in an article in the Irish periodical *Feasta* in 1960 (Ó Cathasaigh 2002: 178).

17. During his years of imprisonment, Tómas Ó hEanáin refused to accept prison visits because he was not permitted to speak Irish during visits by the authorities. He remained one of Belfast's most prominent language activists until his death in the early 1990s (interview with Mac Seáin, 26 July 2006).

18. Billy's brother John Kelly was a leading IRA figure during the border campaign and later played a central role in the famous Arms Trial in 1970, in which members of the 26-county government were implicated in smuggling guns to the north for the IRA (see Bowyer Bell 1990: 370–3). John died in 2007.

19. See MacEoin (1997).

## CHAPTER 5

1. In September 1983, 38 republican prisoners, including one of the narrators in this research, staged a mass breakout from Long Kesh prison in what became known in republican circles as the 'Great Escape' (McKeown 2001).

2. The 'B' Specials were formed in 1920 by the Ulster Special Constabulary as an armed, part-time loyalist police force and were especially feared in the nationalist and republican community in the six counties (Farrell 1983).

3. While initially, following the Loyalist pogroms, the IRA were in disarray, they began to reorganise following a formal split in their ranks in January 1970. For details on the split, see Bowyer Bell (1990), Coogan (2002) and English (2003). When internment began, the leadership of the newly formed provisional IRA had prior intelligence of the swoop and thus largely evaded arrest (see Bowyer Bell 1990, Coogan 2002 and English 2003).

4. These female prisoners organised themselves in the same republican tradition with a military-style structure and similarly engaged in such activities as education classes and social events, including concerts and Irish dancing, during the special category status period (D'Arcy 1981; Murray 1998).

5. Songs like 'The Men behind the Wire' became well-known national ballads during this period (McKeown 1998).

6. The cages of Long Kesh were burned on 15 October 1974 by the sentenced prisoners over dissatisfaction relating to prison conditions, etc. (see McKeown 1998). A more detailed account can be found in Faul and Murray's (1974) compilation of prisoner accounts of events relating to the fire, its background and aftermath, which included the British army murder of internee Hugh Gerard Cooney on 6 November. Meanwhile in Armagh women's prison, the prisoners took the jail's governor and three other prison personnel hostage in support of republican prisoners who had burned their cages in Long Kesh. See D'Arcy (1981) and Murray (1998).

7. For an in-depth discussion on the theoretical, ideological and strategic debate and internal wrangling that took place in the sentenced cages between older

traditional activists and the newer more radical breed of activist to emerge in the mid to late 1970s, see McKeown (1998, 2001) and O'Hearn (2006).

8. For an in-depth analysis of the internal debate amongst prisoners in both the cages and the Blocks in relation to taking part in formal prison education, see McKeown (1998, 2001).

## CHAPTER 6

1. The RUC (Royal Ulster Constabulary) was the police force of the Northern Ireland state from its formation until 2001, when it was renamed the PSNI under the Patten reform proposals emanating from the Good Friday Agreement in 1998. The UDR (Ulster Defence Regiment) was formed after the disbandment of the 'B' Specials and was recruited from the local loyalist and unionist community in the north, with many of its members employed on a part-time basis.

2. 'Protesting' H-Blocks refers to those blocks where prisoners were on the blanket protest; there were also 'conforming' wings or blocks, where many republican and loyalist prisoners conformed to the prison system, wore the prison uniform and carried out prison work (McKeown 2001).

3. These wings shifts and attempts to isolate prisoners and divide command structures had a number of outworkings, according to McKeown (2001: 67): they forced a multiplicity of people into leadership roles who had not previously held them, thus leading to a more horizontal organisational ethos, which brought the republican prisoner leadership into contact with one another and allowed them to discuss the strategy in relation to the protest.

4. Though beyond the scope of this book, it is worth noting the inevitable long-term psychological effects on prisoners who were subjected to such degrading forms of torture and humiliation while on the Blanket protest. For in-depth research on the psychological consequences of the protest, see Hamber (2005).

5. Republican prisoners Gerry Kelly, Hugh Feeney and the Price sisters, Marion and Dolores, were transferred to Long Kesh and Armagh prisons in the six-counties. Two IRA prisoners died on hunger strike in Britain during this period: Michael Gaughan (June 1974) and Frank Stagg (February 1976).

6. Female republican prisoners in Armagh prison had also embarked on the hunger strike in early December 1980, and a further 23 joined on 15 December shortly before the hunger strike was called off (Collins 1987).

7. For a comprehensive account of this new phase in the prisoners' campaign to achieve their goals, see McKeown (1998; 2001).

## CHAPTER 7

1. This clause of the Public Health and Local Council Act was finally removed in 1992 after years of campaigning (Committee on the Administration of Justice, 1993).

2. Gaelscoil na bhFál was the second Irish-medium primary school to be formed in Belfast, in 1986 (O'Reilly, 1999).

## CONCLUSION

1. O'Reilly's (1999) categories arguably misinterpret the political and ideological resonance of many core elements to the Irish cultural revival. For example,

she fails to recognise the decolonising methodology of Hyde and the Gaelic League and categorises them within 'apolitical' cultural discourse despite the fact that they campaigned politically on many rights-based Irish-language issues. Similarly, she includes the activists of the Shaw's Road Gaeltacht in this 'cultural' bracket despite the fact that their consciously radical 'decolonising' activism planted the seeds for a highly politicised community revival.

## EPILOGUE

1. Canavan was the head of the Central Community Relations Unit and the senior civil servant charged with responsibility for the Irish language. Canavan's document only came to light after the signing of the Good Friday Agreement, having been leaked to the press on 22 April 1998 by DUP Belfast city councillor Nelson McCausland (Muller 2010: 70).
2. Ulster Scots is a dialect of Lowland Scots. Although there are no universally accepted criteria for distinguishing languages from dialects, most scholars of linguistics in Ireland agree that the linguistic, historical and social status of Scots proves that it doesn't constitute a distinct language. Certain sections of political unionism in the north of Ireland have promoted Ulster Scots as a language and key element of 'British–Unionist' culture since the signing of the GFA.
3. The St Andrews Agreement is an international political agreement that was signed in October 2006 by both the British and Irish governments and the respective political parties in the north of Ireland.
4. This was clear in the game of brinkmanship between the British government and the main unionist party, the DUP, in the lead-up to the 26 March 2007 deadline for restoring devolution in the north of Ireland. A few days earlier, the British secretary of state for Northern Ireland, Peter Hain, had warned the DUP that failure to agree to devolution at the end of March would mean the enactment of an Irish Language Act and the scrapping of academic selection, whereas an agreement to share power with republicans would grant them a veto in both cases, because both questions would become 'devolved matters' and subject to a cross-community vote in the assembly (Hain 2007; McCausland 2007).
5. Janet Muller (2010: 52) questions the chief inspector's 'assertion' that 'a slowdown in the growth of the Irish Medium primary sector' has 'allowed for consolidation' by pointing out that it is difficult to state with certainty 'whether a more pro-active developmental approach to the sector in the same period could have yielded similar levels of consolidation whilst also allowing for the expanded rate of growth'. In addition, veteran language activist Seamas Mac Seáin estimated in his recent autobiography (2010: 278) that Gaeloiliúnt, the voluntary predecessor to Comhairle na Gaelscolaíochta, had founded 21 schools between 1991 and 2000 compared with Comhairle na Gaelscolaíochta's six schools between 2000 and the present. Mac Seáin raises the question, 'Is it that the same demand isn't there and the ceiling has been reached or could it be that funding has fostered bureaucracy and that the energy and diligence has been extinguished under the burden of minutes and highbrow titles? Does being part of the system mean surrendering to the limits it imposes and losing your core?
6. It is worth noting that the d'Hondt system in place at Stormont requires cross-community support for executive decisions, a fact which allows a veto for both unionist and nationalist political parties within power-sharing structures.

7. A few months into the DUP reign in the DCAL ministry, Campbell caused outrage amongst Irish speakers when he mocked spoken Irish in the assembly by stating, 'Were I were a satirist, I might begin my question to the Minister with the words "Cora my Yogi Bear, a can coca colya"' (this was taken as a mock on the common phrase used by some nationalist politicians when thanking the speaker of the house, 'Go raibh maith agat a Cheann Chomhairle'). Forbairt Feirste director Jake Mac Siacais lodged an official complaint with the speaker of the house, William Hay, calling for Campbell to be disciplined on the basis that the 'deeply offensive' remarks contravened the GFA's call to recognise 'the importance of respect, understanding and tolerance of linguistic diversity' (*AN* 2007). Campbell's remarks and a draconian motion to ban the use of Irish in the NI Assembly proposed by UUP MLA David McNarry the following month prompted Irish-language campaigning group ACHT to organise a protest at Stormont to 'oppose cultural racism'. ACHT spokesperson Ciarán Mac Giolla Bhéin called for support at the protest by stating, 'The use of indigenous languages is an internationally recognised human right that can't be held to ransom by anti-Irish racism or party political posturing' (*Irish News* 2007).

8. Following the failure of the second development proposal, the school's founding principal, Cathal Ó Donnghaile, who played a central role in the campaigning years of Meánscoil Feirste as a founding teacher, wrote a letter in the *Irish News* on behalf of the school community stating: 'I was well accustomed to stone-walling, as we made our case for Gaelic education, under the old regime of the DENI hardliners and, while our experiences over the past two years have been different, the result is the same – no-can-do. There was still the traditional smile and handshake at meetings, but this time it was from friends whom we had believed to be genuine and who we thought would do the business. The whole wider Irish-medium fraternity, as well as the general nationalist community, were disillusioned and found it difficult to accept that Coláiste Speirín had not been given the opportunity to come in out of the cold, as it were. Possibly, we were too naive in thinking, because the decision makers were mostly people from a similar background to ourselves, that all would be well' (Ó Donnghaile 2008).

9. Líofa 2015 was also questioned because of the lack of resources allocated to it 'by a department with a statutory obligation to do so' (Mac Ionnrachtaigh 2011b). Those who sign up to Líofa are directed to 'a variety of Irish Language classes and other learning materials that are available in their locality' and will be contacted 'occasionally' by the DCAL between 2011 and 2015 'to see how their journey towards fluency is progressing' (DCAL 2011).

10. The North–South Ministerial Council was set up under the GFA and comprises ministers of the Northern Ireland Executive and the Irish government (see www. northsouthministerialcouncil.org).

11. The Irish government passed a financial plan that proposed cutting the annual budget of the Department for Gaeltacht and Rural Affairs from £105 million in 2010 to £30 million by 2016 in order to meet 'important economic and social priorities in other areas of capital expenditure' (Walsh 2011b: 49).

12. Civil society groups that have emerged in recent times, though not all explicitly radical, include Claiming our Future, We the Citizens, The People's Convention (An Chomhdháil Phobail) and New Vision (Walsh 2011b: 51).

13. The Basque Korrika also involves a sponsored run across all the Basque Provinces. It began in 1980 and now has upwards of 600,000 people taking part every two years; it raises over £1.5 million for grassroots Basque language projects.

# References

Alexander, Neville (2003) *The African Renaissance and the Use of African Languages in Tertiary Education* (Cape Town).

AN (2007) 'Campbell facing censure for remarks during Irish debate', *Andersontown News* (12 September).

— (2008) '*LÁ Nua* a victim of "dispensation of power-sharing"', *Andersonstown News* (17 December).

— (2011) 'Buses, buses everywhere but not even a single one for Falls Road Irish Language College', *Andersonstown News* (26 February).

Anderson, Benedict (1991) *Imagined Communities: Reflections on the Origin and Spread of Nationalism* (London).

— (1994) 'Imagined Communities', in Hutchinson and Smith 1994: 89–96.

Andrews, Liam S. (1991) 'The Irish Language in the Education System of Northern Ireland: Some Political and Cultural Perspectives', in R.M.O. Pritchard (ed.) *Motivating the Majority: Modern Languages in Northern Ireland* (London): 89–106.

— (1997) 'The Very Dogs in Belfast Will Bark in Irish: The Unionist Government and the Irish Language, 1921–43', in A. Mac Póilin (ed.) *The Irish Language in Northern Ireland* (Belfast): 49–94.

— (2000) 'Northern Nationalists and the Politics of the Irish Language', in J.M. Kirk and D.P. Ó Baoill (eds) *Language and Politics: Northern Ireland, the Republic of Ireland, and Scotland* (Belfast): 44–63.

Bardon, Jonathan (1992) *A History of Ulster* (Belfast).

BBC (2007) 'Brown's web bid to boost English' (17 January), <news.bbc.co.uk/1/hi/uk_politics/7193681>.

Becker, H.S. (1967) 'Whose Side Are We on?' *Social Problems*, 14/3: 239–47.

Beresford, Tom (1987) *Ten Men Dead: The Story of the 1981 Irish Hunger Strike* (London).

Betts, F. (1998) *Decolonisation* (London).

Bourdieu, P. (1991) *Language and Symbolic Power* (Cambridge).

Bowyer Bell, J. (1990) *The Secret Army: A History of the IRA 1916–1979* (London).

— (1991) *The Gun and Irish Politics: An Analysis of Irish Political Conflict 1916–1986* (London).

Boyce, George D. and Alan O'Day (eds) (1996) *The Making of Modern Irish History: Revisionism and the Revisionist Controversy* (London).

Bradley, Finbarr and James J. Kennelly (2008) *Capitalising on Culture, Competing on Difference: Innovation, Learning and Sense of Place in a Globalising Ireland* (Dublin).

Brennan-Whitmore, William J. (1917) *With the Irish in Frongoch* (Dublin).

Buntman, Fran Lisa (2003) *Robben Island and Prisoner Resistance to Apartheid* (London).

Caherty, T., M. Garvin, M. Molloy, C. Ruane and A. Storey (eds) (1992) *Is Ireland a Third World Country?* (Belfast).

Canny, Nicholas P. (1973) 'The Ideology of English Colonization from Ireland to America', *William and Mary Quarterly*, 30: 575–98.

Carroll, Claire and Patricia King (eds) (2003) *Ireland and Postcolonial Theory* (Cork).

Castells, Manuel (1997) *The Power of Identity* (Oxford).

Caute, David (1970) *Fanon* (London).

Chatterjee, Partha (1983) *Nationalist Thought and the Colonial World: A Derivative Discourse* (London).

Chomsky, Noam (1979) *Language and Responsibility* (London).

— (1999) *Latin America: From Colonisation to Globalisation, in Conversation with Heinz Dieterich* (New York).

— (2004) *Hegemony or Survival: America's Quest for Global Dominance* (London).

Clarke, Thomas J. (1970) *Glimpses of an Irish Felon's Life* (Cork).

Clayton, Pamela (1998) 'Religion, Ethnicity and Colonialism as Explanations of the Northern Ireland Conflict', in D. Miller (ed.) *Rethinking Northern Ireland* (London): 40–54.

Cleary, Joe (2003) '"Misplaced Ideas?" Colonialism, Location, and Dislocation in Irish Studies', in Carroll and King 2003: 16–46.

— and C. Connolly (eds) (2005) *The Cambridge Companion to Modern Irish Culture* (Cambridge).

Clemmer, Donald (1958) *The Prison Community* (New York).

Cohen, S. and L. Taylor (1972) *Psychological Survival: The Experience of Long-Term Imprisonment* (Middlesex).

Collins, Kevin (1990) *The Cultural Conquest of Ireland* (Dublin).

Collins, Tom (1987) *The Irish Hunger Strike* (White Island).

Comerford, R.V. (2003) *Inventing the Nation: Ireland* (London).

Committee on the Administration of Justice (1994) 'The UK Government Approach to the Irish Language in Light of the European Charter for Regional or Minority Languages'.

Connolly, James (1983) *Labour and Irish History* (Dublin).

Conradh na Gaeilge (2008) 'What was in the paper this week in 1981', *Andersonstown News* (18 August): 37.

Coogan, Tim Pat (1980) *On the Blanket: The H-Block Story* (Dublin).

— (2002) *The IRA* (New York).

Cosgrove, Art (1990) 'The Writing of Irish Medieval History', *Irish Historical Studies*, 27/106 (November): 97–111.

Crowley, Tony (1996) *Language in History: Theories and Texts* (London and New York).

— (2000) *The Politics of Language in Ireland, 1366–1922: A Sourcebook* (London and New York).

Crystal, David (1994) *The Cambridge Encyclopedia of Language* (Cambridge).

Cummins, J. (1995) 'The Discourse of Disinformation: The Debate on Bilingual Education and Language Rights in the United States', in T. Skutnabb-Kangas and R. Phillipson (eds) *Linguistic Human Rights: Overcoming Linguistic Discrimination* (Berlin): 159–77.

Curtis, Liz (1984) *Nothing but the Same Old Story: The Roots of Anti-Irish Racism* (London).

— (1994) *The Cause of Ireland: From the United Irishmen to Partition* (Belfast).

Curtis, Mark (2003) *Web of Deceit: Britain's Real Role in the World* (London).

D'Arcy, Margeretta (1981) *Tell Them Everything* (London).

Davis, Thomas (n.d.) *Selections from his Prose and Poetry* (London).

DCAL (2007) 'Submissions on proposed Irish Language Legislation' (March), www. dcalni.gov.uk.

— (2011) 'Minister outlines way forward for Irish language', press release (5 September).

De Baróid, Ciaran (2000) *Ballymurphy and the Irish War* (London).

De Brún, Fionntán (ed.) (2006) *Belfast and the Irish language* (Dublin).

Devlin, Paddy (1993) *Straight Left* (Belfast).

Dorian, Nancy (1998) 'Western Language Ideologies and Small-Language Prospects', in L. Grenoble and L. Whaley (eds) *Endangered Languages: Language Loss and Community Response* (Cambridge): 3–21.

Dudley-Edwards, Ruth (2006) 'Why does Ken Loach loathe his country so much?' *Daily Mail* (30 May): 18.

Durkheim, Émile (1984) *The Division of Labour in Society* (London).

Eccleshall, Robert (1992) 'Introduction: the World of Ideology', in Eccleshall et al. 1992: 7–37.

— Alan Finlayson, Vincent Geoghegan, Michael Kenny, Moya Lloyd, Iain MacKenzie and Rick Wilford (1992) *Political Ideologies* (London).

Edwards, John (1985) *Language, Society and Identity* (London).

English, Richard (2003) *Armed Struggle: The History of the IRA* (London).

Fanon, Frantz (1961) *The Wretched of the Earth* (Harmondsworth).

— (1970) *Black Skins, White Masks* (Suffolk).

Fairclough, Norman (2001) *Language and Power*, 2nd edn (Essex).

Farrell, Michael (1976). *The Orange State* (London).

— (1983) *Arming the Protestants: The Formation of the Ulster Special Constabulary and the Royal Ulster Constabulary 1920–1927* (London).

— (1985) *Sheltering the Fugitive: The Extradition of Irish Political Offenders* (Cork).

Faul, Denis and Raymond Murray (1974) *The Flames of Long Kesh: The Murder of Hugh Gerard Coney, Internee* (Dungannon).

Feldman, Allen (1991) *Formations of Violence: The Narrative of the Body and Political Terror in Northern Ireland* (Chicago).

Fennell, Desmond (1989) *The Revision of Irish Nationalism* (Dublin).

Figgis, Darrell (1917) *A Chronicle of Jails* (Dublin).

Fishman, Joshua (1989) *Language and Ethnicity in Minority Sociolinguistic Perspective*, Multilingual Matters 45 (Clevedon, England).

— (1991) *Reversing Language Shift: Theoretical and Empirical Foundation of Assistance to Threatened Languages* (Clevedon, England).

— (2005) 'The Soft Smile and the Iron Fist', prefatory remarks in D. Ó Néill (ed.) *Rebuilding the Celtic Languages: Reversing Language Shift in the Celtic Countries* (Wales).

Foras na Gaeilge (2007) *Oidhreacht Feirste: An Ghaeilge i mBéal Feirste.*

Foster, Roy F. (1988) *Modern Ireland, 1600–1972* (London).

Foueraker, Joe (1995) *Theorizing Social Movements* (London).

Fox, G. Richard and Orin Starn (1997) *Between Resistance and Revolution: Cultural Politics and Social Protest* (USA).

Freire, Paulo (1972a) *Pedagogy of the Oppressed* (London).

— (1972b) *Cultural Action for Freedom* (England).

— (1992) *Education for Critical consciousness* (New York).

Gaelscéal (2011) 'Bua cúirte do Choláiste Feirste agus an Ghaelscolaíocht', *Gaelscéal* (28 October).

Gellner, E. (1983) *Nations and Nationalism: New Perspectives on the Past* (Oxford).

Gibbons, Luke (1996) *Transformations in Irish Culture* (Cork).

Githens-Mazer, Jonathan (2006) *Myths and Memories of the Easter Rising: Cultural and Political Nationalism in Ireland* (Dublin).

Gledhill, John (2000) *Power and Its Disguises: Anthropological Perspectives on Politics* (London).

Graham, Colin, and Richard Kirkland (eds) (1999) *Ireland and Cultural Theory: The Mechanics of Authenticity* (London).

Gramsci, Antonio (1971) *Selections from the Prison Notebooks* (London).

Greed, Clara (1990) 'The Professional and the Personal: A Study of Women Quantity Surveyors', in Stanley 1990: 145–55.

Greene, David (1966) *The Irish Language* (Dublin).

Hain, P. (2007) Press release from Secretary of State's Office (20 March).

Hall, S. and P. Scraton (1981) 'Law, Class and Control', in M. Fitzgerald, G. McLennan and J. Pawson (eds) *Crime and Society: Readings in History and Theory* (London): 460–79.

Hall, S., C. Critcher, T. Jefferson, J. Clarke and B. Roberts (1978) *Policing the Crisis* (London).

Hamber, Brandon (2005) '"Blocks to the future": A Pilot Study of the Long-Term Psychological Impact of the No Wash/Blanket Protest', report written and published by Brandon Hamber and Associates on behalf of *Cúnamh* (Derry).

Harris, Jerry (2007) 'Bolivia and Venezuela: The Democratic Dialectic in New Revolutionary Movements', *Race and Class: A Journal on Racism, Empire and Globalisation*, 49 (July–September): 1–25.

Herman, E.S. and N. Chomsky (1988) *Manufacturing Consent: The Political Economy of Mass Media* (New York).

Hill, Christopher (1970) *God's Englishmen: Oliver Cromwell and the English Revolution* (London).

Hillyard, Paddy (1987) 'The Normalisation of Special Powers: From Northern Ireland to Britain', in P. Scraton (ed.) *Law, Order and the Authoritarian State* (Milton Keynes): 279–312.

Hindley, Reg (1990) *The Death of the Irish Language: A Qualified Obituary* (London).

Hobsbawm, Eric (1990) *Nations and Nationalism since 1780* (Cambridge).

— and T. Ranger (eds) (1983) *The Invention of Tradition* (Cambridge).

Hourigan, Niamh (2006) 'Movement Outcomes and Irish Language Protest', in L. Connolly and N. Hourigan (eds) *Social Movements and Ireland* (Manchester): 124–44.

Hroch, Miroslav (1985) *Social Preconditions of National Revival in Europe: A Comparative Analysis of the Social Composition of Patriotic Groups among Smaller European Nations* (Cambridge).

Hudson, B.A. (1993) *Penal Policy and Social Justice* (London).

Hughes, A.J. (2006a) 'The Ulster Gaelic Society and the Work of MacAdam's Irish Scribes', in De Brún 2006: 65–100.

— (2006b) 'Robert MacAdam and the Nineteenth-Century Revival', in De Brún 2006: 43–64.

Hutchinson, J. (1987) *The Dynamics of Irish Cultural Nationalism: The Gaelic Revival and the Creation of the Irish Free State* (Dublin).

— (1994) 'Cultural Nationalism and Moral Regeneration', in Hutchinson and Smith 1994: 122–31.

— and A.D. Smith (1994) *Nationalism* (Oxford).

*Irish News* (2007) 'Unionists' ban plan anti-Irish says group', *Irish News* (9 October).

— (2011) 'PSNI officers sign up for Irish lessons', *Irish News* (6 September).

Jackson, Alvin (1999) *Ireland 1798–1998* (USA).

Jay, Richard (1992) 'Nationalism', in Eccleshall et al. 1992: 185–217.

Jones, Steve (2006) *Antonio Gramsci* (London and New York).

Kachuk, Patricia (1993) 'Irish Language Activism in West Belfast: A Resistence to British Cultural Hegemony' (unpublished Ph.D. thesis, social anthropology, University of British Columbia).

Kiberd, Declan (1992) 'Ireland and the Third World: Some Parallels', in Caherty et al. 1992: 29–37.

— (1995) *Inventing Ireland: The Literature of the Modern Nation* (London).

Khleif, Bud B. (1979) 'Language as Identity: Toward an Ethnography of Welsh Nationalism', *Ethnicity*, 6: 346–57.

— (1985) 'Issues of Theory and Methodology in the Study of Ethno-Linguistic Movements: The Case of Frisian Nationalism in the Netherlands', in E. Tiryakian and R. Rogowski (eds) *New Nationalism of the Developed West: Toward Explanation* (Boston): 176–99.

Kirby, Peadar (2011) 'Domhandú, Eacnamaíocht agus Féiniúlacht: Cás na hÉireann', in B. Mac Cormaic (éag) *Féiniúlacht, Cultúr agus Teanga i Ré an Domhandaithe* (BÁC): 254–68.

Klein, Naomi (2007) *The Shock Doctrine: The Rise of Disaster Capitalism* (London).

Kleinrichert, Denise (2001) *Internment and the Prison Ship Argenta, 1922* (Dublin).

Krauss, Michael (1992) 'The World's Languages in Crisis', *Language*, 68/1: 4–10.

Laffan, Michael (1999) *The Resurrection of Ireland: The Sinn Féin Party, 1916–23* (Cambridge).

Larrain, Jorge (1979) *The Concept of Ideology* (London).

— (1989) *Theories of Development: Capitalism, Colonialism and Dependency* (USA).

— (1991) *Marxism and Ideology* (England).

Lebowitz, Michael A. (2006) *Build it Now: Socialism for the Twenty-First Century* (New York).

Lee, Joseph (1989a) *The Modernisation of Irish Society 1848–1918* (Dublin).

— (1989b) *Ireland 1912–1985: Politics and Society* (Cambridge).

Lennon, Colm (1994) *Sixteenth-Century Ireland: The Incomplete Conquest* (Dublin).

Lloyd, David (2003) 'After History: Historicism and Irish Postcolonial Studies', in Carroll and King 2003: 46–63.

Lyons, F.S.L. (1973) *Ireland since the Famine* (London).

MacArdle, Dorothy (1951) *The Irish Republic* (Dublin).

MacAtasney, G. (2004) *Seán Mac Diarmada: The Mind of the Revolution* (Leitrim).

MacEoin, Uinseann (1997) *The IRA in the Twilight Years 1923–48* (Dublin).

Mac Ionnrachtaigh, Feargal (2011a) 'Ón Bhun Aníos: Resisting and Regenerating through Language in the North of Ireland', in J.M. Kirk and D.P. Ó Baoill (eds) *Sustaining Minority Language Communities: Northern Ireland, the Republic of Ireland, and Scotland* (Belfast): 132–56.

— (2011b) 'Language doesn't decline in powerful communities', *Andersonstown News* (17 September).

— (2011c) 'Samhain Nua Mhaoinithe: ár seirbhísí i mbaol', *Andersonstown News* (15 October).

— (2011d) 'Bua do chearta daonna', *Andersonstown News* (5 November).

Mac Póilin, Aodán (ed.) (1997a) *The Irish Language in Northern Ireland* (Belfast).

— (1997b) 'Plus ça change: The Irish Language and Politics', in Mac Póilin 1997a: 31–48.

— (1997c) 'Aspects of the Irish Language Movement', in Mac Póilin 1997a: 171–89.

— (2006) 'Irish in Belfast, 1892–1960: From the Gaelic League to Cumann Chluain Ard', in De Brún 2006: 114–35.

Mac Seáin, Seamus (2006) 'Century of Irish language growth', *Andersonstown News* (9 October): 4.

— (2010) *D'imigh sin agus tháinig seo: Scéal oibrí fir i mBéal Feiste a linne* (BÁC).

Mac Siacais, Jake (1981) Untitled communication to Jack Brady (circa March).

Mac Síomóin, Tomás (1994) 'The Colonised Mind: Irish Language and Society', in Ó Ceallaigh 1994a: 42–71.

— (2006) *Ó Mhársa go Magla: Straitéis nua don Ghaeilge* (BÁC).

— (2007) 'An náisiúnachas: Ball laige an tsóisialachais', in *Faoin Bhratach Dhearg: aistí sóisialacha* (BÁC): 108–25.

— (2011) 'Nua-Éireannachas: Namhad don Ghaeilge', in B. Mac Cormaic (éag) *Féiniúlacht, Cultúr agus Teanga i Ré an Domhandaithe* (BÁC): 236–54.

Maguire, Gabrielle (1990) *Our Own Language: An Irish Initiative* (Clevedon).

— (2006) (Nig Uidhir, Gabrielle) 'The Shaw's Road Urban Gaeltacht: Role and Impact', in De Brún 2006: 136–47.

Mackie, Robert (ed.) (1980) *Literacy and Revolution: The Pedagogy of Paulo Freire* (London).

Mandela, Nelson (1994) *Long Walk to Freedom: The Autobiography of Nelson Mandela* (Boston).

Marcuse, Herbert (1972) *One-Dimensional Man* (London).

Marx, Karl (1979) 'The Eighteenth Brumaire of Louis Bonaparte', in K. Marx and F. Engels, *Collected Works, vol 2* (New York): 99–197.

May, Stephen (2002) *Language and Minority Rights: Ethnicity, Nationalism and the Politics of Language* (Essex).

Mayo, Marjorie (1997) *Imagining Tomorrow: Adult Education for Transformation* (London).

McAlister, Siobhán, Phil Scraton and Deena Haydon (2009) *Childhood in Transition: Experiencing Marginalisation and Conflict in Northern Ireland* (Belfast).

McCausland, Nelson (2007) 'Act is a shillelagh to coerce unionists into Stormont', *News Letter* (14 March): 11.

McCluskey, Fergal (2011) *Fenians and Ribbonmen: The Development of Republican Politics in East Tyrone, 1898–1918* (Manchester).

McConville, Seán (2003) *Irish Political Prisoners, 1848–1922: Theatres of War* (London and New York).

McCoy, Gordon (1997) 'Protestants and the Irish Language in Northern Ireland' (unpublished Ph.D. thesis, Faculty of Arts, Queen's University Belfast).

— (2001) 'From Cause to Quango? The Peace Process and the Transformation of the Irish Language Movement', in J. Kirk and D.P. Ó Baoill (eds) *Linguistic Politics: Language Policies for Northern Ireland, the Republic of Ireland, and Scotland* (Belfast): 205–19.

McEvoy, Kieran (2001) *Paramilitary Imprisonment in Northern Ireland: Resistance, Management and Release* (Oxford).

McGee, Owen (2005) *The IRB: The Irish Republican Brotherhood, from the Land League to Sinn Féin* (Dublin).

McGuffin, John (1973) *Internment* (Tralee).

McKearney, Tommy (2011) *The Provisional IRA: From Insurrection to Parliament* (London).

McKeown, Laurence (1998) 'Unrepentant Fenian Bastards: The Social Construction of an Irish Republican Prisoner Community' (Ph.D. thesis, Faculty of Arts, Queen's University, Belfast).

— (2001) *Out of Time, Irish Republican Prisoners Long Kesh 1972–2000* (Belfast).

— B. Campbell and F. O'Hagan (eds) (1994) *Nor Meekly Serve My Time: The H-Block Struggle 1976–81* (Belfast).

McKittrick, David, S. Kelters, B. Feeney and C. Thornton (eds) (1999) *Lost Lives: The Stories of the Men, Women and Children who Died as a Result of the Northern Ireland Troubles* (Edinburgh).

McRobbie, Angela (1982) *Feminism and Youth Culture: From* Jackie *to* Just Seventeen (Basingstoke).

Memmi, Albert (1965) *The Colonizer and the Colonized* (Orion Press).

Moane, Geraldine (2002) 'Colonialism and the Celtic Tiger: Legacies of History and the Quest for Vision', in P. Kirby, L. Gibbons and M. Cronin (eds) *Reinventing Ireland: Culture, Society and the Global Economy* (London): 109–24.

Muller, Janet (2010) *Language and Conflict in Northern Ireland and Canada: A Silent War* (Hampshire).

Murray, Raymond (1998) *Hard Time: Armagh Gaol 1971–1986* (Dublin).

Naíonra na Fuiseoige (1988) *Naíonra na Fuiseoige* (Belfast).

Nairn, Tom (1994) 'The Maladies of Development', in Hutchinson and Smith 1994: 70–6.

Ngugi Wa Thiong'o (1997) *Decolonising the Mind: The Politics of Language in African Literature* (London).

Nic Craith, Mairéad (2001) *Culture and Identity Politics in Northern Ireland* (Dublin).

Nimni, E. (1995) 'Marx, Engels, and the National Question', in W. Kymlicka (ed.) *The Rights of Minority Cultures* (Oxford): 57–75.

Ní Phóilin, Aoife (1998) 'An Ghaelscolaíocht i dtuaisceart Éireann: Cúlra, Forbairt agus Teoiric (unpublished BA thesis, University of Ulster).

Nkrumah, Kwame (1964) *Consciencism: Philosophy and Ideology for Decolonisation and Development with Particular Reference to the African Revolution* (London).

— (1965) *Neo-Colonialism: The Last Stage of Imperialism* (London).

Ó Briain, Diarmuid (1979) *Traolach Mac Suibhne* (BÁC).

Ó Cadhain, Máirtín (n.d.) 'The Language Movement: A Movement Astray', translated from the original Irish by Seosamh Ó Díochan (Communist Party of Ireland pamphlet).

Ó Cathasaigh, Aindrias (2002) *Ag Samhlú troda: Máirtín Ó Cadhain 1905–1970* (BÁC).

— (2011) 'The Left and the Language', *Red Banner: A Magazine for Socialist Ideas*, 46 (Dublin): 24–30.

Ó Ceallaigh D. (ed.) (1994a) *Reconsiderations of Irish History and Culture: Selected Papers from the Desmond Greaves Summer School* (Dublin).

— (1994b) 'Reconsiderations', in Ó Ceallaigh 1994a: 5–26.

Ó Conaire, Breandán (1986) *Language, Lore and Lyrics* (Blackrock).

Ó Croidheáin, Caoimhín (2006) *Language from Below: The Irish Language, Ideology and Power in Twentieth-Century Ireland* (USA).

Ó Cuív (ed.) (1969) *A View of the Irish Language* (Dublin).

— (1975) 'The Irish Language in the Early Modern Period', in T.W. Moody and F.X. Martin (eds) *A New History of Ireland: Early Modern Ireland 1534–1691, vol.3* (Oxford): 500–12.

Ó Donnghaile, Cathal (2008) 'Coláiste Speirín: A Watershed in the Revival of the Gaelic Order', *Irish News* (10 October).

O'Donovan Rossa, Jeremiah (1967) *My Years in English Jails* (Tralee).

O'Dowd, Liam (1992) 'Colonial Dimensions: Settler–Native Mentalities', in Caherty et al. 1992: 15–28.

O'Fearaíl, Pádraig (1975) *The Story of Conradh na Gaeilge* (Dublin).

Ó Fiaich, Tomás (1969) 'The Language and Political History', in Ó Cúiv 1969a: 101–11.

Ó Gadhra, Nollaig (1989) *An Chéad Dáil Éireann (1919–1921) (agus an Ghaeilge)* (BÁC).

Ó Giolláin, Diarmuid (2000) *Locating Irish Folklore: Tradition, Modernity, Identity* (Cork).

Ó hAdhmaill, Feilim (1985) *Report of a Survey Carried out on the Irish Language in West Belfast* (Glór na nGael).

— (2011) 'The Revival of the Irish Language? Let's open up the debate' *Andersonstown News* (8 October).

O'Hagan, Feilim (ed.) (1991) *Éirí na Gealaí: Reflections of the Culture of Resistance in Long Kesh* (Belfast).

Ó hAilín, Tomás (1969) 'Irish Revival Movements', in Ó Cúiv 1969a: 91–100.

Ó hÉallaithe, Donncha (2004) 'From Language Revival to Language Survival', in C. Mac Murchaidh (ed.) *'Who Needs Irish?' Reflections on the Importance of the Irish Language Today* (Dublin): 159–85.

O'Hearn, Denis (2006) *Nothing but an Unfinished Song: Bobby Sands, the Irish Hunger Striker Who Ignited a Generation* (New York).

Ó Huallacháin, Colmán (1994) *The Irish and Irish: A Sociolinguistic Analysis of the Relationship Between a People and Their Language* (Dublin).

Ó hUid, Tarlach (1960) *Ar Thóir mo Shealbha* (BÁC).

— (1985) *Faoi Ghlas* (Maigh Eo).

O'Mahony, Seán (1987) *Frongoch: University of Revolution* (Dublin).

O'Malley, Ernie (1978) *The Singing Flame* (Dublin).

Ó Maoileoin, Seamás (1958) *B'fhiú an broan fola* (BÁC).

Ó Maolbhríde, Seán (1981) 'Máirtín Ó Cadhain', *Feasta*, 34 (Deireadh Fomhair): 17–20.

Ó Maolchraoibhe, Pádraig (1985) 'The Importance of Learning Irish', in Pádraig Ó Maolchraoibhe, *Learning Irish: A Discussion and Information Booklet* (Belfast): 3–7.

— (1986) 'The Role of the Language in Ireland's Cultural Revival', in *The Role of the Language in Ireland's Cultural Revival* (Belfast): 1–11.

Ó Muirthile, Seosamh (1967) *Tréithe Thomáis Ághas* (BÁC).

Ó Murchú, Máirtín (1971) 'Language and Community' ('Urlabhra agus Pobal'), Occasional Paper No.1 (Dublin).

Ó Néill, Eoghan (1990) 'NIO eases Irish language ban as legal pressure mounts', *Andersonstown News* (15 September): 2.

— (2008) 'Cá bhfuil sibh, a chairde sa Chúirt?' *LÁ Nua* (28 Eanair).

O'Reilly, Camille (1999) *The Irish Language in Northern Ireland: The Politics of Culture and Identity* (London).

Ó Riagáin, Dónall (2006) 'An Ghaeilge agus an Saol Eacnamaíoch: Athmhachnamh' (to be published).

Ó Snódaigh, Aengus (ed.) (1998) *Fealsúnacht, Feall agus Fuil: aistí ar ghnéithe de Stair '98* (Dublin).

— (2006) 'An Teanga agus an Réabhlóid', *An Phoblacht* (16 March): 12.

Ó Snódaigh, Pádraig (1995) *Hidden Ulster: Protestants and the Irish Language* (Belfast).

— (2006) *Na Priompalláin: 1916 agus athscríobh na staire* (BÁC).

Ó Tuathaigh, Gearóid (2005) 'Language, ideology and national identity', in Cleary and Connolly 2005: 43–58.

— (2007) 'Máirtín Ó Cadhain, An Stair agus An Pholaitíocht: Athmhachnamh', in *Saothar Mháirtín Uí Chadhain: Léachtaí Chomh Cille XXXVII* (Maynooth): 166–208.

— (2011) 'An Stát, an Féiniúlacht Náisiúnta agus an Teanga: Cás na hÉireann', in B. Mac Cormaic (éag) *Féiniúlacht, Cultúr agus Teanga i Ré an Domhandaithe* (BÁC): 76–113.

Olesen, Virginia, and E. Whittaker (1967) 'Role Making in Participant Observation: Processes in the Researcher–Actor Relationship', *Human Organisation*, 26/4: 273–81.

Parekh, B. (1995) 'The Concept of a National Identity', *New Community*, 21: 255–68.

Parenti, Michael (1995) *Against Empire* (USA).

Pearse, P.H. (1986) *The Murder Machine and Other Essays* (Cork).

Phillipson, R. (1992) *Linguistic Imperialism* (Oxford).

Pilger, John (2006) *Freedom Next Time* (London).

Rahman, T. (2001) 'Language-Learning and Power: A Theoretical Approach', *International Journal of the Sociology of Language*, 152: 53–74.

Rees, Russell (1998) *Ireland 1905–25* (Down).

Ross, David (2002) *Ireland: History of a Nation* (Scotland).

Rowthorn, Bob and Naomi Wayne (1988) *Northern Ireland: The Political Economy of Conflict* (Cambridge).

Rudé, George (1980) *Ideology and Popular Protest* (London).

Ryder, Chris (2001) *Inside the Maze: The Untold Story of the Northern Ireland Prison Service* (London).

Said, Edward, W. (1993) *Culture and Imperialism* (London).

— (2002) 'Thoughts about America', *Al-Ahram Weekly* (2 March).

— (2003) 'Afterword: Reflections on Ireland and Postcolonialism', in Carroll and King 2003: 177–85.

Sands, Bobby (1975) 'Ag Bunú Gaeltachta', in *Ar nGuth féin* (prison magazine).

— (1998) *Bobby Sands: Writings from Prison* (Cork).

Schubert, Michael (1986) 'Political Prisoners in West Germany: Their Situation and Some Consequences Concerning Their Rights in respect of the Treatment of Political Prisoners in International Law', in B. Rolston and M. Tomlinson (eds) *The Expansion of the European Prison Systems* (Belfast): 184–94.

Scott, Alan (1990) *Ideology and the New Social Movements* (London, 1990).

Scraton, Phil (2007) *Power, Conflict and Criminalisation* (New York).

— and K. Chadwick (2001) 'Critical Research', in E. McLaughlin and J. Muncie (eds) *The Sage Dictionary of Criminology* (London).

— Joe Sim and Paula Skidmore (1991) *Prisons under Protest* (Buckinghamshire).

Shirlow, Peter, J. Tonge, J. Mcauley and C. McGlynn (eds) (2010) *Abandoning Historical Conflict? Former Political Prisoners and Reconciliation in Northern Ireland* (Manchester).

Smyth, Gerry (1999) 'Decolonialisation and Criticism: Towards a Theory of Irish Critical Discourse', in Graham and Kirkland 1999: 29–49.

Stanley, L. (1990) *Feminist Praxis* (London).

Swartz, David (1997) *Culture and Power: The Sociology of Pierre Bourdieu* (London).

Sykes Gresham, M. (1958) *The Society of Captives* (New Jersey).

Tollefson, James W. (1991) *Planning Language, Planning Inequality: Language Policy in the Community* (London and New York).

Tomlinson, Mike (1980) 'Reforming Repression', in L. O'Dowd, B. Rolston and M. Tomlinson (eds) *Northern Ireland: Between Civil Rights and Civil War* (London): 187–96.

— (1995) 'Imprisoned Ireland', in Mick Ryan (ed.) *European Prison Systems: A Critical Perspective* (London): 240–48.

Townshend, Charles (1998) *Ireland in the Twentieth Century* (London).

Tuhiwai Smith, Linda (1999) *Decolonizing Methodologies: Research and Indigenous Peoples* (London and New York).

Wall, Maureen (1969) 'The Decline of the Irish Language', in Ó Cuív 1969: 101–11.

Walsh, John (2011a) *Contests and Contexts: The Irish Language and Ireland's Socio-Economic Development* (Bern).

— (2011b) 'An Ghaeilge mar acmhainn forbartha in am na géarchéime', in B. Mac Cormaic (éag) *Leas na Gaeilge, Leas an Stáit* (BÁC): 32–56.

Walters, R. (2003) *Deviant Knowledge: Criminology, Politics And Policy* (Cullompton) .

Watson, Iarfhlaith (2008) 'The Irish Language and Identity', in C. Nic Pháidín and S. Ó Cearnaigh (eds) *A New View of the Irish Language* (Dublin): 66–75.

Waxman, Chaim I. (ed.) (1968) *The End of Ideology Debate* (New York).

Williams, Colin (1994) *Called unto Liberty: On Language and Nationalism* (Clevedon).

— (2000) 'Development, Dependency and the Democratic Deficit', in W. Thomas and J. Mathias (eds) *Developing Minority Languages: The Proceedings of the Fifth International Conference on Minority Languages, July 1993* (Cardiff): 14–38.

Williams, G. (1992) *Sociolinguistics: A Sociological Critique* (London).

Williams, Raymond (1977) *Marxism and Literature* (Oxford).

— (1980) *Problems of Materialism and Culture* (Oxford).

Whelan, K. (2003) 'Between Filiation and Affiliation: The Politics of Postcolonial Memory', in Carroll and King 2003: 92–109.

— (2004) 'The Revisionist Debate in Ireland', *boundary 2*, 31/1 (Spring 2004): 179–205.

— (2005) 'The Cultural Effects of Famine', in Cleary and Connolly 2005: 137–54.

Whyte, John (1990) *Interpreting Northern Ireland* (Oxford).

Wright-Mills, C. (1959) *The Sociological Imagination* (New York).

# Narrator Biographies

What follows is a list of the names of those who participated as narrators in this research and some brief biographical notes describing them; their names are listed chronologically, in terms of time-periods spent in prison or years active in the Irish-language movement, instead of alphabetically. While it is worth noting that not all of the narrators listed below have their contributions cited in the book, they're nevertheless acknowledged as activists who gave up their time to be interviewed for the purposes of this book.

- *Eddie Keenan* – Eddie was from Belfast and was interned without trial in Crumlin Road Jail in Belfast in 1941 before famously escaping from prison and eventually being re-arrested in Dublin and sent to the Curragh camp in Kildare, where he was held without trial from 1943 to 1945 and subsequently learned the Irish language. Upon his release, he lived and worked in England for many years before returning to Belfast to raise a family. He became and remained a well-known Irish-language activist and traditional singer. Eddie passed away in 2009.

- *Willie-John McCorry* – Willie-John was a prominent republican activist from Belfast and one of the longest serving internees in the Curragh camp, where he was held from 1940 to 1945. He shared a hut with and learned Irish from Máirtín Ó Cadhain. Upon his release, he remained involved in republican activism and was eventually re-interned in Long-Kesh in 1971 while in his fifties. When released, he was the chairperson for the Irish Republican National Graves Association. Willie-John passed away after a short illness in 2006, aged 86.

- *Liam Ó Stiobhaird* – Liam is from Belfast and was a prominent republican activist when arrested and interned in Crumlin Road Jail from 1942 to 1945. He learned Irish and became a fluent speaker during imprisonment. On release, he continued as a republican activist throughout the 1950s, including cultural activism such as the organisation of language classes and *céilithe*.

- *Billy Kelly* – Billy was from Belfast originally and comes from a well-known republican family. From 1957 to 1960, he was interned without trial in Crumlin Road Jail, where he learned the Irish language. He remained active in the republican movement throughout his life and was interned without trial again in Long Kesh in 1973. Billy passed away in 2010 after a short illness.

- *Larry McGurk* – Larry is from Belfast and was interned without trial in Crumlin Road Jail from 1957 to 1960. He learned Irish in prison and became a well-known Irish-language activist in Cumann Chluain Ard upon his release. He remains active in Irish-language circles in Belfast to the present, centring around Cultúrlann MacAdam Ó Fiaich on the Falls Road.

- *Jim McCann* – Jim is a well-known republican from Belfast who was sentenced to the cages of Long Kesh from 1971 to 1979. He has written three very popular and comical autobiographical memoirs about his time in Long Kesh, including *The Boys Behind the Wire* (2001). He has been heavily involved in political activism since his release, including playing an influential role in setting up a *gaelscoil* in the Upper Springfield area of west Belfast and highlighting the human rights abuses inflicted on Long Kesh prisoners who are still suffering the ill-effects of CR/CS gas used by the British Army after the fire in Long Kesh in 1974.

- *Eibhlín Collins* (née Brady) – Eibhlín is from a well-known Belfast republican family; her father, Jack Brady, was a famous republican and Irish-language activist who was central to the development of the language as a prisoner in Crumlin Road Jail in the 1940s. She was sentenced and imprisoned in Armagh prison from 1971 to 1977 and began learning Irish in prison before continuing it on the outside. Upon her release, she completed a degree and qualified as a teacher while working voluntarily in Belfast's first *naíscoil* in Cumann Chluain Ard. She worked for many years as a primary school teacher in Scoil an Lonnáin on the Falls Road in Belfast before taking early retirement.

- *Francie Brolly* – Francie is from Dungiven in County Derry and learned Irish in secondary school. He was interned without trial in 1972 and imprisoned in the cages of Long Kesh until 1975. While imprisoned, he taught Irish and promoted Gaelic games. He returned to republican activism upon his release and was also a well-known singer and songwriter, who wrote the famous H-Block song, 'I'll wear no convict's uniform'. He has continued his work in Irish-language activism and spent many years as an elected Sinn Féin MLA for South Derry; he was Sinn Féin's Irish-language spokesperson before retiring in 2010.

- *Terry Enright* – Terry is from Belfast and from 1973 to 1975 was interned without trial in Long Kesh, where he learned the Irish language. Upon his release, he became involved in political activism and community development and was also a founder member of Sinn Féin's Roinn an Cultúir (Cultural Department), which played a crucial role in the 1980s language revival. He continued to play an important role in community politics in the west Belfast area and is also well-known as an environmentalist who is central to the 'Save the Black Mountain' anti-quarrying campaign. He is the current vice-chair of the Upper Springfield Development Trust and a long-standing trade-union and human-rights activist who sits as the community representative on the Equality Coalition and Human Rights Consortium.

- *Séanna Breathnach* – Séanna is from Belfast and learned Irish in school before becoming fluent while sentenced to the cages of Long Kesh from 1973 to 1976. He was released and arrested a short time later and imprisoned in the H-Blocks of Long Kesh from 1976 to 1984, where he was OC following the hunger strike in 1981; he was arrested and jailed in the H-Blocks for the third time from 1988 to 1998, when he was centrally involved in Irish-language development in the prison. He has been working as an Irish-language activist since his release and is the head of Sinn Féin's Roinn an Chultúir. Séanna was chosen by the leadership of IRA to read out their statement ending their armed campaign on 28 July 2005. He also sits as elected board member on Foras na Gaeilge's national board.

- *Daithí Mac Adhaimh* – Daithí is from a well-known Belfast republican family and learned Irish during three separate phases in prison. He was sentenced to the cages from 1974 to 1976, imprisoned in the H-Blocks from 1978 to 1982, and was arrested for the third time in 1994 and imprisoned until the prison eventually closed in the year 2000. Upon his release, he worked as a radio presenter with Belfast Irish-language radio station, Ráidió Fáilte. He also acted in numerous Irish-language dramas promoted by Irish-language Theatre Company Aisling Ghéar, including 'Dialann Ocrais', in which he played the main part of a Long Kesh hunger striker. He now works as a full-time social worker in Belfast.

- *Diarmuid Mac an tSionnaigh* – Diarmuid is from Belfast and between 1974 and 1990 completed a life sentence in the cages of Long Kesh, where he learned the Irish language. Upon his release, he completed a degree in Celtic studies and politics at Queen's University, Belfast. He has been involved in Irish-language activism since his release, working first for Glór na nGael before taking up a post as a professional Irish-language translator and senior executive officer for the CCEA (Council for the Curriculum, Examinations and Assessment).

- *Cyril Mac Curtain* – Cyril is from Limerick; he learned Irish in school and moved to Belfast in 1971 having been inspired by political events. He was arrested in 1974 and sentenced to the cages of Long Kesh until 1979. There he played a central role in the setting up of the Gaeltacht hut. He was released and re-arrested in 1981 and imprisoned in Portlaoise prison until 1986, where again he played a prominent role in setting up a Gaeltacht wing. He now lives and works in Limerick, where he remains very active on Irish-language issues.

- *Jake Mac Siacais* – Jake is from Belfast and was sentenced to the cages of Long Kesh, where he learned the Irish language, from 1975 to 1977. Shortly after his release, he was re-arrested and sentenced to the H-Blocks of Long Kesh, where he was imprisoned from 1977 to 1982. During this period he played a central role in Irish-language development in the prison. Following his release, he has been very active in Irish-language and community development in Belfast. He worked as a sub-editor with the *Andersonstown News* and *LÁ* newspapers before taking up his current post as Director of Belfast Irish-language Development Agency, Forbairt Feirste, which is centrally involved in the development of the Gaeltacht quarter in west Belfast.

- *Caoimhín Corbett* – Caoimhín is from north Belfast and was sentenced to the cages of Long Kesh from 1976 to 1984, where he became fluent in Irish. Upon his release he involved himself in Irish-language activism and played an instrumental role in the setting up of north Belfast's first nursery school, Naíscoil Ard Eoin, in 1984. He was re-arrested in 1988 and sentenced to the H-Blocks of Long Kesh from 1988 to 1993. He recently successfully completed a degree in Irish and Celtic Studies at Queen's University Belfast and works with north Belfast Irish-language group Glór an Tuaiscirt.

- *Seán Mag Uidhir* – Seán is from Belfast and learned Irish at school in St Malachy's College, before becoming fluent while sentenced in the cages of Long Kesh from 1976 to 1984. Since his release Seán has been very active in Irish-language circles and played a central role in the setting up of Naíscoil Ard Eoin in 1986. He sits on the board of Iontaobhas na Gaelscolaíochta and spent many years as editor of the *North Belfast News*. He now works for Community Restorative Justice in Ardoyne in north Belfast.

- *Liam Ó Maolchluiche* – Liam is from Belfast and learned Irish while sentenced to the cages of Long Kesh from 1976 to 1984. Upon his release, he was centrally involved in Irish-language activism in the Upper Springfield area of west Belfast, including the development of Irish-medium education in the area. He moved to Galway for a few years, completing a degree in Irish-language studies and history and an MA in sociology at Galway University. Liam later returned to west Belfast and played a key role in community development in the area. He now works as youth development co-ordinator for Irish-language youth organisation FEACHTAS.

- *Donncha Mac Niallais* – Donncha is from Derry City and learned Irish in school before becoming fluent while imprisoned in the H-Blocks of Long Kesh from 1976 to 1986. He was instated as Irish-language officer for the camp in 1982, a post he held for a considerable time. Since his release, he has been a central player in Irish-language activism in Derry City, where he is now based; he was a full-time development worker for Irish-language development agency An Gaelarás and was instrumental in the setting up of Cultúrlann Uí Chanáin.

- *Eoghan Mac Cormaic* – Eoghan 'Gino' Mac Cormaic is originally from County Derry; he was sentenced to life imprisonment in the H-Blocks of Long Kesh, where he was imprisoned from 1976 to 1991. He learned Irish while imprisoned and became a highly proficient writer and translator. He was central to Irish-language development in the prison and in 1989 brought a court case against the prison authorities and the NIO on grounds of cultural discrimination against prisoners. When released he completed an Irish-language degree at Galway University and also successfully stood as president of the students' union there. He spent a period as head of Sinn Féin's Roinn an Chultúir and also held senior positions in Conradh na Gaeilge. He has had numerous literary works published, including, *Caipín an Phápa*, and has also translated two of Gerry Adams's books into Irish, *Cás a 11* and *An tSráid agus scéalta eile*. He now lives in Galway, working full-time for the All-Ireland Irish-language organisation Glór na nGael, and is a member of Foras na Gaeilge's national board.

- *Dr Laurence McKeown* – Laurence is from Randalstown, County Antrim and was sentenced to life imprisonment in the H-Blocks of Long Kesh from 1976 to 1992, where he learned Irish. He went on hunger strike in 1981 and survived 70 days. He was involved in the development of education programmes in the prison and was co-founder of An Glór Gafa (The Captive Voice) and co-edited the book *Nor Meekly Serve My Time: The H-Block Struggle 1976–1981*. He was also vice OC of the H-Blocks from 1987 to 1989. He completed an Open University BA honours degree while imprisoned and after his release went on to complete a Ph.D. with the social sciences department in Queen's University Belfast in 1998. His doctoral thesis, *Unrepentant Fenian Bastards: The Social Construction of an Irish Republican Prisoner Community*, was published as a book, *Out of Time*, in 2001. He also co-wrote the film *H3* which was based on the Long Kesh prison struggle and released in 2001. He has spent most of his time since his release working as a development officer for Coiste na n-Iarchimí. He now lives and works as a writer and dramatist in Dundalk.

- *Máirtín Ó Maolmhuaidh* – Máirtín is from Strabane, County Tyrone and was imprisoned in the H-Blocks of Long Kesh from 1976 to 1984, where he learned Irish. He involved himself in Irish-language activism in Strabane before being re-arrested and imprisoned in the H-blocks from 1988 to 1998. He was adjutant of the H-Blocks from 1994 to 1996 and played a pivotal role in the setting up of the Irish-speaking wing in the prison, Gaeltacht na Fuiseoige, in 1995. On his release he involved himself in Irish-language activism and was instrumental in pioneering Irish-medium provision in Strabane. He spent a period working as a development officer for Cumann na Fuiseoige, an organisation set up in 1999 to promote the skills of republican ex-prisoners amongst the Irish-language-speaking community. He now works as full-time development officer for Strabane Irish-language group Gaelphobal.

- *Dr Ciarán Dawson* – Ciarán is from Belfast and learned his Irish in school and in the H-Blocks of Long Kesh, where he was imprisoned from 1976 to 1984. Ciarán went back into full-time education upon his release and gained a degree in Irish-language studies from the University of Ulster in 1988. He successfully completed a Ph.D. on the life and work of Peadar Ó Gealeacáin in 1995. Until 1997 he worked on various projects in the University of Ulster, before moving to Cork, where he now works as a lecturer and teacher in University College Cork's Ionad na Gaeilge Labhartha.

- *Antóin De Brún* – Antóin is from Derry City and learned his Irish in the H-Blocks of Long Kesh, where he was imprisoned from 1976 to 1988. He completed his O levels and A levels while in prison and went into full-time education upon his release. He gained a degree in Irish-language studies from the University of Ulster and went on to become a qualified teacher. He was centrally involved in Irish-language activism in Derry, including the development of Irish-medium education there. He currently teaches in Gaelscoil Éadáin Mhóir in the Bogside area of Derry City.

- *Peadar Ó Cuinneagáin* – Peadar is from Belfast and was imprisoned in the H-Blocks of Long Kesh from 1977 to 1985, where he learned Irish. He re-involved himself in political activism on his release and was re-arrested a few years later and imprisoned from 1989 to 1998. During this period he was instrumental in promoting Irish-language development in the prison, including the formation of Gaeltacht na Fuiseoige in 1995. Since his release he has been prominent as an Irish-language activist; he spent spells working as a development officer for both Comhairle na Gaelscolaíochta and Foras na Gaeilge before returning to full-time postgraduate study at Queen's University Belfast.

- *Garaí Mac Roibeáird* – Garaí is from Belfast and was sentenced to life imprisonment in the H-Blocks of Long Kesh from 1977 to 1991. He learned Irish in prison and was also one of the 38 prisoners who escaped from Long Kesh as part of the Great Escape in 1983, though he was quickly caught and re-imprisoned. Garaí completed a degree in Celtic studies and history at Queen's University Belfast upon his release. He qualified as a teacher and spent many years as principal of Coláiste Feirste, the first Irish-medium secondary school in the six counties, before moving to his current post as senior advisor for Irish-medium education with the Education and Skills Authority on behalf of the Department of Education.

- *Pádraic McCotter* – Pádraic is from a long-standing republican family in Belfast and his father was a well-known republican and Irish-language activist who both learned and taught Irish while imprisoned in Crumlin Road Jail in the 1940s. Pádraic was imprisoned in the H-Blocks of Long Kesh from 1977 to 1979, where he learned Irish. He was re-arrested in 1986 and sentenced to the H-Blocks where he was imprisoned until 1996. He was a member of the prison camp staff when the Gaeltacht na Fuiseoige was formed in 1995. Pádraic has continued with his political activism since his release and spent a period working full-time for Coiste na n-Iarchimí as training officer and tour guide for their political tours programme. He is also now a member of socialist republican political party éirígí and recently stood for election to Belfast City Council in the 2011 elections.

- *Pilib Ó Ruanaí* – Pilib is from Belfast and learned his Irish while imprisoned in the H-Blocks from 1977 to 1984. Upon his release, he became a full-time Irish-language activist in the south and east Belfast area, while successfully completing his degree in Celtic studies and English at Queen's University Belfast. He was centrally involved in the first *naíscoil* in the east of the city in Short Strand and its eventual development into Scoil an Droichid on the Ormeau Road in south Belfast. He also oversaw its development as part of An Droichead cultural centre, and spent many years as its chairperson. He also works full time as chief executive of the Irish-Medium Trust Fund, Iontaobhas na Gaelscolaíochta.

- *Michael Liggott* – Michael comes from a well-known Irish-language-speaking family in north Belfast. He was incarcerated in Crumlin Road Jail from 1978 to 1981, where he taught Irish to prisoners on remand in preparation for their language classes in the H-Blocks of Long Kesh when they were sentenced. He has been involved in community development since his release and now works as a community worker in north Belfast.

- *Michael Culbert* – Michael is from Belfast and was sentenced to life imprisonment in the H-Blocks of Long Kesh, where he was incarcerated from 1978 to 1993. He learned Irish there and was centrally involved in the development of welfare system for prisoners inside the prison; he also completed a piece of research on the subject of formal and informal education programmes for prisoners for an Open University course. Since his release, he has been active in community development and has spent much of that time working full-time for republican ex-prisoner umbrella organisation Coiste na n-Iarchimí, of which he is now director.

- *Caoimhín Mac Mathúna* – Caoimhín is from Belfast and learned his Irish in the Gaeltacht wing in Portlaoise prison in county Laois, where he was imprisoned from 1980 to 1986. He was arrested and imprisoned again in the H-Blocks of Long Kesh from 1989 to 1999 and was instrumental in the setting up of Gaeltacht na Fuiseoige in the prison. He successfully completed an Open University degree during this period and qualified as a teacher upon his release. He subsequently moved to Gaoth Dobhair in the Donegal Gaeltacht where he is very active on Irish-language issues as well as teaching full-time in the *gaelscoil* in Gort a' Choirce.

- *Marcas Mac Ruairí* – Marcas is from Downpatrick in County Down and learned Irish in school, at night classes and in prison. He was arrested and held on remand in Crumlin Road Jail from 1982 to 1984 before being sentenced to the H-Blocks from 1984 to 1988. Marcas has been a full-time Irish-language activist since his release and played a central role in bringing Irish-medium education to the Downpatrick area. Marcas also worked full-time as a journalist with Irish-language newspaper *LÁ* before working as senior research development officer with Irish-language organisation POBAL for a number of years. He now works full-time with All-Ireland Irish-language organisation Glór na nGael and sits on Foras na Gaeilge's national board.

- *Seán Ó Loingsigh* – Seán is from Lisnaskea in County Fermanagh and was imprisoned in the H-Blocks of Long Kesh from 1986 to 1998. Seán was vice OC of the H-Blocks from 1992 to 1994 and OC from 1994 to 1996. He played a key role in overseeing the setting-up of the Irish-speaking wing in the prison, Gaeltacht na Fuiseoige, in 1995, where he would later learn his Irish. Shortly after his release he was instrumental in the setting up of County Fermanagh's first Irish-medium nursery, Naíscoil an Traonaigh, which in 2004 developed into Bunscoil an Traonaigh, where Seán still functions as chairperson of its committee. Seán also worked as the project co-ordinator with the Fermanagh ex-prisoners and dependents group in Lisnaskea. He now works full time for Sinn Féin and is a councillor and MLA for County Fermanagh.

- *Dr Déaglán Ó Mochain* – Déaglán is from County Monaghan and was arrested and imprisoned in the H-Blocks of Long Kesh from 1989 to 1997. He learned Irish in the Gaeltacht wing of the prison and also successfully completed an Open University social sciences degree while incarcerated. Upon his release, he was very active in Irish-language circles as well as going back to full-time education and successfully completing an MA in the social sciences in Queen's University Belfast. He continued with his studies and in 2011 completed a Ph.D. into post-hunger-strike resistance amongst republican political prisoners in Long Kesh. He also successfully completed a course with Acadamh na hOllscolaíochta Gaeilge in television and film-making through the medium of Irish in Gaoth Dobhair, Donegal and has since worked on a number of Irish-language television programmes. He now works full-time in Cultúrlann Uí Chanáin in Derry City with Irish-language film-making company Dearcán.

- *Mícheál Mac Giolla Ghunna* – Mícheál is a prominent Irish-language activist from Belfast who successfully completed a degree in Celtic studies from Queen's University and worked full-time for Glór na nGael in Belfast. He was arrested and sentenced to the H-Blocks from 1990 to 1997; he completed an Open University political science degree while imprisoned and was to the forefront of Irish-language development in the prison's Gaeltacht wings and the development of theatre and creative writing groups. Upon his release, he spent a period as head of Sinn Féin's Roinn an Chultúir and completed an MA in Irish-language studies from the University of Ulster before qualifying as a teacher. He now works in Coláiste Feirste in Belfast as school principal.

- *Rosa Mac Lochlainn* – Rosa is from Letterkenny, County Donegal and moved to Belfast to study physics at Queen's University. She successfully completed her degree and learned Irish with the Cumann Gaelach in the university. She qualified as a teacher before being arrested and imprisoned in Maghaberry from 1994 to 1996, where she taught Irish to fellow prisoners. She spent many years working in Belfast as a teacher in Coláiste Feirste, before taking up her current post as educational advisor for the Western Education and Library Board in the north-west.

- *Jamesey Ó Muireagáin* – Jamesey is from Belfast and was imprisoned in the H-Blocks of Long Kesh from 1991 to 1998. He learned his Irish on the Gaeltacht wing and successfully completed his GCSE and A level Irish while imprisoned. Upon his release he re-involved himself in Irish-language and community activism and taught Irish on a number of different accredited BIFHE courses. He now works full-time in Coláiste Feirste as school caretaker.

- *Rosie McCorley* – Rosie is from Belfast and was imprisoned in Maghaberry prison from 1990 to 2000. She was OC of the female republican prisoners in the prison for a long period and also began learning and teaching Irish there before taking this further following her release. She successfully completed an Open University degree while in prison and recently completed the MA in Irish translation studies with Queen's University. She worked as a development officer for Coiste na n-Iarchimí until recently and also played a pivotal role in the development of Bunscoil an Traonaigh in Fermanagh. She now works as a political advisor for Sinn Féin in Stormont, with specific responsibility for Irish-language affairs.

- *Dr Feilim Ó hAdhmaill* – Feilim is a prominent Irish-language activist from Belfast who learned his Irish in school and at night classes as a teenager. He was very active in the 1980s Irish-language revival and carried out a piece of research for Glór na nGael in Belfast titled 'Report of a survey carried out on the Irish Language in West Belfast' in 1985. He completed a degree in social sciences in the University of Ulster before going on to complete a Ph.D. with the same department in 1990 titled *The Function and Dynamics of the Ghetto: A Study of Nationalist West Belfast*. He was later arrested and jailed in England in 1994. In 1996 he was moved to the H-Blocks, where he remained until the prison closed in 2000. He was to the forefront of Irish-language development in the prison during his incarceration and has been active as a full-time Irish-language activist since his release, working in various posts in the Irish-language sector in Belfast. He now lives in Cork, where he lectures full-time for the department of social sciences and social policy in University College Cork.

- *Seamás Mac Seáin* – Seamás is from Belfast and is one of the founding fathers of the contemporary Irish-language revival in the north of Ireland. He learned his Irish in school and in Cumann Chluain Ard and was one of the key founders of the Shaw's Road Urban Gaeltacht in the 1960s and the north's first Irish-medium primary school, Bunscoil Phobal Feirste, in 1971. He also founded west Belfast's first community newspaper, the *Andersonstown News*, and directed it for many years. Seamás was also central to the setting up of the first six-county Irish-language secondary school, Meánscoil Feirste (now Coláiste Feirste) in 1991, Cultúrlann MacAdam Ó Fiaich and many other such cultural projects. His autobiography, *D'imigh sin agus tháinig seo*, was released in 2010. He lives in Belfast and continues to be as active as ever in Irish-language circles as chairperson of Taca, the fundraising charity for Irish-medium education.

- *Pádraig Ó Maolchraoibhe* – Pádraig is from South Armagh and learned his Irish at school and at Queen's University Belfast where he achieved a degree in Celtic Studies and Spanish in the 1960s. He qualified as a teacher and lived and taught in the Basque country before returning to Ireland in the early 1970s and moving to Belfast, where he taught Spanish in St Mary's Christian Brothers School on the Glen Road. Pádraig was centrally involved in the Bunscoil Phobal Feirste project and was its chairperson for many years. He was also Sinn Féin's first councillor for Lisburn and spokesperson for its Roinn an Chultúir for many years. He speaks six languages fluently and now divides his time between Belfast and Ecuador, the native home of his wife. He recently translated the smuggled transcript of a Columbian political prisoner from Spanish into Irish, *Mo Scéal Féin: Diego*, published as a book.

- *Aodán Mac Póilin* – Aodán is from Belfast and learned his Irish in Cumann Chluain Ard and was educated by the Christian Brothers and at the University of Ulster. He is a member of the Shaw's Road Gaeltacht community and has been an Irish-language activist since the early 1970s. He qualified and worked as a teacher for many years and is also a former chairman of Bunscoil Phobal Féirste. He was the Irish-language editor of the literary journal *Krino* and the author of two pamphlets on broadcasting. He was also editor of *The Irish Language in Northern Ireland* (1997) and co-editor of *The Selected Poems of Padraic Fiacc* (1994) and *Styles of Belonging: The Cultural Identity of Ulster* (1991). He currently works as director of six-county cross-community Irish-language agency Iontaobhas Ultach.

- *Máirtín Ó Muilleoir* – Máirtín is from Belfast and learned his Irish at school and in Cumann Chluain Ard. He completed a Celtic Studies degree at Queen's University Belfast and began working full-time as a journalist with the *Andersonstown News*. He was also a very prominent Irish-language activist who spent time as head of Sinn Féin's Roinn an Chultúir and as a councillor for west Belfast. He is also a well-known author who has written numerous books both in Irish and in English, including *Comhad Comhairleora* (1990), *Krauts* (1992) and *Belfast's Dome of Delight: City Hall Politics 1981–2000* (2000). He spent time as editor of the *Andersonstown News* before taking up his current post as overall managing director of the *Belfast Media Group*. He was also re-elected as a Sinn Féin councillor for Balmoral in the council elections of 2011.

- *Bairbre De Brún* – Bairbre is from Dublin originally and learned her Irish in school and at university before moving to Belfast to become active during the anti-H-Block campaigns. She became a prominent Irish-language activist and was central to Sinn Féin's Roinn an Chultúir. She also qualified as a teacher and taught French in Meánscoil Feirste in Belfast for many years. She currently divides her time between Belfast and Brussels, where she works full-time as Sinn Féin MEP for the six counties.

- *Jim Herron* – Jim is from Belfast and learned his Irish at home and in school at St Malachy's. He was educated at Queen's University Belfast, where he completed a degree in Celtic studies before qualifying and working as an Irish secondary school teacher at St Patrick's Grammar School, Armagh. He also worked as an Irish teacher via the formal Long Kesh prison education system and taught night classes to republican political prisoners in Long Kesh from 1985 to 1995. He remains active today in Irish-language and GAA circles and now works as vice-principal at St Patrick's.

- *Eoghan Ó Néill* – Eoghan is from Belfast and learned his Irish in school and in the Cumann Chluain Ard and was educated at Queen's University Belfast. He has been a very prominent Irish-language activist ever since and a co-founder of *LÁ* newspaper and Ráidio Fáilte in the early 1980s. He spent time as editor of *LÁ* and works as an Irish-language radio broadcaster for Ráidio Fáilte and BBC Radio Ulster. He's also a founder of web-based Irish-language news service Nuacht 24 and writes a weekly column in national Irish-language newspaper *Gaelscéal*. His autobiographical travel diary *Cathracha* was also published in Irish.

- *Ciarán Mac Giolla Bhéin* – Ciarán is from Belfast and is a product of the 1980s revival who was educated in Bunscoil Phobal Feirste and Meánscoil Feirste. He went on to complete a degree in Irish and Celtic studies and history from Queen's University Belfast as well as an MA in Irish and Celtic studies. He is prominent in the city as an Irish-language activist and spent time as a development worker with Forbairt Feirste before moving to his current post as national youth officer with Foras na Gaeilge. He sits on the national executive of Conradh na Gaeilge and chairs Irish-medium youth network Foram na nÓg, and was formerly chairperson of Irish-language campaigning group ACHT.

# Appendix

Personal communication written in Irish by Jake Mac Siacais to 'Moscow Jack Brady' on cigarette paper during the 1981 hunger strike in an attempt to lobby the Irish language community to attend the rallies.

# Index